D0208704

The Rise and Fall of Management

This book is written with thanks to Jack Clyde, my one-time mentor, boss and friend, who offered both encouragement and example as a professional manager of huge competence, experience, wisdom and integrity and who made working with him and for him, fulfilling, profitable and fun.

The Rise and Fall of Management

A Brief History of Practice, Theory and Context

GORDON PEARSON

GOWER

Gower Applied Business Research
Our programme provides leaders, practitioners, scholars and researchers with thought provoking, cutting edge books that combine conceptual insights, interdisciplinary rigour and practical relevance in key areas of business and management.

Published by
Gower Publishing Limited
Wey Court East
Union Road
Farnham
Surrey, GU9 7PT
England

Ashgate Publishing Company
Suite 420
101 Cherry Street
Burlington,
VT 05401-4405
USA

www.gowerpublishing.com

British Library Cataloguing in Publication Data
Pearson, Gordon.
  The rise and fall of management : a brief history of
  practice, theory and context.
  1. Industrial management--History.
  I. Title
  658'.009-dc22

  ISBN: 978-0-566-08976-3 (hbk)
      978-0-566-08977-0 (ebk)

Library of Congress Cataloging-in-Publication Data
Pearson, Gordon J., 1939-
  The rise and fall of management : a brief history of practice, theory, and context / by Gordon Pearson.
      p. cm.
  Includes bibliographical references and index.
  ISBN 978-0-566-08976-3 -- ISBN 978-0-566-08977-0 1. Management--History.
  2. Industrial management--History. 3. Industrialization--History. I. Title.
  HD30.5.P43 2009
  658.009--dc22

                                                                2009024530

Mixed Sources
Product group from well-managed
forests and other controlled sources
www.fsc.org Cert no. SA-COC-1565
© 1996 Forest Stewardship Council

Printed and bound in Great Britain by
MPG Books Ltd, Bodmin, Cornwall.

Contents

Acknowledgements

I have referenced many illustrious writers and practitioners to whom I am obviously indebted. The text has also been hugely improved through the friendly criticism and advice given by various extremely generous individuals. They notably included Peter Armstrong, Jack Clyde, John Cole, Stuart Fraser, Malcolm Joels, Peter Lawrence, Simon Lilley, Terry O'Neill, Martin Parker, Toni Reed, Alan Surgey and Ian Wilson, none of whom can be blamed for the end result.

My original interest in the subject matter goes back to GCE 'A' levels in economics and economic history which I took to gain entry to a BSc in management science at Warwick University, financed by my then employers, Mills & Rockleys Ltd. As a management practitioner, I reached moderately interesting levels in three groups of companies and after around 20 years in industry I won a Tom Lupton scholarship to read for a PhD at Manchester Business School looking at what facilitates and inhibits innovation in industry. This absorbing study rendered me apparently unemployable as a practitioner, so I joined academe, teaching what I knew and writing what I was continuing to learn. I am grateful to all those who I worked with over those years and who helped develop my interest in the fascinating subject of management.

Finally, I am grateful also to Gower's Martin West for his knowledgeable support and interest throughout this book's commissioning.

Gordon Pearson

Prologue

The main focus of this brief history is on the management of business organizations operating for profit in freely competitive markets. Such business organizations are important because it is from the fruits of their operations, either directly or indirectly, that a nation pays for its health, education, defence and social services as well as its government. And their management is important because it, or they, largely determine the effectiveness of business operations, usually measured in terms of taxable profitability and growth, and therefore the potential generosity of the national services referred to, which are some measure of the degree to which a society might be regarded as civilized.

The story of capital accumulation and its investment in industrial enterprise has been one of ever rising standards of living, albeit with the occasional step backwards along the way. But it is also a story that has always seemed inequitable. In the beginning, peasant farmers were dispossessed of their meagre strips of land so that it might be enclosed for the economic advantage of tenant farmers and their landlords. The dispossessed then joined a reserve army of labour to be accessed as needed by the capital accumulating industrialists.

Ricardo's later explanation of capital as the accumulated surplus value expropriated from labour clearly had some general justification even if his detailed argument appears somewhat arcane.

However, industrial development has also been a story of impecunious members of the labouring class, through their own ingenuity and energy, becoming masters of industry and possessors of substantial wealth. There had always been some such social mobility, but it substantially increased with the process of industrialization.

Those who presided over the distribution of the surpluses produced by industry could, if so minded, discharge those responsibilities with fairness and 'frugality', to use Adam Smith's word. But Smith argued that the economy as a whole depended on quite different behaviour if it were to grow and prosper.

'It is not from the benevolence of the butcher, the brewer, or the baker, that we expect our dinner, but from their regard for their own interest. We address ourselves not to their humanity but to their self-love.'[1]

Smith argued that the efforts of these many individuals working purely to maximize their own wealth in competitive markets largely freed from government regulation and interference, would maximize the aggregate wealth of the population. And, so far, his theory has worked better than any alternative in delivering that object. Despite their vulnerability to sentiment and sometimes even hysteria, markets work better in the delivery of economic goods and commodities than the alternative systems of central planning and control.[2]

But maximizing aggregate wealth does not necessarily imply equity in its distribution. The emerging gap between employers and employed and more particularly the unemployed, sometimes highlighted by the ostentatious consumption of the few in the faces of the insecure many, fuelled continuous aggravation and from time to time open conflict and occasionally bloody revolution. And quite apparently it may do so again. This inequity lies at the heart of the management task.

Throughout its history, industrial enterprise has been shaped, both directly and indirectly, through the actions of government guided by the prevalent economic theory. While variations have occurred at different times, economic theories, from Marx to Keynes and Friedman, share both a common root in Adam Smith and a more or less complete incomprehension of business enterprise and its management.

Alfred Chandler started his account of the twentieth-century American management revolution, with the assertion that the visible hand of management had replaced Adam Smith's invisible hand of market forces. Modern business enterprise had become:

'the most powerful institution in the American economy and its managers the most influential group of economic decision makers.'[3]

1   Smith, A., (1776), *An Inquiry into the Nature and Causes of the Wealth of Nations* , Book 1, Chapter 2, p. 22. *Wealth of Nations* was republished as a selected edition in 1993 with an introduction and notes by Kathryn Sutherland in the Oxford World's Classics imprint by Oxford University Press. In references from *Wealth of Nations* page numbers are quoted from this Oxford edition unless stated otherwise.
2   Parker, M. and Pearson, G., (2005), 'Capitalism and its Regulation: A Dialogue on Business and Ethics', *Journal of Business Ethics*, Vol. 60, No 1, pp. 91–101.
3   *The Visible Hand: The Managerial Revolution in American Business* (1977), Cambridge, Mass: The Belknap Press of Harvard University Press, p. 1.

Nevertheless, he noted that economists had excluded management from their theory of the firm:

> *'Any theory of the firm that defines the enterprise merely as a factory or even a number of factories, and therefore fails to take into account the role of administrative coordination, is far removed from reality.'*[4]

Moreover:

> *'Historians as well as economists have failed to consider the implications of the rise of the modern business enterprise. … they have paid almost no notice at all to the managers who … play a far more central role in the operations of the American economy than did the robber barons, the industrial statesmen, or financiers.'*[5]

Nevertheless economic theory influences the thinking not just of management but of all enterprise stakeholders: customers, employees, shareholders, suppliers, money lenders, tax authorities, legislators, politicians, local communities and the wider environment which will be the home of future generations. They all now share the dismal science's perspective on the amoral, self-interested role of management. It has become the taken-for-granted assumption that almost everyone has about management. It is in the culture of organizations, governments and social groups of all kinds and it is what is taught to business school students of management. It has bred such cynicism, that if a business were to act with integrity, it would simply be regarded as engaging in good public relations, rather than it being the product of a deeply embedded organizational culture which determines 'the way we do things around here'.

Some account of economic theory is therefore unavoidable in an examination of management. Here it is limited to what has significantly influenced business and management. Repeatedly over the past two hundred and thirty-odd years since Smith's *Wealth of Nations*, economists have produced broad general accounts of economic activity which appear logical, stand up to practical scrutiny and seem to work. Then, repeatedly, theorists have sought to examine and explain in detail the foundations of those broad truths and have come up with theories and propositions which appear absurd if not factually wrong, and so serve to undermine, rather than support, the broad analysis. In this account, the detail of economic theory is largely omitted.

---

4   Ibid, p. 490.
5   Ibid, p. 490–1.

All history is a compromise; a brief history an even greater one. Broad generalizations have been made in the narrative of management's emergence, rise, fall and possible renewal. This is clearly not the whole truth; there have always been those prepared to swim against the tide. But the rise and fall generalization nevertheless appears to be a valid picture of the broad trends. Similarly so with the treatment of the various tides of economic theory; attention has been concentrated on the broad trends.

The brevity is further strained by the necessity with this subject to straddle the Atlantic. The initial focus was in England where industry and the management process first emerged. But since the late nineteenth century, management practice and theory has been dominated by the United States. This history is therefore essentially Anglo-Saxon in its analysis, both of the development of management and of economic theory in its political context. The British reality has been closely entwined with that of the United States and that proximity is reflected in these pages which largely exclude non-Anglo-Saxon contributions to the story. The most regrettable omissions are the Japanese and German more technologically oriented contributions, both demonstrably more successful than Britain in their post Second World War industrial development.

A final compromise that had to be made in a brief history of this kind was in the selection and balance between the different strands which make up the history: management practice, management theory, economic theory, the political context and the education of management. The normal respect for chronology is somewhat compromised by this entwining of strands. The first part covers a period from around the beginning of the eighteenth century to somewhere around 1870 when the United States economy overtook those of the old world. The second part deals with the following hundred years or so up to the time when 'Keynesian economics' ceased to be the accepted orthodoxy. Part III then takes the story from the late 1970s through to the new millennium. Part IV is written from a 2008–9 perspective.

The new context substantially raises the stakes for management. It is now generally agreed that, driven by world population growth and the unceasing quest for better standards of living, the earth's resources are being depleted at an unsustainable rate, its atmosphere polluted and its climate undermined through the industrial activities of the developed and developing world. Management can no longer simply aim to 'make as much money as possible for stockholders'. All our futures depend on management espousing higher aims than that and largely achieving what they aim for, and doing so before it is too late.

PART I
The Emergence of Management

The full history of the skills and competencies which later became known as management may have started back in 5000 BC with the Sumerian temple priests, whose tax system involved the amassing of worldly goods for which records had to be maintained; or in 4000 BC with the building of the pyramids, which must clearly have involved some understanding of organization among the Egyptians. Evidence on Moses suggests the Hebrews had some management awareness around 1500 BC and similarly, so did the Chinese from 1100 BC. And there are well-documented military antecedents from the fourth century BC in both Greece and China, with references now included in the modern literature. Since then the literature of pre-industrial management relates almost exclusively to the military and to the management of the sovereign state, with some limited references to the organization of the Christian church and overseas trading monopolies. These sources may be of some academic interest, but the history of management as it is now understood really starts with the creation of an economic surplus and the subsequent introduction of industrial manufacturing in eighteenth-century England.

This opening part is concerned with that first revolutionary century of practice and its reflection in the economic theory expounded by Adam Smith and others. It sees the decisions, processes and responsibilities now associated with management starting to emerge first in the new agriculture and pre-industrial businesses and subsequently in the development of the first transportation infrastructure, the canals and turnpike roads, and only then in the process of industrialization itself.

Smith recognized the revolutionary changes that might be enabled by the cost reductions that could be achieved by the division of labour into specialized tasks. Such reduced costs would bring what were previously luxury commodities within the reach of a far greater number. Thus a virtuous cycle could be established which was limited only by the size of markets. He therefore argued against the old protectionist systems of trade and commerce which limited the size of markets; all such government intervention could only inhibit economic growth.

Industrialization, based on the division of labour and the accumulation and investment of capital, resulted in an explosion of industrial factory building and the creation of whole new urban populations. It changed everything both for the better and for the worse. It created great wealth and great misery. It supported an explosion in population and established an unprecedented and ever expanding level of consumption simultaneously with the creation of an underclass of paupers and workers who from time to time became the unemployed as the economy progressed through booms and slumps.

Smith did not live to see the poverty and disease of the new industrial towns. It was left to his successors to observe such inequity and consider ways to organize better the industrial system of economics and governance. Some suggested the misery had to be accepted if the increase in wealth was to be achieved. Others violently rejected that proposition. Thus from the beginnings of industrialization there was a fundamental divide between employers and employed, between rich and poor, capitalists and labour. The management responsibility began to emerge as a separate and partly autonomous category. Those who carried that responsibility were recognized by labour simply as the agents of the capitalists, while the capitalists came to suspect them of maximizing their own self-interest at the expense of capital. But management, by definition neither capital nor labour, was in the front line of economic development, and in a position to influence its course for good or ill.

1

Creating the First Economic Surplus

Industrialization depended on the prior generation of an economic surplus and the establishment of ways of working for which management, as we now refer to it but didn't then, was primarily responsible. Industrialization improved the standards of living, health and longevity of industrializing people but it had negative effects as well as positive.

Prior to industrialization, life in England for the vast majority was fairly short and uncomfortable, if not 'brutish'. The English population remained at around five and a half million through the first half of the eighteenth century, held there by recurrent harsh climatic conditions (1708–10, 1725–29 and 1739–42), poor harvests resulting in famine, poor public hygiene resulting in disease (notably dysentery, smallpox and consumption) as well as much alcoholic excess – output of spirits reached eight million gallons in 1742–43, six times higher than in the early years of the century, and didn't fall till after 1750 when taxes on alcohol were substantially raised. Infant mortality ran at one in 15 for most of the first half of the century. The population lived in poverty and for the majority life was a struggle against the odds. It was no golden age.

In the last four decades of the century, as industrialization was beginning, conditions overall improved substantially. More productive agriculture resulted in the elimination of famine and improved diet for the masses. Greater supplies of coal for domestic heating, improved ventilation, more soap and washable garments contributing to improved hygiene, improvements in medical practice and surgery with the creation of hospitals and dispensaries and the adoption of the smallpox inoculation, all contributed to the reduction and elimination of disease. As a result England's population grew by around two thirds to over nine million by the end of the century, infant mortality fell almost eightfold to one in 118 and life for the majority became progressively less precarious, though not for all.

The improvements which enabled industrialization to take off were only achieved by the intelligence, diligence and energy of large numbers of people and perhaps the genius of a small number, all motivated to create something better than had been previously known.

Assuming such people were motivated solely by their own self-interest, or greed, is an inadequate proxy for the truth. There had to be something less dismal within man which motivated such heroic achievement.

Human Needs: Engine of Economic Growth

The fundamental idea which underpins much of economic thought is that of 'economic man', the utterly rational, amoral, self-interested individual identified by Adam Smith and eternally associated with his name. Writing in 1776, he identified the 'self-love' of producers and tradesmen, rather than their concern for any social ends, as the solid foundation of economic activity and growth:

> 'By pursuing his own interest he frequently promotes that of the society more effectually than when he really intends to promote it. I have never known much good done by those who affected to trade for the public good.'[1]

This is the simple, direct Adam Smith that survives most explicitly in economic thinking today, but his examination of what motivated people was actually rather more nuanced than just that of economic self-interest.

He recognized that economic growth depended on people being motivated to satisfy certain needs and 'conveniences'. He suggested a progression of needs, starting from childhood with those arising from hunger and thirst, heat and cold.

> 'The preservation and healthful state of the body seem to be the objects which nature first recommends to the care of every individual ... The first lessons which he is taught by those to whom his childhood is

---

1   Smith, A., (1776), *Wealth of Nations*, Book 4, Chapter 2, Part II, p. 292.

entrusted, tend, the greater part of them, to the same purpose. Their principal object is to teach him to keep out of harm's way.'

Smith expressed these needs in adulthood as desire, firstly for food (for which desire is 'limited by the size of a man's stomach'), and then for satisfying:

'the other wants and fancies of mankind. Cloathing and lodging, household furniture and what is called Equipage'[2] (equipage being identified as articles for personal ornament and use and a carriage etc.).

These wants may be unlimited, clearly extending to what was later referred to by Thorstein Veblen as 'conspicuous consumption'.[3] These were the human needs and wants driving economic growth.

Smith also identified the desire to save as the ultimate human need. By saving, rather than consuming all, a person could accumulate capital in order to 'improve' themselves. While others objected that immediate consumption on pleasure, vice and luxury, would be the more effective driver of economic progress, Smith argued that 'frugality' was more powerful than vice and luxury. Frugality which enabled people to become:

'proper objects of this respect, of deserving and obtaining this credit and rank among our equals, is, perhaps, the strongest of all our desires, and our anxiety to obtain the advantages of fortune is accordingly much more excited and irritated by this desire. Than that of supplying all the necessities and conveniences of the body, which are always very easily supplied.'[4]

Adam Smith therefore had a richer appreciation of human motivation than is now widely assumed. More recent contributors have added to, rather than replaced, Smith's model. The much quoted Maslow proposed a hierarchy of human needs[5] starting with physiological needs (food, sleep, shelter, sex, etc.) at the lowest level, rising through safety needs, love needs, esteem needs and finally, at the top level, which would be salient once the lower level needs were

2   Smith, A., (1776), *Wealth of Nations*, Chapter 11, Part II, p. 152.
3   Veblen, T., (1899), *The Theory of the Leisure Class: An Economic Study in the Evolution of Institutions*. New York: Macmillan.
4   Smith, A., (1759), *The Theory of Moral Sentiments*, Part VI, Section I, republished in the Dover Philosophical Classics imprint by Dover Publications Inc of New York in 2006, pp. 213–4.
5   Maslow, A., (1943), 'A Theory of Human Motivation', *Psychological Review*, Vol. 50, pp. 370–396.

satisfied, the need for self-actualization (which was exampled as 'a musician must make music'). Maslow's model appeals intuitively and seems sound common sense even though it was not based on empirical evidence.

Less elegant approaches, such as Murray's original work in the 1930s,[6] later enhanced by Atkinson[7] and McClelland,[8] suggested there were more than 20 intrinsic human needs, any one or more of which might be potent at any one time. Moreover, there was not necessarily a hierarchical relationship between needs, no structured progression from one need to the next and no indication that the various needs were necessarily of equal importance. This less structured account offers some diversity and flexibility as well as the messiness of reality.

Alderfer[9] produced a simplified model suggesting just three basic human needs: existence, relatedness and growth. Existence can be taken as similar to Maslow's physiological and safety needs. Relatedness is similar to Maslow's love and esteem needs and also to McClelland's need for affiliation. Alderfer's growth need is equivalent to Maslow's self-actualization and McClelland's needs for achievement or as Smith suggested, the need to become a 'proper object of respect'.

There is therefore some basic consistency among many theoreticians, more or less independent of their era, about the human needs which might motivate behaviour: basic needs (existence, food, shelter, clothing, safety, etc.), social needs (love, esteem, affiliation, relatedness, 'wants and fancies', etc.) and growth needs (achievement, self-actualization, 'frugality', etc.).

To this simple model Adams added the idea of equity,[10] i.e. the concepts of fairness and justice. This is not an absolute measure, but is a comparative one. An individual perceives his or her own treatment and compares it with the apparent treatment of others and so assesses the equity of their own treatment.

Growth needs appear to be the most powerful motivators once the basic needs have been satisfied. But growth means different things to different

---

6   Murray, H.A., (1938), *Explorations in Personality*, Oxford: Oxford University Press.
7   Atkinson, J.W., (1964), *An Introduction to Motivation*, London: Van Nostrand.
8   McClelland, D.C., Atkinson, J.W., Clark, R.A. and Lowell, E.L, (1953), *The Achievement Motive*, London: Van Nostrand.
9   Alderfer, C.P., (1972), *Existence, Relatedness and Growth*, New York: Free Press.
10 Adams, J.S., (1965), 'Inequity in Social Exchange', *Advances in Experimental Social Psychology*, Vol. 62, pp. 335–343.

individuals. For example, growth may, as Maslow indicated, lead certain individuals to make music, or paint or write poetry. These creative outlets are recognizable as satisfying the need for self-actualization. Others may feel more motivated to the achievement of quite different outcomes, such as great buildings, or feats of civil engineering, such as the bridges and tunnels of railway lines, or even the lines themselves. For others the creation and development of a new enterprise, contributes directly to, and involves in many various ways, the lives of other people.

Any such projects may be the focus of the growth needs for some individuals. For others the focus may be rather less heroic. Examples of Smith's amoral, self-interested 'economic man' certainly existed and for them the focus may well be on the acquisition of money and power. And as Smith suggested with some disdain, they may well be motivated by the ability to display their power or money in front of a wide audience with the expectation that they will be accorded respect, if not love, for their celebrity.

Lower level needs, including the need for equity, are likely to fall into the category of what Herzberg called hygiene factors which do not themselves motivate behaviour, but could well demotivate or aggravate if unsatisfied.

Using this simple model as the backdrop it seems clear that, initially at least, as Adam Smith suggested, it was the basic set of human needs which led people to initiate and accept the developments in agriculture which resulted not only in the population being more reliably fed but also the generation of an agricultural surplus simultaneously with the disadvantaging of some. Similarly, social needs, including the need for esteem from peers, would explain the unlimited market potential for all kinds of commodities, while growth needs among some sections of the population must have driven the accumulation of capital and the process of industrialization. At the same time, the lack of satisfaction of basic and social needs among other sections, and the obvious lack of equity, was clearly the cause of considerable and continuing discontent.

The rational, amoral, self-interested 'economic man' was always an inadequate substitute for this richly varied reality which encompasses human beings who also exhibit courage, generosity and kindness, as well as corruptibility, characteristics which economics is simply not equipped to address and therefore excludes from its analysis.

Agricultural Development

Prior to industrialization the main purpose of economic activity was to satisfy man's basic needs, that is, to provide food, shelter and clothing to support a subsistence society. Most activity was essentially localized, with each village being largely self-sufficient, having little need for long-distance communications. One of the critical prerequisites to breaking out of this subsistence economy was the creation of an agricultural surplus. Formerly the dominant notion had been that a farm should be just big enough to support a family. In motivational terms that would mean satisfying basic survival or subsistence needs. Such a unit would achieve satisfaction except in dearth years when poor harvests might result in hunger and disease or even famine. There would therefore be some motivation for the farmer to achieve an additional surplus and accumulate it as capital against more needy times.

Capital accumulation by the few also provided the funding to invest in new scientifically based methods which substantially raised productivity. But concomitant with this benign development was the conversion of the peasant subsistence farmer into the landless waged agricultural labourer who may from time to time find himself unemployed.

England's experience of this process was different from that on continental Europe, where the ancient rights of the peasant farmer were protected and still influence today's Common Agricultural Policy. The process in England was more ruthless. Though it culminated in the eighteenth century with larger landlords dispossessing the peasant by enclosing his land, the process of dispossession had actually started much earlier.

The breakdown of the old manorial system whereby the peasant worked his few strips of land and shared in labouring for the lord of the manor had started in England before 1348–49 when the Black Death gave it further impetus by killing off more than a third of the population. After the Black Death the lord of the manor was left without tenants to work his land and if he tried to buy in labour to do the job he found it in short supply and expensive, despite the Statute of Labourers which was intended, but failed, to fix wages at pre-Black Death rates. Without tenants and labour the lords of the manor were driven to give up agriculture themselves and to lease out their land for what they could get. By the fifteenth century, English agriculture was based to a significant extent on lease-holding tenant farmers and their labourers.

Major changes followed in English agriculture in the sixteenth century with sheep farming significantly replacing arable. The price obtainable for corn was controlled by the State in the interests of the consumer and its export was similarly restricted so returns to the farmer were limited and beyond his control. On the other hand there was a ready market for English wool which was long fibred and suitable for making into fine cloth for which there was also an unregulated and buoyant export market. Moreover sheep farming was less labour intensive than arable, making it viable when labour was in short supply, so it subsequently contributed to the re-emergence of a labour surplus. However, it could not be conducted on the old manorial system of scattered strips of land, requiring instead the creation of large sheep runs. This could be achieved by rationalizing and consolidating land holdings and enclosing them behind fences, walls, hedges and ditches.

The sixteenth-century enclosure movement dispossessed many of the remaining peasant farmers who joined the bands of unemployed roaming the countryside seeking work or begging. The eighteenth- century enclosure movement was therefore only the final completion of the process which turned the English peasant farmer into an agricultural labourer.

Enclosures enabled agricultural improvement which supported a growing population and the early development of larger-scale manufacture. In this buoyant economy, the prices of agricultural produce rose making it feasible for waste land to be brought under cultivation. At the same time common land which had not previously been enclosed and was still being used for peasant farmer subsistence, was enclosed to grow food for the market. From 1760 to 1800 there were 2,000 enclosures by Act of Parliament whereas in the previous 60 years there had been very few. The enclosure movement was significant in its economic effects but also as a rallying symbol of the dispossession of England's yeoman farmer. Enclosures were not achieved without substantial upheaval and some insurrection.

Common land could be enclosed either by buying up the rights of common right holders or by Act of Parliament, either of which was expensive. Sometimes such enclosure, for example, by an estate owner reasserting ancient rights which had been long ignored, could cause great resentment. Defoe in his 1722 *Tour through England and Wales* reported one such case, a Buckinghamshire landowner:

> *'Presuming upon his power, set up his pales, and took in a large parcel of land call'd Wiggington common ... the cottagers and farmers opposed it, by their complaints a great while; but finding he went on with his*

work, and resolv'd to do it, they rose upon him, pulled down his banks,
and forced up his pales, and carried away the wood, or set it on a heap
and burnt it; and this they did several times ...'[11]

Such aggravated action was widespread.

In addition to the enclosure movement there had also been a marked decline in small farms.

'The land tax evidence ... shows ... The major decline of small owners
and of small farmers in general must have occurred before 1760,
probably between about 1660 and 1750.'[12]

The reasons for that decline were various. Alternative occupations in trade, industry and the professions were growing making small farms less attractive both as an occupation and as an investment; many such small farms and land holdings were bought up by larger land owners. These effects applied unevenly across the country with small farms remaining strong in some areas where incomes were augmented by industrial earnings.

The dispossession of the yeoman farmer peasantry by the landowners and their tenants completed through the later eighteenth century was a significant part of the march of capital in English agriculture.

By the mid-eighteenth century, tenant farmers were managing bigger farm units that could benefit from the division of labour as well as various technical innovations, some of which required the application of more capital. For example, fertility was increased dramatically through the application of inventions such as the deep plough, the drill sower and machine hoe. Also a new crop rotation system was introduced based on the alternation of cereal crops with artificial grasses and winter roots such as turnips, swedes, etc., replacing the old system which required the land to be left fallow every third year. Not only did the new system effectively increase the land under cultivation by half, but the root crops also provided winter feed for livestock so the autumn cull of surplus animals, which had previously taken place on all farms across the country, became unnecessary. Livestock breeding was also hugely improved

---

11 Defoe, D., (1722), *A Tour Through England and Wales, Vol. 2*, J.M. Dent & Sons Ltd, Everyman edition published in 1928, p. 15.

12 Mingay, G.E., (1968), *Enclosure and the Small Farmer in the Age of the Industrial Revolution*, Studies in Economic History Series, London: Macmillan, p. 51.

by a more scientific approach. The development of breeds of sheep and cattle, enabled by enclosures, saw the doubling in weight of the main breeds in not much more than half a century. Such 'scientific' inputs to farming dramatically increased the efficiency and overall output of agriculture.

The main produce was in grain-stuffs and livestock which were the staple food, and barley which was the staple drink. Rye and oats were used to make bread and meal for the poor as well as feed for cattle and horses. With a surplus production over and above subsistence needs, agriculture was also able to support the development of other industries. For example, wheat was supplied to corn millers, bakers, distillers and starch makers. The corn millers supplied not only bakers but stationers, bookbinders, linen printers, trunk makers and paper hangers. Similarly, barley was supplied to distillers and brewers for the production of beer and ale and rye meal was supplied to the leather tanning industry.

Livestock supplied similarly broad end markets. Sheep supplied the wool textile industry and cattle supplied hides for tanners and various leather based industries. Fat from sheep and cattle supplied soap boilers and candle makers. Horns were used by cutlers and bones by glue manufacturers.

The development of agriculture demonstrated much that was good and bad about capital accumulation as well as some early examples of what might be referred to as commercial management. A whole class of people were dispossessed of their original land birthright but were compensated as wage earners so that, initially at least, they were significantly better off, though it was from their ranks that the homeless unemployed emerged and were often treated rather more as criminals than victims.

The immediate and long-term beneficiaries, the landlords and tenant farmers, were able to invest some of their surplus in improving their land and holdings, sometimes with a long-term perspective from which they themselves would be unable to benefit, for example the long-term plantation of trees on which the British navy depended up to and beyond the Battle of Trafalgar. Others, becoming the newly rich land owning class, became major investors in the new capital projects, including the transportation systems and newly emerging manufactures. These sections of the population, motivated by growth, addressed themselves to the management problems of forecasting and planning, command and control. Their success produced the surplus to invest without which the ensuing benefits could never have accrued.

Transportation Infrastructure

Another strand in the pre-industrial change, and a vital prerequisite to industrialization, was focused on internal travel and transportation: the development of the turnpike road system and canals, the turnpikes for personal transport and higher value goods, the canals for industrial freight, such as coal, stone, slate, clay and grain, which were all low-cost, heavy items uneconomic to transport by road.

Previously, the chief highway of England had been the sea, but travel was a long slow process. Ashton quotes an example of a pig iron load being delivered from Horsehay in Shropshire to Chester.[13] Its journey started by being transported by road a few miles to the river Severn. It was then loaded onto a barge and sent down river to Bristol where it was unloaded and put on a freight coaster ship to go round the Welsh coast to the river Dee where it was loaded onto a river barge and thence upstream to Chester. The journey was around 250 miles, involved four loadings and unloadings and took many weeks to accomplish even if the weather conditions remained fair. Many cargoes were lost as ships foundered in storms at sea and sometimes even in the rivers. Opening up the canals reduced the journey to 50 miles, eliminated any interference by bad weather, cut out most of the double handling and reduced the time in transit from an average of just less than three months to five days. This was not only much cheaper but also freed up huge amounts of cash tied up in goods in transit that could be invested in fixed capital.

Few of the English rivers were naturally navigable and most were also blocked by corn mill dams and other obstacles to shipping which charged for their opening. In the seventeenth century a number of rivers had been 'improved' and made navigable and this process continued apace in the early eighteenth century by the formation of navigation companies largely financed by merchants who stood to gain from their development. Improvements included the removal of weirs and dams, the deepening of channels, the building of locks and also the shortening of routes by digging new 'cuts'. From this it was a short step to the great capital-consuming enterprise of canal building which started in the 1750s.

Canals were not new. The Romans built the Fossdyke from Lincoln to the River Trent, for both drainage and navigation, in around AD 50. The Grand

---

13   Ashton, T.S., (1955), *An Economic History of England: The Eighteenth Century*, London: Methuen & Co, p. 71.

Canal of China was completed in the tenth century and the 150-mile long Canal du Midi in France which connected the Mediterranean to the Atlantic via the Garonne River was completed in 1681. Nor was canal lock technology new. The pound lock was invented by the Chinese in AD 983 and the still familiar V-shaped mitre gate held together by the water pressure is generally attributed to Leonardo da Vinci. What was new was the creation of a whole system of canals.

The Duke of Bridgewater started the canal mania when he employed James Brindley to build a canal connecting his coal mines at Worsley to the coal consuming city of Manchester. The project involved building an aqueduct and various tunnels into the mines. The reduced cost of delivery to the end users in Manchester substantially lowered the price of coal and demonstrated the viability of canal transport. There followed a number of long distance navigations, with Brindley as the leading canal engineer of his time. He largely built the so-called 'Grand Cross' of canals which linked the four great river basins of England: the Thames, Severn, Humber and Mersey.

Building major infrastructure projects like this involved facing a number of what we would now refer to as management problems that had not been previously confronted. The canal engineers faced all the practical details of surveying the route and estimating the costs likely to be involved. It was necessary also to draw up a petition for an Act of Parliament to be passed approving the project. This was expensive as was bribing objectors to the proposed canal and compensating private land owners through whose territory the canal would go, as well as sometimes compensating navigation owners for their loss of toll income. Funds had to be raised to finance the project, mainly by the sale of company shares. It usually took several years for a canal to be completed and so companies necessarily raised further funds by mortgages and issues of bonds or promissory notes. The ingenuity with which capital funding was raised was one of the major contributions of the canal movement to the capital accumulation and industrialization project.

In addition the engineers, either resident engineer or clerk of works, had to procure supplies of material and equipment, assemble large numbers of 'navvies' (short for navigation labourers, i.e. pick and shovel men) often in remote places, arrange their board and lodging and supervise their work. Managing 500 or so unskilled hard drinking men scattered over miles of countryside no doubt presented some new problems for the engineer. Brindley's approach was to devolve responsibility for specific projects such as locks or bridges, down to contractors who were paid a fixed price for each item. For the main cuts it was normal to agree with groups of men a price per cubic yard of earth and stone removed. As well as pick and shovel labourers there were large numbers of brick makers, quarrymen, bricklayers, miners and tunnellers as well as different groups of skilled artisans. The division of labour between different specializations considerably exceeded that required in agriculture. In addition canal building involved many specialized tools and items of equipment. Bridgewater had barges fitted out as masons', carpenters' and blacksmiths' shops so that work could proceed as the project progressed. From the start of the project to its completion and the commencement of its ability to earn and pay back, a substantial investment of capital was absorbed, far in excess of that required by any earlier enterprises such as the overseas trading companies.

Similar problems were confronted with the building of turnpikes. Previously the road system had just about been good enough for the local farmer, or pedlar or for a packhorse laden with woollen or linen goods. But they didn't serve satisfactorily as main roads between major cities. Their foundations were weak, drainage extremely limited, the narrow wheels of carriages made deep ruts and cattle further damaged the surface in wet weather. Personal transport by road, other than on horseback, was extremely slow. Ashton reports a Roderick Random wishing to go from Newcastle to London first looked for passage by ship.[14] He was persuaded by the perils of the sea to go by road on foot and overtook a wagon that had set out on the same journey two days before him.

The problem was largely one of organization. Maintenance and upkeep of roads was legally the responsibility of each local parish that generally employed out-of-work and unpaid paupers on road maintenance. National legislation was mainly focused on defining the sorts of traffic allowed which was largely concerned with the width of wheels, and the relative tolls that could be charged. Wider wheels were less damaging to the road, but narrower wheels faster and more comfortable for the traveller. By the mid-eighteenth century, however, it was clear that attention should be focused on the road itself rather than its traffic.

Improvements were initially achieved following enclosures of agricultural land permitting new routes to be established and often paid for by the proprietors of coal mines and other burgeoning industrial enterprises in order

---

14 Ashton, T.S., (1955), *An Economic History of England: The Eighteenth Century*, London: Methuen & Co, p. 78.

to improve the transport of their goods to market. The turnpikes, established by Acts of Parliament, transferred responsibility for the maintenance of roads from the parishes to trusts which took responsibility for the whole length of a road through many parishes and which charged the road's users for its building and maintenance. The new turnpikes were established with gates at each end where users were charged tolls and with fences or walls at the side of the road to ensure users were not able to avoid the toll gates.

Building the new turnpikes involved many processes similar to those of canal building. They were major projects involving substantial investment and a prolonged time delay before they were able to generate any income in return. The engineers involved, such as Telford and Macadam, faced many of the same issues confronting the canal builders, planning the routes, estimating the costs, solving the engineering problems presented by the particular terrain, negotiating with parliament and local landlords and authorities, managing large teams of navvies, semi-skilled and skilled workers and artisans as well as raising the funds for the whole project.

Canals and turnpikes were great infrastructural projects which absorbed huge amounts of capital. The roads had to be supplied with fences, gates, bridges and tollhouses and canals with reservoirs, locks, sluices, towpaths, bridges and quays. All of which building needed not only labour and skilled craftsmen, but also new tools and equipment. New types of craft and vehicles were needed, as well as new inns, stables and warehouses. They added nothing immediately to the supply of goods for consumption. But they created substantial employment for others including the satisfaction of the navvies' demands for food, drink, clothing and shelter.

These new infrastructural projects, as the new agriculture had also, substituted capital for labour. Phillips noted how, for example, standing at Brindley's Barton aqueduct over the Irwell navigation, you could see at the same time:

> 'seven or eight stout fellows labouring like slaves to drag a boat slowly up the Irwell, and one horse or mule, or sometimes two men at the most, drawing five or six of the Duke's barges linked together, at a great rate upon the canal.'[15]

15 Phillips, J., (1792), *History of Inland Navigation*, p. 87, quoted in Ashton T.S., (1955), *An Economic History of England: The Eighteenth Century*, London: Methuen & Co, p. 85.

The substitution of capital had consolidated the dispossession of the peasantry into an unskilled waged or unemployed pool of labour. Whilst a long way short of the deployment of robots in modern manufacture, it was the beginning of the process which first created the pool of labour and then displaced that labour from the process of manufacture. Nevertheless the process of capital accumulation and labour substitution improved immeasurably the degree to which most people were able to satisfy their basic needs, as can be seen in the records of mortality, health and population growth previously cited.

Pre-industrial and Domestic Manufacturing

At the start of the eighteenth century manufacturing all over England was only accomplished through small-scale operations as had been done for preceding centuries. There were no large-scale manufacturing operations and no large units of employment. Coal getting, for example, was by shallow bell pits employing only small numbers, typically no more than thirty, and usually aiming only to provide for local consumption rather than sending to more distant markets. There were no large-scale deep coal mines and the application of capital in mining was limited. The same was true of brick manufacture and also for iron founding. Abraham Darby's foundry and forges at Coalbrookdale had worked on a small scale through the early eighteenth century making domestic iron pans. It was not till the last two to three decades of the century that significant expansion was achieved following the successful development of coke iron-making. And it was not till 1795 that Matthew Boulton and James Watt commenced construction of the Soho Foundry which was to establish the precision and accuracy of metal finishing that enabled them to produce the reliably working pistons and cylinders, critical components of steam engine manufacture.

It was that other basic of a subsistence society, clothing, which led the industrialization process. The textile industries had long been major employers, but most of the enterprises were small with only a few employing large numbers of workers. Even among the larger employers, nearly all the employees worked from their own homes where they operated domestic-scale equipment. The machinery had to be small enough to be sited in the kitchen or possibly in purpose-built spinsters' cottage lofts. Overall the capital involved in the textile industries was not substantial by later standards and its ownership was spread thinly. The acquisition of a spinning machine or loom was not completely out of reach of the one who operated it though mostly they were owned by the employer.

The textile industry employed many supply chain middle men. For example, a fustian dealer, fustian being the basic coarse cotton fabric, might employ a country manufacturer to put out raw cotton and yarn to carders, spinners and weavers. The country manufacturer would be charged for the materials and he paid the wages of the people he put the work out to. He was then repaid for the completed materials plus a commission for his own expertise and labour in organizing, putting out the work, paying of wages and collecting finished materials at depots rather than the cottage door. Raw fibre was collected by spinsters (traditionally women and girls) from the depot and they took it home and spun it into yarn, returned it to the depot and were paid by the piece. Similarly, yarn was collected by the weavers (usually male) who took it home and wove it into fabric before returning it to the depot for payment.

The country manufacturer, who also played a limited role as owner at least of working capital, had no responsibilities for employing people or keeping them in work. There was no need for large central premises and overhead costs beyond the setting up of a small depot for the distribution and collection of material.

The dealer's prime task was to sell the finished product and to be an effective buyer and seller of materials so that a reasonable margin could be earned between the two transactions. He could expand his business simply by buying more raw fibre and having it distributed to more spinners and weavers so long as he had a ready market for the product he was handling.

Superficially at least there were considerable advantages for the home workers in this domestic system of production. They had greater control over their lives, over when and how fast they worked, and their children working at home were less susceptible to the abuse and exploitation they later experienced under the factory system. But there were downsides. Because the output from the system was so small the workers were paid very little and were not far above the breadline even when working full time. There are many contemporary accounts from Defoe and others which suggest their lives were far from idyllic.

This flexible way of organizing business required the dealer to focus on three issues which we now recognize as problems of management. Firstly, it was vital to manage logistics efficiently so as to eliminate any cash being tied up unnecessarily in work in progress. He would require the manufacturer to operate timely collection by, and delivery from, the spinners and weavers which would have played a significant part in the manufacturer's controllable costs. Secondly, the dealer, and therefore also his manufacturer, would also be responsible for ensuring the work was completed at the required quality of workmanship which meant developing close relationships of trust with the highly skilled independent spinners and weavers. Finally, it was also vital for the dealer and manufacturer to create and maintain effective relationships with the various other parties to the business such as customers and suppliers as well as the spinners and weavers. All these relationships determined the quality, cost, price and availability of finished product. If they were not well managed the dealer and his manufacturer would fail. If they were well managed then any or all the middle men would be able to earn a surplus profit and be able to accumulate some capital for future investment and growth.

Elements of Management

Economic activities generally entail some aspects of management for their effective completion. Farming, once it had progressed beyond simple subsistence, required the accumulation of some capital to invest in new equipment and machinery, the development of new and better ways of doing things and the identification of how to sell the surplus produce for wider food markets or new industrial uses.

The development of the internal transport infrastructure with canals and turnpikes produced a whole new set of management problems. The canal and road engineers needed to be accomplished managers, envisaging a completely new scale of project and having to plan their profitable completion as well as control their actual implementation. The scale of the projects and therefore of the funding required for their completion was completely new, as was the long-term delay before the commencement of any income and therefore return to the providers of capital. In addition they had to arrange the procurement of all the necessary materials and other resources including, most importantly of all, the people who would do the actual work building the canal or road. And they had to devise practical ways of recruiting, organizing and rewarding that new form of migrant labour and controlling their work so that it was completed in conformity with required quality standards and on time. The technical engineering problem that had to be overcome along the way was completely without precedent. The funding of such projects required planning and control over costs and timing in order to generate returns to the providers of funds.

The entrepreneur played the key role in pre-industrial textile manufacture. It was the French economist, Jean Baptiste Say, who introduced the term 'entrepreneur' to describe the role which combined management with some element of ownership in the creative, developmental role understood today. The element of ownership might start off quite small, but from that toehold in ownership the entrepreneur would seek to grow and accumulate an increasing share of the surplus and consolidate their position in ownership. Identification with the best long-term interests of the business was crucial to the entrepreneur concept. It was a quite different role from that of, for example, the travelling salesman who was not expecting to revisit the same territory. Such a salesman, being an amoral 'economic man', would naturally seek, by fair means or foul, to squeeze every ounce of advantage for himself out of every sale. The entrepreneur, on the other hand, would focus on a continuing relationship with customers and be concerned to demonstrate his worthiness of their trust.

In pre-industrial textiles the entrepreneur might have been the dealer who started the process in motion and who also sold finished product, or the country manufacturer who was the one with direct contact with the spinners and weavers. His task required foresight and planning as well as some command and control in achieving an essentially innovative and profitable result.

Logistics and quality control, as well as stakeholder relations, were key to the entrepreneur's success. Profitability was also of crucial importance as without it there would be no surplus to reinvest to ensure the organization's survival and future prosperity. But the necessary retention of surplus could only be achieved by strictly controlling all costs including, most importantly of all, the wages paid to the workers.

All these problems were to present themselves when the development of the factory system of manufacturing was undertaken, but by then they were not completely new. They had already been confronted and means of their solution identified.

2

An Economic Theory of Industry and Commerce

The generation of an economic surplus came after millennia of, at best, subsistence living. The explanation of why it happened when and where it did remains incomplete, though theories abound. Adam Smith wrote *An Inquiry into the Nature and Causes of the Wealth of Nations* just as the very first examples of industrial development were being established. His theory of economics was developed further as a consequence of industrialization and became in its turn influential on governments in shaping that process. More recently economic theory has played an overwhelmingly influential role in shaping the job of management itself.

Smith probably started his investigations prior to 1760; his experience in France up to 1766 clearly added a more cosmopolitan flavour to his work and especially informed his attack on mercantilism. He finally published in 1776. He did not live to see the impoverishment and misery of life in the factories, mills and mill towns of nineteenth-century England. That was left to his successors, Ricardo, Malthus, Say and others. Nevertheless, he acknowledged aspects of the dehumanizing impact of the division of labour.

Smith laid out the territory of economic theory and established its basic logic. The subsequent innovations and changes to the main thrust of his model have been relatively minor even though the industrial and economic world the model seeks to explain has changed beyond recognition.

The emergence and development of what came to be known as classical theory had substantial influence on the development of management though that influence was not immediately obvious. The early industrializers were probably unaware of economic theory, though the importance of Smith's work was publicly acknowledged in 1792 by Pitt the Younger addressing parliament:

> (Smith's) *'extensive knowledge of detail and depth of philosophical research will, I believe, furnish the best solution to every question connected with the history of commerce and with the question of political economy.'*[1]

Economic theory and political and industrial practice were interdependent from the beginning of industrialization and remain so today, perhaps more powerfully than ever.

Mercantilism and Trade Protection

During the period of achieving an economic surplus and its initial investment in infrastructure and manufacturing, government's role in those economic activities was essentially piecemeal and discontinuous. It was more concerned with the matter of trade and commerce. England had long seen itself as competing with the other European states, especially France and Spain, for a finite amount of trade with Africa, Asia and America. Governments sought to regulate that trade through tariffs and subsidies so as to enrich themselves and become more powerful.

Spain acquired precious metals from its South American colonies and its accumulated bullion was accepted as a measure of that nation's wealth. This led to a rather curious exaggeration of the importance of bullion which still persists in some quarters today. To compete, in the absence of gold and silver mines, England had to accumulate a surplus of exports over imports. This favourable balance of trade was seen as crucial. So government's aim was simply to impose tariffs to limit imports and offer subsidies to stimulate exports.

Domestic industries and agriculture were protected from overseas competition and subsidies were paid to producers who made a surplus for export. Initially these trade balances were considered for the individual industry but later it was agreed that what mattered was the overall balance of trade, with imbalances allowed in particular industries. The simple belief, which was later

---

1   William Pitt the Younger, parliamentary speech introducing 1792 budget, quoted in Galbraith, J.K., (1987), *A History of Economics*, London: Hamish Hamilton, p. 61.

referred to as mercantilism, was that governments had a duty to intervene in trade so as to grow the national wealth at the expense of 'competing' nations.

By the late seventeenth century the wool trade, for example, was protected by heavy import tariffs and wearing certain imported cloths was forbidden by law. Laws were also passed to make the use of English cloth mandatory for some uniforms and, in 1667, there was even a law which ordered the dead be buried wrapped in English wool cloth. Moreover, the emigration of skilled artisans was forbidden in case they should give any industrial secrets away to foreign competitors and the export of machinery was made similarly illegal.

Foreign trade was also directly forbidden in some instances. Import of French wines, brandies, linen and paper was illegal, while trade with Portugal, which was thought to be in favourable balance, was encouraged. Transporting goods between England and overseas possessions had to use English ships. The colonial trade produced significant surpluses, with the English heavily involved in trade in spices and also the trade in slaves kidnapped in Africa and sold in America.

Government also involved itself in awarding monopolies both in commodities and also in geographical areas to the great trading enterprises which were set up as joint stock companies, initially with stockholders acquiring a share of the financial responsibility and profits of individual expeditions. These were risky projects; many such expeditions were unprofitable and in some cases the ships simply did not return. Protection in the form of a royal charter granting monopoly rights provided some compensation for the assumption of such risk.

This interventionist approach to trade, which had long informed government policy, was firmly in place when industrialization first began. Although there had been some energetic objections to various individual trade limitations, notably the prohibitions on French trade – especially wine and brandy – there had been no assault on the mercantilist system itself until Adam Smith pressed the argument in favour of free trade.

Accumulation of Capital

Smith's prime concern was with the progress of society and he saw industrialization and the wealth it created as a key turning point. At the same time, he recognized the inequality industrialization caused and the fundamental need to do something to alleviate it. He expounded a simplistic model of society's progress, identifying four ages of man defined according to how they earned their subsistence.[2]

First, the age of the hunter-gatherer, who was innocent of the notion of private property and government.

Second, the age of the shepherd, who necessarily owned property in the form of flocks and herds and so had some simple notions of property, justice and government.

Third, the age of agricultural man, who owned private property and had a relatively complex legal system to protect it and government to enact and oversee the law. Justice was corrective in that it punished those who harmed another person, their property or their reputation, rather than being distributive, that is ensuring an equitable distribution of riches.

Finally, the age of commercial man which was the phase then being entered. The growth of capital and inequality raised the question of why citizens should be obedient to government or should respect authority acquired through wealth.

Smith's crude fable emphasized the progression of inequality as the consequence of economic progress with the property owners developing government and a protective legal system to permit continued economic development and further inequality.

Such a model might accept that society may always have been hierarchical – hierarchy exists even in animal groups – but a critical development was when the hierarchy became based on the ownership of property, the distribution of which generally had little to do with justice. The old aristocracy and landed gentry usually came by their possessions for no better reason than that they or their ancestors happened to be on the winning side. When land was plentiful it was cheap and of limited use beyond subsistence. It was owned but it was not energetically exploited because there was no market for surplus produce. Over the centuries landed and landless had co-existed in a generally accepted inequitable interdependence.

---

2   Smith, A., (1776), *Wealth of Nations*, Book V, Chapter 1, Part First.

However, when the economy stirred, some of the landed gentry discovered they had untold wealth under their feet. The Duke of Bridgewater, for example, found he was the owner of rich seams of coal and built his canal to get it cheaply to market. Others of the old aristocracy enjoyed similar riches, but in aggregate their wealth was wholly insufficient to fuel industrialization. That had to be funded from within the industrial process itself

Richard Arkwright, for example, who built the world's first cotton mill, was the son of a tailor. He was the youngest of seven children, without the funds even to pay for schooling. He was trained as a barber and subsequently a wig maker. With no money to invest in industrial development, he learned about the possibilities of a new spinning machine, joined forces with some of the inventors, managed to borrow the money to invest in a prototype machine, perfected it and then managed to engage the interest of other investors to finance the building and equipping of the first cotton spinning mill.

Borrowing by entrepreneurs such as Arkwright was duly made easier by the establishment of banks. Initially banks were merely safe places for the deposit of money in its various forms and all the money so deposited was kept solely for the disposal of the depositor. Payment of a debt would be accomplished by the movement of money from one deposit to the other. Bankers were therefore holding deposits of money which were largely inactive and in due course they began to lend a proportion of those deposits to borrowers who wanted to invest in projects which would otherwise have been far beyond their reach. It was unlikely that all depositors would require their money back at the same time, unless of course word got out that the bank was insecure. So the proportion of deposits that banks could afford to lend out was a matter of fine judgment: lending too large a proportion might be too risky, but lending too little meant they would be turning down opportunities to do good business and, more importantly, restricting the amount of new funds available for investment.

Investors in an industrial project had to be persuaded of its viability and the likelihood of it generating a sufficient return to make their investment worthwhile. The project had to earn a surplus having paid all its expenses including its employees' wages. Wages were ever in contention both in practice and in the curious theories developed to justify them being kept at subsistence levels. Beyond these expense items the firm needed to earn a surplus for the entrepreneur to either retain or to invest in the firm's future development. From this retained profit, entrepreneurs like Arkwright accumulated considerable personal wealth, which was a prime source of capital funding for the new industries.

Division of Labour

Human beings have always divided work so that different individuals specialize in particular jobs and become more proficient at their completion. Without speculating on the ways of the hunter-gatherers of pre-history, at least as early as ancient Greece, specialization was a well-established way of life. Plato not only refers to the system, but justifies it on the grounds that:

> 'no two of us are born exactly alike. We have different natural aptitudes which fit us for different jobs.'[3]

He goes on to describe division of labour between the farmer, the weaver and the shoe maker, and the smiths and craftsmen needed to make their various tools and equipment.

The degree of specialization increased as economies developed and an ever larger surplus was produced. Petty, born 100 years before Adam Smith, noted the division of labour used in Dutch shipyards. In English shipyards workers would build ships in sequence, finishing one before starting the next. The Dutch used several groups of workers, completing the same specialized tasks on each ship. He subsequently applied the same principles in his Irish survey splitting the workload into skilled and unskilled jobs, passing the unskilled jobs to untrained workers.[4] He also gave the example of watch manufacture in which the division of labour between the various watch components reduced the cost, enabling the price of watches to be reduced thereby increasing demand. The principle is quoted as applying quite generally to all trades.

> 'The Labourer will still have as much wages, and will consequently be enabled to purchase more Conveniences of Life; so that every interest in the Nation would receive a Benefit from an Increase of our working People.'[5]

---

3   Plato, (~ 375 BC), *The Republic*, translated by D. Lee, Penguin Classics, Part II, Book II, p. 57.
4   Petty, W., (1691), *Political Anatomy of Ireland* based on his experience in 1672 and published posthumously.
5   Hughes, J., (1711), 'Nihil largiundo gloriam adeptus est', *The Spectator*, No 232, 26 November, available at: http://meta.montclair.edu/spectator/text/1711/november/spectator232.xml

Similarly Mandeville in 1728:

> *'If one will wholly apply himself to the making of Bows and Arrows, whilst another provides Food, a third builds Huts, a fourth makes Garments, and a fifth Utensils, they not only become useful to one another, but the Callings and Employments themselves will in the same Number of Years receive much greater Improvements, than if all had been promiscuously follow'd by every one of the Five...'*[6]

Hume also refers to the 'partition of employments' drawing attention to the benefits on a broader front, including not only the increase in manpower and skills, but also to reduced exposure to accidents.

> *'Tis by this additional force, ability, and security, that society becomes advantageous'.*[7]

The ideas of specialization and its many benefits were clearly well understood by 1776 when Smith famously elaborated it in *Wealth of Nations*. His first sentence reads:

> *'The greatest improvement in the productive powers of labour, and the greater part of the skill, dexterity, and judgment with which it is anywhere directed, or applied, seem to have been the effects of the division of labour.'*

His particular example was pin making, which he himself described as a 'very trifling manufacture'. Smith emphasized the benefits from specialization of labour separately from those gained through the application of capital which had not then become as decisive as it was later to become. Whereas one man making a pin from beginning to end would perhaps make one a day, 'and certainly could not make twenty', by the division of labour, ten men could make 'upwards of 48,000 pins in a day'.

> *'One man draws out the wire, another straights it, a third cuts it, a fourth points it, a fifth grinds it at the top for receiving the head'*[8] and so forth.

---

6 Mandeville, B., *The Fable of the Bees,* available within *The Enlightenment Fable* by E.J.Hundert (1994), Vancouver: University of British Columbia.

7 Hume, D., (1729), *A Treatise of Human Nature* republished in 2004 by the Dover Philosophical Classics imprint of Dover Publications Inc of New York, p. 345.

8 Smith, A., (1776), *Wealth of Nations*, Book 1, Chapter 1, 'Of the Division of Labour', p. 12.

The benefits in terms of output and cost were clear. The further benefits for society at large in terms of reduced prices and therefore raised living standards were also obvious. But that was only the beginning. Benefits accrued in terms of increasing expertise and matching that expertise with specialized tools and equipment. The more specialized a job could be defined, the greater the specialized expertise that could be developed leading to technical innovations in the form of more efficient and sophisticated tools and equipment as well as improved methods of working.

Smith, as others before him, recognized the universal applicability of the benefits of specialization across all human activity, including even 'philosophy or speculation', in which, as in every other sphere, the result would be improving 'dexterity and saving time'. Somewhere between pin making and philosophy, the idea of specialization could also be applied to the labour of management itself.

A consequence of even the most primitive forms of division of labour was that individuals reduced their own self-sufficiency and therefore needed to trade and barter. As specialization increased and with it the benefits in terms of productivity, reduced prices and raised standards of living, so the degree of self-sufficiency diminished and thus the areas over which people needed to trade increased, so markets became more important. Markets, initially physical locations where trade and barter took place, developed and diffused so that the term market came to have a less specific, more abstract meaning.

Regulation of markets, or interference in their free operations, as was done by governments under the mercantilist system, only served to constrain and inhibit their development and ultimately limit their size and therefore restrict the degree to which labour could be specialized and the cost of production reduced. Thus, classical theory derived from Smith rejected the idea of regulation or interference with markets since that could only reduce the rate of economic growth.

However, the division of labour was not automatic; labour did not necessarily specialize in particular tasks, or do so by mutual consent or by some democratic process. The process and the consequent investment in, and application of, specialized tools and equipment provided from accumulated capital, had to be initiated and directed by those responsible. Moreover, those responsible were also in a position, should they be so minded, to see that the division of labour and the distribution of its benefits were accomplished equitably.

For all its manifest benefits Smith himself was also concerned by some of the ill effects of the division of labour, warning that it leads to a 'mental mutilation' in workers:

> 'The man whose whole life is spent in performing a few simple operations, of which the effects are perhaps always the same, or very nearly the same, has no occasion to exert his understanding or to exercise his invention in finding out expedients for removing difficulties which never occur. He naturally loses, therefore, the habit of such exertion, and generally becomes as stupid and ignorant as it is possible for a human creature to become. The torpor of his mind renders him not only incapable of relishing or bearing a part in any rational conversation, but of conceiving any generous, noble, or tender sentiment, and consequently of forming any just judgment concerning many even of the ordinary duties of private life. Of the great and extensive interests of his country he is altogether incapable of judging, and unless very particular pains have been taken to render him otherwise, he is equally incapable of defending his country in war. The uniformity of his stationary life naturally corrupts the courage of his mind, and makes him regard with abhorrence the irregular, uncertain, and adventurous life of a soldier. It corrupts even the activity of his body, and renders him incapable of exerting his strength with vigour and perseverance in any other employment than that to which he has been bred. His dexterity at his own particular trade seems, in this manner, to be acquired at the expense of his intellectual, social, and martial virtues. But in every improved and civilised society this is the state into which the labouring poor, that is, the great body of the people, must necessarily fall, unless government takes some pains to prevent it.'[9]

Smith's proposal was to counterbalance these effects of such work by attending to the education of the workers. His concern for aspects of social welfare has largely been forgotten by his Friedmanite successors. He had previously explained his basic sympathy:

> 'How SELFISH soever man may be supposed, there are evidently some principles in his nature, which interest him in the fortune of others, and render their happiness necessary to him, though he derives nothing from it, except the pleasure of seeing it. Of this kind is pity or compassion, the

---

9   Smith, A., (1776), *Wealth of Nations*, Book V, Chapter 1, Part III, Article II: 'Of the Expense of the Institutions for the Education of Youth', p. 429.

emotion which we feel for the misery of others, when we either see it, or
are made to conceive it in a very lively manner.'[10]

The conflict of interest between those who accumulated capital and those who were dispossessed of what little they had was multiplied many times over by the industrialization process. Whilst citing the citizens' pure self-interest as the solid foundation of economic progress Smith nevertheless acknowledged, and had sympathy for, all humanity including especially those who were inevitably disadvantaged by industrialization.

While he counselled against governments interfering directly in free markets, he nevertheless advocated a progressive taxation system whereby the rich pay proportionately more of their wealth and income than the less rich, and the taxes be deployed to benefit the poor, for example, through their education.

> 'The subjects of every state ought to contribute towards the support of
> the government, as nearly as possible, in proportion to their respective
> abilities; that is, in proportion to the revenue which they respectively
> enjoy under the protection of the state ... It is not very unreasonable that
> the rich should contribute to the public expense, not only in proportion
> to their revenue, but something more than in that proportion.'[11]

The more recent Friedmanite interpretation of Smith's economics which dominated government thinking well into the twenty-first century arguing for low non-progressive taxation was clearly in contravention of Smith's own approach.

Markets, Trade and Comparative Advantage

The division of labour resulted in reduced prices and consequently increased the amount of goods that could be bought. The resultant diversified economy depended for its prosperity on an increasing level of trading between its members, each, according to the theory, acting from self-interest to achieve the most favourable outcome for themselves. As productive output grew, so the size of markets also had to grow if they were to absorb the increased output. The growth in markets could only be maintained by reducing prices and that

---

10   Smith, A., (1759), *The Theory of Moral Sentiments*, Part VI, Section I, p. 3.
11   Smith, A., (1776), *Wealth of Nations*, Book V, Chapter 2, Part 2, 'Of Taxes', p. 451.

was made possible by increased division of labour and the application of accumulated capital to the newly specialized tasks. The lower the price of a product, the more it would be bought. The more that could be produced and sold, the greater the justified investment in plant and equipment and thus the feasible extent of the specialization of labour and the greater the resultant cost savings.

Such a virtuous cycle was limited only by the size of markets. The bigger the market, the greater the investment that could be justified and the greater the consequent opportunity to specialize. Therefore it was crucial to eliminate anything which inhibited or restricted the freedom to trade or distorted the effect of market forces. Thus Smith's advocacy of unrestricted free trade was clear, both domestically and internationally, and his direct attack justified on mercantilism and its tariffs and protections which interfered directly with open markets.

Free-market economics, based on the 'economic man' assumption, proved perhaps to be the most influential of Smith's contributions. It suggested that the combined efforts of many amoral 'economic men', working purely to maximize their own wealth in competition with each other, served to maximize the aggregate wealth of the population.

Freedom was essential to enable the unrestricted competition to produce cost reductions and the means by which prices would be forced to a minimum for the benefit of the general population. But Smith was mindful of the fact that those self-interested competitors would seek to place limitations on competition:

> 'People of the same trade seldom meet together, even for merriment and diversion, but the conversation ends in a conspiracy against the public, or in some contrivance to raise prices. It is impossible indeed to prevent such meetings, by any law which either could be executed, or would be consistent with liberty and justice. But though the law cannot hinder people of the same trade from sometimes assembling together, it ought to do nothing to facilitate such assemblies; much less to render them necessary.'[12]

Any associations that might result in fixing prices, or any cartel arrangements, were anathema to Smith. And he was profoundly opposed to monopoly which

---

12 Smith, A., (1776), *Wealth of Nations*, Book I, Chapter 10, Part 2, p. 129.

was the extreme case of such limitations on competition. Under mercantilism, monopolies were routinely granted by government as charters to the trading companies, granting unique legal rights to trade. Not only did such monopolies limit the development of markets, but they were also disadvantageous to the monopolizing nation which thus cut itself off from the real source of economic success which was competition. The only economically justifiable argument for monopoly was of a limited term such as when a new and dangerous overseas trade was being opened up. The argument for that was exactly similar to the justification for a limited-term patent protection. But when the limited term was completed, free-market competition should ensue for the benefit of the general population.

There is some incoherence within Smith's work. What survives most powerfully today is the clear and simple 'greed is good', amoral philosophy which proscribes interference with or hindrance of market forces and seeks to protect the total freedom to compete and trade on the grounds that such a system ensures maximum economic growth and aggregate wealth. What has survived less securely is his recognition of inequality as an inevitable result of economic growth and his argument that its worst effects should be offset by a more than proportionately progressive system of taxation which should fund further social progress of the poor.

Further understanding of how markets worked was achieved by Smith's successors, David Ricardo and Jean-Baptiste Say, both born as *Wealth of Nations* was being published. They had the great advantage of living through the industrialization process and seeing the immense changes to the economy and to society that resulted.

Say was a fearless advocate of free markets and his famous contribution to economic theory was a 'law of markets' which stated that there would always be demand for any level of supply. This was because every item produced and sold would provide a return to the producer which would have to be spent or saved, and if saved it would be invested and subsequently spent. Thus the supply of goods would create the funds to satisfy its own demand. There could never be an oversupply of goods.

From time to time there was clear evidence of oversupply in particular industries, with the resulting discontinuities, increases in unemployment and consequent further reductions in demand. However, Say's law was applied at the level of the whole economy: in aggregate there could be no shortage of demand for products and full employment would therefore be maintained. When there appeared to be general oversupply and the resulting unemployment appeared to exist across the whole economy, it was explained away as a temporary situation to which there would be a natural adjustment after which normal supply and demand rules would again apply. Thus business cycles became part of the generic economic model. Say's law clearly did not work in practice, but it nevertheless remained a key concept of classical economics till well into the twentieth century.

The importance of Say's law of markets was that it suggested the economic system was self-regulating and therefore it served to reinforce the classical idea of unrestricted free markets. The free market had within it the means of its own optimization. If sufficient demand was assured, then attempts to interfere or regulate markets would merely produce a sub-optimal result.

Ricardo elaborated the treatment of monopolistic markets and the dangers they posed to the common good. He distinguished between resources which were reproducible (i.e. copiable), which would be priced according to their labour value, and those that were not, which would be priced according to their scarcity value. The non-copiable resources were the basis of monopolistic markets in which the monopolist could achieve higher prices and rates of profit at lower levels of output than would be achieved in a competitive market. Ricardo noted that in fact almost everything was reproducible and so the evils of monopoly were limited. The only exceptions he noted were:

> 'rare statues and pictures, scarce books and coins and wines of a peculiar quality which can be made only from grapes grown on a particular soil.'[13]

These concepts of monopoly were rather different from the simple idea of monopoly granted and protected by law. The creation of monopolistic markets, or at least the limitation of free competition, as referred to by Ricardo, is familiar in today's markets with their emphasis on differentiated and branded products which command a premium price.

Ricardo broadened the theory of competitive markets to international trade, focusing on the comparative costs enjoyed in different countries and the gains that could be made from trade between countries with different inherent costs. He used

---

13 Ricardo, D., (1817), *The Principles of Political Economy and Taxation*, republished in 2004, with an introduction by F.W. Kolthammer, by Dover Publications Inc of New York, p. 6.

the example of Anglo-Portuguese trade. Portugal could produce wine cheaper than England, i.e. it had a comparative advantage, while England had a comparative advantage in the production of woollen cloth. It would therefore be profitable for Portugal to specialize in the supply of wine and sell some to England for less than it would cost England to produce, while England could supply cloth to Portugal for less than it would cost to produce in Portugal. Thus both nations benefit from the trade. If all countries specialized in the goods where they enjoyed a comparative advantage, the generation of wealth across the world would increase.

Thus Ricardo's law of comparative advantage, like Say's law, reinforced the argument in favour of free unregulated trade.

Alternative views did exist. Malthus, for example, challenged Say's Law that supply would create its own demand and regarded markets as naturally unstable. Producers may well focus on securely establishing their businesses rather than consuming all, which would reduce funds available for demand. Thus overproduction and subsequent economic recession was perfectly feasible, if not inevitable, from time to time.

The theory suggested that competitive markets, with competitors seeking only to maximize their own profit, would result in aggregate social welfare being maximized. However, the theory did not address the distribution of social welfares, which in practice was quite obviously unequal. If participants adhered to the self-interested model, as theory taught them they should, the theoretical result would inevitably be that the strong would exploit the weak. And that was also the practical outcome.

Remunerating Labour and Capital

The division of labour and the consequent need to barter and trade, the inequitable accumulation of capital and its subsequent investment which multiplied the inequity, and the unedifying portrayal of man as amoral, eternally self-interested and competitive, are all aspects of classical economic theory. Despite Smith's recognition of the complexity of human motivation, it was on the 'economic man' caricature that the classical model based its explanation of how prices and wages were established and justified.

Smith initially struggled with a labour theory of value which asserted that the value of a commodity was equal to the amount of labour involved in its production. A commodity's price was therefore dependent on the cost of its production, but Smith was less than definitive about how costs were to be identified. They were incurred on labour, capital and land, agriculture being yet a dominant economic activity, and the rent returned to the landlord still loomed large in their considerations. Each of these had to be remunerated.

Subsistence theory held that wages should be just sufficient to maintain the labour force in existence, sufficient to pay for the labourer and his family at simple subsistence level. The remuneration of capital and land was less straightforward for Smith. Having identified the labour theory of value – that the value of anything was equal to the labour incurred in its production – he left the obvious inference for others to pick up that the returns to the owner of capital were in effect wages withheld from labour. He left the question of rent open, being undecided whether it was a cost or a residual item after other costs had been paid for.

Ricardo, Malthus and others tightened up the theory and defended it from attack. Malthus further examined the subsistence theory of wages. He saw that population depended on the means of its subsistence, that it would grow when the means of subsistence permitted and it would grow geometrically while food supplies would only grow arithmetically, and therefore population would ultimately be limited by hunger and starvation, unless previously limited by war, plague, or disease. Thus subsistence was all that the labouring classes could hope for unless, he later added, they would exercise 'moral constraint'. Any benign attempt to improve the lot of the labouring masses would simply result in an excess of procreation which would drag them back to subsistence level. This was a powerful argument against any such benevolence.

Ricardo reinforced the subsistence theory, arguing that wages would be naturally at a level:

> *'which is necessary to enable the labourers, one with another, to subsist*
> *and to perpetuate their race, without either increase or diminution.'*[14]

Thus it was inevitable – an 'iron law' – that workers would remain living at subsistence level. Their continued misery was an essential of the system.

How capital should be remunerated was less clear. The distinction between risk-free investment remunerated by interest and risky investment rewarded by

---

14   Ibid, p. 52.

uncertain levels of profit was not fully made till the twentieth century. Ricardo, like Smith, had recourse to the labour theory of value, which could be applied equally to the capital items required for production so they were similarly valued as equal to the labour involved in their production. Thus any surplus value that accrued when a commodity was sold, value which was taken by the provider of capital, was in truth the value that should have been paid to labour including those previous generations who produced the capital items.

To this potentially explosive idea, Sismondi[15] added the notion of two quite separate social classes: the rich and the poor or as later termed: the bourgeoisie and the proletariat.

The early theorists who developed this system, which was apparently clinical in its objectivity, accepted that achieving the greatest degree of economic advancement would inevitably result in the unfair treatment of some. The theoreticians themselves recognized the unfairness of the system and sought in different ways to ameliorate its worst effects. For example, Smith advocated a redistributive taxation system with the tax revenue deployed to benefit the poor. And Ricardo sought to soften the interpretation of subsistence by including 'conveniences' which became a habitual part of life, so that the labouring class might justify an improving standard of living as the economy grew, which he foresaw continuing indefinitely.

Classical theory was prescriptive about how businesses and governments should behave, but there were clearly differences of view as to how the obvious unfairness of the classical system should be offset. It was widely recognized that the unfairness was unsustainable in the long term and such recognition suggests a vulnerability in the system which might bring about its downfall with a reduction of benefit to all. The system worked but it was unfair and the unfairness needed to be ameliorated. Such amelioration was partly in the hands of government and partly in the hands of those on the ground who determined the balance in the employer/employee relationship, i.e. management.

Management and Classical Theory

The many practical examples and anecdotal evidence included in Adam Smith's account suggest his inclination was to be, as far as possible, empirical.

---

15 Sismondi, J.C.L. de, (1819), *Nouveaux Principes d'économie politique, ou de la Richesse dans ses rapports avec la population*, Paris: Delaunay.

However, as he predated the worst excesses of industrial misery, the evidence for his observation was incomplete. The large-scale mills and mill towns only emerged three or four decades later, to be observed by Ricardo and Malthus and then to become a stage further grotesque when reported by Engels.

The pin factory was a nice example of a small-scale workshop of the time which made use of worker specialization without much capital investment in specialized plant and equipment. For Smith, it had to suffice as the example of industrial development on which economic growth depended. New wealth was created through the aggregate activities of all such workshops competing against each other in free, unregulated markets for the benefit of the consumer. These small-scale enterprises were for the most part owner-managed, which was the organizational form espoused by classical theory. The idea of professional managers controlling a business, but not owning it, was unacceptable to Smith and the classical theorists.

> 'The directors of such companies, however, being the managers rather of other people's money than of their own, it cannot well be expected, that they should watch over it with the same anxious vigilance with which the partners in a private copartnery frequently watch over their own. ... Negligence and profusion therefore must always prevail, more or less, in the management of the affairs of such a company.'[16]

Smith could not have been more wrong in his assessment of management as was subsequently shown by their achievement in terms of productivity, innovation and efficiency. Galbraith, writing in 1987, commented:

> 'Returning today, he (Smith) would be appalled at a world where, as in the United States, a thousand corporations dominate the industrial, commercial and financial landscape and are controlled by their hired management.'[17]

Maybe he would have been appalled; maybe he would have been surprised and fascinated. His suspicion of the corporation controlled by hired management was a symptom of the era in which he lived. At that time, the leading examples of such corporations were the trading companies, legally set up and protected as monopolies, of which he was duly sceptical. He did not give much credit to the major infrastructural projects, such as the canals and turnpikes, which were

---

16   Smith, A., (1776), *Wealth of Nations*, Book V, Chapter 1, Part 3, Article 1, original edition p. 506.
17   Galbraith, J.K., (1987), *A History of Economics,* London: Hamish Hamilton, p. 71.

effectively managed by the engineers rather than the shareholder owners. And he was, of course, innocent of the publicly owned, management controlled, limited liability competitive businesses which came to be dominant in the later nineteenth and twentieth centuries.

Smith's successors were also more fully informed as to the inequity industrialization caused, but their responses were largely justifications of the established system. Malthus' argument was that the working class, if circumstance ever let them escape poverty, would always breed their way back to subsistence living, so the subsistence level of wage was inescapable. Ricardo accepted a similar analysis and even pointed out that the working classes were being dispossessed of their fair wages by the owners of capital.

The decisions as to what might be done about this inequity were in reality in the hands of the management who controlled how the factors of production were to be deployed to generate wealth and how the surpluses generated were to be distributed.

Although economic theory may not initially have impinged greatly on how management worked, it was nevertheless contributing to the culture of the times. It was probably not pure coincidence that, though there were exceptions, the exploitation of workers by the mill owners and industrialists accorded so precisely with the archetype defined by classical theory. Moreover, this archetype was subsequently justified by utilitarian moral philosophers such as Bentham and Mill, arguing that though economic progress involved considerable hardship for some, the aggregate was an increase in 'happiness' – which economists necessarily interpreted as wealth – and the hardships must therefore be borne in order to achieve the greatest happiness for the greatest number.

Industrial management in those early days, largely the entrepreneur owner-managers, may or may not have been susceptible to such arguments. They may or may not have seen themselves as 'economic men' with the duty to seek only to maximize their own self-interest, so that the greater good could result. Or they may have been motivated to act in the best interests of their business organization, concerned for its survival and long-term prosperity and so to preside over a just and equitable distribution of benefits. Both breeds of management have existed from the beginning of industrialization.

Management was beginning to emerge as a separate category, neither capital nor labour, and classical economic theory had some difficulty accounting for its peculiarly independent position.

3

Industrialization and Management Responsibilities

Industrialization began in England but spread quickly through Europe and to America. The textile industries were at the forefront of the process and the first to establish factory units employing large numbers of people in the same plant. Other industries quickly followed. Metal working, brick making and coal getting were already beginning to expand by the mid-eighteenth century, establishing small factories and workshops which were rapidly to grow in scale following the precedent set in textiles. Industrialization quickly extended beyond the subsistence industries related to food, shelter and clothing.

Smith's pin factory bore little resemblance to these industrial factories. It made little use of capital equipment and none of power-driven machinery. There was no requirement for the essential discipline of factory working, only some recognition of the mind-deadening effects of the simple repetitive tasks defined by the division of labour.

Smith set out his theory of industry ahead of the practice being established, unaware of the unforeseen consequences of industrialization: its misery and despair. For him, the inevitable inequalities were largely theoretical and necessarily justified by theoretical argument. Succeeding generations of economic theorists saw the negative impacts of industrialization as well as the positive, and were in a position to develop a means of offsetting the one against the other. However, their general approach was less progressive than Smith's advocacy of redistributive taxation.

Those responsible for industrial management were in a position to implement the industrial process with fairness and justice even if many failed to do so, at least initially. By mid to late nineteenth century, when management became recognized as an autonomous category, their practice had improved for the benefit of employees, customers, suppliers and the local community as well as shareholders.

The Industrial Factory System

The first industrial-scale textile factory, a silk mill, had been built by John Lombe in Derby, England, in 1717. A smaller mill had been built earlier by Thomas Cotchett of Mickleover, perhaps the first germ of the industrial revolution, but Cotchett's machinery could not achieve consistent quality of thread and his mill never developed into a major employer. Lombe, who had worked for Cotchett, had illicitly taken drawings of some successful Italian silk machinery for winding, twisting and doubling fine raw silk and he built twelve such machines in the Derby factory. He was the first of many textile machinery 'inventors' accused of stealing their ideas for which his brother, Thomas, later obtained patents. Lombe predated Arkwright by almost 50 years though literature accords Arkwright the accolade 'father of the factory system', possibly because of the greater importance of the cotton industry in the subsequent industrial revolution. During that fifty-year period the great infrastructural projects were forging ahead, devising new ways of raising capital and managing large-scale employment. Arkwright had the benefit of that prior experience, but it was Lombe who really pioneered the factory system.

The Derby mill employed around 300 people working at machines driven by a seven-metre diameter water wheel turned by the River Derwent. No such 'manufactory' had ever been built before. To be first required some innovative and courageous commitments. The power of water wheels to drive large numbers of machines was well understood. Such power could not be exploited driving domestic machinery sited in cottages spread around the area. Bringing them all together on one site would clearly enable water power to be used efficiently. Lombe had to confront various problems of management: he needed to estimate the costs involved in this new sort of building, in equipping it with the newly devised machinery, estimating how long it would take before it could be brought into production, raising the necessary funds to support the development, recruiting the necessary skilled workers, training the others, investigating the market opportunities in terms of volume and price and making some estimates of the eventual profitability of the enterprise and therefore the scale and probability of a return on the funds invested.

The project was revolutionary. If it had failed Lombe would have been finished. But he got it right, as Defoe later noted:

> *'One hand will twist as much silk as before could be done by fifty and that in a finer and better manner.'*[1]

The silk mill was a success and others followed in England as well as overseas in Europe and America. It is unclear why the son of a Norfolk weaver and merchant should have foreseen the potential for this new enterprise. Perhaps the basic economics were so overwhelmingly favourable that had Lombe not done it when he did, then someone else would very soon afterwards have done so on the basis of the most crude calculations.

If that were so, the case for building Arkwright's cotton mill in Cromford, some 25 miles north of Lombe's silk mill, was even more timely. The agricultural surplus was already achieved and development of the internal transport infrastructure, canals and turnpikes, was well underway by 1771 when Arkwright's first mill opened. Unlike silk, cotton was in practically limitless supply from America, already being shipped into Liverpool from where it could be brought to Cromford in Derbyshire initially by packhorse but planned shortly to utilize the new canal system.

Arkwright equipped his cotton-spinning mill with newly invented machinery, in his case the water-frame spinning machine, which in effect mass-produced cotton thread. The true provenance of the water frame is in doubt; Arkwright, Samuel Crompton and Thomas Highs probably all contributed but Arkwright gained the patent and made the effective modifications to bring the machine to production performance. Compared to domestic spinning wheels, the output of standard thread was revolutionary in terms of both quantity and consistent quality.

But Arkwright, like Lombe before him, had more to contend with than the simple matter of invention and innovation. To raise the finance to build the first large-scale cotton mill he had to estimate the capital cost of building and equipping the mill, forecast the amount of cotton thread he could sell at the price he estimated he could afford as well as how much he could produce at the cost for which he could produce it, under market conditions substantially influenced by his proposed new factory system. His estimations must have

---

1   Defoe, D., (1722), *A Tour Through England and Wales, Vol. 2*, J.M. Dent & Sons Ltd, Everyman edition published in 1928.

been that the cost reductions from mass-producing would create new mass markets for cotton textile justifying the cost of building and equipping the new mill. Similar issues were faced 150 years later by Henry Ford planning the mass-production of his Model T. Arkwright also faced problems of location – there were no people in the areas where climatic conditions were most suitable, so he had to build a company village to accommodate his workers.

Having no money himself, he had to borrow what he could and also persuade those with money to invest in his hair-raising scheme. Arkwright's problem was not merely the formulation of his plan, though given its ground-breaking nature that was problem enough. He also had to deal with what is now recognized as the much greater problem of implementation: developing new machines, getting them to work efficiently, building the mill, recruiting and housing the people, sourcing the raw materials and finding new markets for finished product.

Whether Arkwright was an inventor is in doubt, but certainly he was an innovator, bringing inventions to commercial fruition and innovating new ways of doing things. Water power made it feasible to use large-scale machinery rather than simple manually operated domestic equipment, and technological developments revolutionized the productivity and output of machines. The dealers, manufacturers, entrepreneurs and newly enriched land owners had progressively accumulated surplus profits to invest in these new capital projects. With water power it was as cheap to drive a bank of large- scale machines as to drive a single machine and so factories were built in which large numbers of people were employed. In a few short years the scale and nature of business organization had been changed forever.

Arkwright's forecasting and planning, no matter how informal or crude, are nevertheless apparent in his building the Cromford mill. Having had his initial projections confirmed or, more likely, far exceeded, he moved quickly to replicate that success. Within a few short years he and his partner, Strutt, had built more than a dozen much bigger mills employing many times the 300-strong original workforce, using hundreds of machines initially driven by waterpower and then by Watt's greatly improved rotary drive steam engine, and creating whole new communities and mill towns, as well as the infrastructure to move bulk materials. His success was quickly copied by many others across Britain, Europe and America.

Arkwright's main legacy, the factory system, gave the employer control over the product and the means and cost of production as well as the organization and command of labour in one specialized workplace. Under the domestic system, though their hours were long and their pay extremely poor, workers had some control over when they worked and when they took breaks. With the factories came the necessity for rules and regulations. The machinery would necessarily all start and finish working at the same time, so times were set each day and workers began to be subservient to machines.

Moreover, there had to be rules which achieved consistency in the quality of work produced. There had to be at least some rudimentary rules related to the safety of working. And there had to be people responsible for seeing the rules were obeyed. Arkwright's organization and co-ordination in the first mill are apparent in the way the mill was designed not only as to its internal specialized departments but also the physical disposition of his own house from where he had a clear view overlooking the mill's main entrance and mill-yard and from where it was surmised he exercised a high degree of command and control.

In addition, with the creation of the factories the nature of the work itself changed. The new steam power-driven machinery resulted in new jobs being created. Traditional highly skilled work was replaced by semi-skilled jobs and an ever increasing number of unskilled jobs. Each generation of new machinery removed the requirement for some element of personal skill by the operator and progressively even craft work became de-skilled. Unskilled labour, often largely concerned with moving material from one work place to the next, involved large numbers of people.

Arkwright himself appears to have been a relatively enlightened employer, providing his workers with good quality housing, allotments and other facilities and in return his workforce showed some loyalty, standing by to defend the mill against the threat from Luddite machine breakers. But there were many employers who were less benign, whose workforces were more exploited and abused.

Arkwright has been adjudged by more recent commentators. Mantoux characterized him as:

> 'neither an engineer, nor a merchant, but adding to the main characteristic of both, qualifications peculiar to himself: those of a founder of great concerns, an organiser of production and a leader of men.'[2]

---

2   Mantoux, P., (1961), *The Industrial Revolution in the Eighteenth Century*, London: Jonathan Cape, p. 233.

And to a historian of management theory, his factory system innovated

> *'continuous production, plant site planning, co-ordination of machines, materials, men and capital, factory discipline, and division of labour'.*[3]

The factory system saw the establishment of semi-autonomous manufacturing 'states' where the employer's power was more or less absolute. The rights and duties of employers and employees had been established in Tudor times but from the early nineteenth century until 1875, as employment relations became increasingly defined by contract, the main impact of the law was to allow for enforcement of employment contracts, with imprisonment for workers' breach of contract. Under such circumstances the industrialist, acting from pure self-interest, could abuse his position of power and mercilessly exploit those less powerful, the workers, who enjoyed no legal protection for acting in concert, in combinations, till the Trade Union Act of 1871. Exploitation of labour became the rule, including women and children. It was 1847 before the Ten Hours Act, for example, protected them from being forced to work all daylight hours.

Moreover, the employer had the personal right to hire and fire any of his employees at any time for any reason. And for the worker the worst of all situations was to be unemployed without income or relief of any kind. For them life was precarious with starvation a continuous and very real threat. The young Friedrich Engels, son of a German textiles magnate, who was sent to England for work experience, recorded that:

> *'During my residence in England at least twenty or thirty persons have died of simple starvation under the most revolting circumstances, and a jury has rarely been found possessed of the courage to speak the plain truth in the matter. Let the testimony of the witnesses be never so clear and unequivocal, the bourgeoisie from which the jury is selected, always find some back door through which to escape the frightful verdict, death from starvation. The bourgeoisie dare not speak the truth in these cases, for it would speak its own condemnation.'*[4]

---

3 George, C.S., (1968), *The History of Management Thought*, Englewood Cliffs, New Jersey: Prentice Hall, p. 52.

4 Engels, F., (1844), *The Condition of the Working Class in England*, republished in 1969 by Panther Books with an introduction by Eric Hobsbawm, p. 59. Reference page numbers for this text refer to the Panther Books edition.

Acceptance of this extreme of inequality stabilized the industrial system and kept the wages of the employed sufficiently low that capital could be further accumulated by those who needed it least and could therefore afford to invest it in further development.

Outcomes from Industrialization

The speed with which industrialization took off was remarkable, rightly earning the label 'revolution'. The British cotton industry, for example, imported 4,760,000lb of raw cotton in 1771, a figure which had been roughly stable for decades. Over the next 30 years, imports multiplied more than 12 times to 60,500,000lb.

Such growth was not restricted to cotton. And it was clearly not just a blip, but the start of a fundamentally different way of life. It created concentrations of working people in the new industrial towns located adjacent to the main deposits of coal. Despite the rapid growth of population their standard of living, after several decades of ups and downs, progressively improved so that the lasting result was one of advance for all, apart perhaps from the unemployed underclass which was largely ignored till the later decades of the nineteenth century.

Whole industries were adopting the factory system, not just individual entrepreneurs. The woollen industry, silk, cotton, coal, iron and transportation, all experienced the same massive growth from adopting industrial-scale operations and the technological innovations that industrialization enabled. Also trade which had traditionally been localized round mainly small market towns, was opened up to whole regions and to export and import. And the capital accumulation which was required to finance this explosion gave rise to a revolution in banking which in effect enabled the creation of new money for further investment. Simultaneously the development of joint stock companies facilitated wider corporate ownership than was previously available.

The inequality between employer and employee was repeated throughout the economy. Inequity, sometimes imposed by exploitative and abusive employers, was endemic, if not absolutely essential, to the industrial system.

Rural populations, rendered landless and unemployed by the changes in agriculture, migrated to the new mill towns which provided the desperately needed employment. But there were other consequences. As work became further specialized and deskilled the workers suffered, as Smith had suggested they would, from the dehumanized work and became, though he didn't use the word, alienated. It was the start of the process which much later was depicted in the Charlie Chaplin film 'Modern Times' showing the dehumanized work on the mass production line.

The factories became places of hardship and despair, exploiting women and children through the imposition of long hours, low wages, and often dangerous working conditions. Working hours were typically from dawn to dusk, six days per week. Wages were set at a level such that entire families, father, mother and children, had to work in order that the family might survive at a bare subsistence level. Even Arkwright's relatively enlightened partner, Strutt, employed children. In 1774 he told a committee of the House of Commons that he employed children from the age of seven but preferred them to be over ten. He criticized those employers who took children as soon as they were 'able to crawl'.

An empirical account of early English industrial working life in the first half of the nineteenth century was provided by Engels. He graphically recorded the appalling life experiences in the new industrial towns and the horrendous living and working conditions in the mills, foundries and factories. The following are extracted from his study of *The Condition of the Working Class in England*:

> 'On the occasion of an inquest held November 14th 1843, by Mr Carter, coroner for Surrey, upon the body of Ann Galway, aged 45 years, the newspapers related the following particulars concerning the deceased: She had lived ... with her husband and nineteen year old son in a little room, in which neither bedstead nor any other furniture was to be seen. She lay dead beside her son upon a heap of feathers which were scattered over her almost naked body, there being neither sheet nor coverlet. The feathers stuck so fast over the whole body that the physician could not examine the corpse till it was cleansed, and then found it starved and scarred from the bites of vermin. Part of the floor of the room was torn up, and the hole used by the family as a privy.' (p. 63)

> '... the filth, debris, and offal heaps and the pools in the streets are common to both quarters, and in the district now under discussion, another feature most injurious to the cleanliness of the inhabitants, is the multitude of pigs walking about in all the alleys, rooting into the

offal heaps, or kept imprisoned in small pens. Here, as in most of the working-men's quarters of Manchester, the pork raisers rent the courts and build pig pens in them. In almost every court one or even several such pens may be found, into which the inhabitants of the court throw all refuse and offal, whence the swine grow fat; and the atmosphere, confined on all four sides, is utterly corrupted by putrefying animal and vegetable substances. ... on rereading my description, I am forced to admit that instead of being exaggerated, it is far from black enough to convey a true impression of the filth, ruin, and uninhabitableness, the defiance of all considerations of cleanliness, ventilation and health which characterise the construction of this single district, containing at least twenty to thirty thousand inhabitants.' (p. 86)

'On Monday, January 15th 1844, two boys were brought before the police magistrate because, being in a starving condition they had stolen and immediately devoured a half cooked calf's foot from a shop. The magistrate felt called upon to investigate the case further, and received the following details from the policeman: the mother of the two boys was the widow of an ex-soldier, afterwards policeman, who had had a very hard time since the death of her husband, to provide for her nine children. ... When the policeman came to her he found her with six of her children literally huddled together in a little back room, with no furniture but two old rush-bottom chairs with the seats gone, a small table with two legs broken, a broken cup and a small dish. ... The poor woman told him she had been forced to sell her bedstead the year before to buy food. Her bedding she had pawned with the victualler for food. In short everything had gone for food.' (p. 63/4)

Engels made early use of the official blue book statistics and reliable secondary sources as well as his own observations. But the outcomes he described were not permanent. His own preface to the 1892 English edition of his book included the following:

'... the repeated visitations of cholera, typhus, small-pox, and other epidemics have shown the British bourgeois the urgent necessity of sanitation in his towns and cities, if he wishes to save himself and family from falling victims to such diseases. Accordingly, the most crying abuses described in this book have either disappeared or have been made less conspicuous...'

Engels clearly implied that such improvements by the 'bourgeois' were not made from any concern for their fellow humans, but purely for their own preservation as would be the case if they were conforming to classical economic theory. Working conditions were also progressively improved, hours reduced and the very worst exploitations largely eliminated. The suggestion was frequently offered that such improvements were made in order to achieve the higher productivity that could be obtained from a healthy workforce. Such interpretations of motive are irrelevant to the economic case. In the early years of industrialization conditions were appalling and inhuman and later they were improved. Whether the original conditions resulted from a conspiracy of employers to exploit their workers or whether it was ignorance of how industrialization would develop without intervention must remain conjecture. Undoubtedly there were mercilessly exploitative employers and there were also some who were more benign and enlightened. There is no universal truth.

It is clear that the employers who were rapidly, like Arkwright, becoming themselves owners of capital, increasingly seen by government as the source of new national wealth, were gaining political power and influence. By contrast, the workers had no political power. When they tried to organize into the first labour unions, they were often outlawed by fearful governments actively supporting the ever increasing inequality. This aggravation was the seed bed of English socialism and the reform movement which later was to focus on the achievement of universal suffrage.

Accounting for Profit and Capital

The focus of much discontent has been on the concepts of profit and capital, both of which warrant some consideration. For some, profit is what has been sequestered from labour's rightful wage and set aside to be accumulated as capital. Profit and capital are sometimes dealt with by theoreticians as though the terms are unambiguous, clear and simple, but their meaning is not without complication. Both profit and capital are published in a company's accounting schedules, the balance sheet and the profit and loss account, and their calculation has long been required to be true and fair, with their truth and fairness audited by professionally qualified third parties. They nevertheless both involve matters of judgment in their valuation and are by no means as clinically precise as they might on the surface appear.

The purpose of the accounting schedules is to provide a public account of management's stewardship of the company over the previous year. The balance sheet provides a picture of the company's net worth – what it owns less what it owes – at the end of the year, while the profit and loss shows how much surplus the company made during the year and how that surplus has been deployed.

Profit is a term which appears several times on the profit and loss account schedule. There is a calculation of profit which is the surplus of the firm's sales revenue less the direct costs of making those items sold. By direct costs is meant the cost of materials and wages involved in production. That calculation is referred to as gross profit. There are other expenses which have to be paid, items which are not attributable directly to production, such things as the rent and rates of buildings, the wear and tear on machinery, and the costs of administration, sales staff, office staff and management. The remaining amount, the net profit, has to cover the interest to be paid on borrowings, the tax to be paid on any profits earned, and the dividends which are paid to shareholders. The remaining amount, if there is any, is the profit which is retained and reinvested in the company.

It is not easy to identify in the above what Ricardo identified as the profit which is the surplus sequestered from labour's wages. Out of the items referred to, dividends are the only items which are not bound to be paid and which do not explicitly and directly contribute to the company's financial strength and viability. Yet if dividends were to be reduced the value of the company's shares may well be affected and the future security of the company threatened and along with it the livelihood of workers. Similar considerations would apply if retained profit were reduced in order to increase wages.

Capital is the other concept which needs some consideration. For some, capital is regarded as simply the accumulation of whatever has been stolen over the years from labour. But the balance sheet has a more objective perspective, though not completely so. Capital appears on the balance sheet in two forms. Firstly, it is the amount of money originally put into the business and subsequently accumulated from its operations. Secondly, capital is also shown on the balance sheet as the assets which have been acquired by the business to make its operations more productive and efficient, such items as specialized machinery and equipment. These are the capital assets on which industrialization depends. They were traditionally separated into two categories: land and buildings, which tended not to lose their value and to wear out only slowly, and plant and machinery, which tended to wear out more quickly. Latterly motor vehicles were added as a separate, even more rapidly wearing category, of 'fixed' capital.

There seems to be little ambiguity in such items and little to cause discontent. Such capital items are essential to industry and there is nothing inherent in them which denotes any particular form of ownership or the means by which ownership has been achieved.

The valuation of such capital items, particularly land and buildings, can be problematic. Far from wearing out, property, over the long term, has substantially appreciated in value, and for many companies its valuation has been critical to the overall value of the company. Moreover, it is perfectly possible within the law for the value of such assets to be understated, or overstated, inadvertently or deliberately, and this can be of critical importance, especially in situations of merger and acquisition.

The company owns the assets already referred to plus it may also own cash and other quickly realizable assets as well as raw materials and consumable items and it may be owed money by its customers. These are its current assets. And the firm will probably owe money to its suppliers, its current liabilities. Current assets less current liabilities are referred to as working capital.

The total net value of all these assets, fixed and working capital, is 'balanced' by the sources of its long-term funding. These sources include the money its shareholders contributed originally when the company was formed and the value they have since accumulated as a result of the company's operations, plus any money borrowed on a long-term basis. The providers of this debt are paid a fixed amount of interest each year irrespective of how well the company has performed, while the shareholders receive a dividend which may vary according to how profitable the company has been. Loan stock therefore carries the lesser risk, and is normally given preferential treatment in the event of the firm being wound up. Shareholders, on the other hand, accept a higher level of risk; if the firm performs badly they may receive no dividend and the value of their shares may fall substantially and if the firm is bankrupt they may lose the whole of their original investment.

This broadly is how industrialization was financed from the beginning and how the great enabling infrastructural projects, the turnpikes and canals, were also financed. There is nothing inherent to the system of capital ownership which determines the nature or motivation of capital owners. They are many and various. Some may be idealists bent on supporting the purpose of the company, others may be other firms, they may be small investors who have put their meagre savings into a company they admire, or they may be super-rich individuals seeking to maximize their take. Today, among the biggest shareholders are the pension funds and other financial institutions which achieve their investing power from, and discharge their management responsibilities to, a wide spread of relatively small members and investors.

Even from this brief review it is clear that the treatment of profit and capital in economic theory is somewhat simplified. An economic theory, such as the labour theory of value, suggested that a proportion of profit earned by labour was not paid to them and must therefore be regarded as stolen from them. This wrong, if such it is, should surely be righted, but it is not at all clear how this can be done in practice. What proportion of profit could be identified as stolen wage? And is it part of the profit distributed to shareholders, or is it part of the profit retained within the company, i.e. its capital? If it is to be taken back from shareholders it would mean reducing or eliminating dividend payments, but this would immediately impact on the share price. And if that fell, would the company become vulnerable to take-over and would that be in the best interests of the employees? Or if it is to be taken from retained profit, how could that be realized without selling off some part of the company with similarly dubious impacts on employees? Decisions would then have to be taken as to how to reduce investment in the company's future development and would that be in the employee's best interests?

Economic theory appears to sidestep practical realities. But these investment and distribution decisions cannot be sidestepped by the management responsible.

Management, Labour and Capital

The remuneration of labour is one important aspect of the relationship between management and labour, but it is by no means the whole story. It is a personal relationship between parties with unequal power. Such conspicuous inequality invited correction by enlightened employers and considerable attention was paid to their efforts, which were exampled by local acts of paternalism. David Dale was one such relatively enlightened employer. He set up textile mills at New Lanark outside Glasgow and employed Glaswegian orphans who he accommodated in his mill village. No doubt their lot was improved but they still worked thirteen-hour days for six days a week till hours were somewhat reduced when the plant was taken over by Robert Owen.

Owen had seen the grim environment in fast industrializing Manchester: bad housing, bad factory conditions, labour exploitation, cyclical unemployment and gross poverty. His meteoric rise commenced at the age of 20 when he managed a mill employing 500. At 25 he became managing partner of Chorlton Twist Co which in 1799 took over the New Lanark Mills from Dale. There he established a benign, if paternalistic, company culture which was at the same time commercially profitable.

Owen himself put his success down to a unique understanding of working people:

> '(I) produced such effects over the workpeople in the factory in the first six months of my management, that I had the most complete influence over them, and their order and discipline exceeded that of any other in or near Manchester; and for regularity and sobriety they were an example which none could then imitate.'[5]

Though allowance must be made for the different language of that era, this nevertheless sounds as though it might be dangerously self-deluding. Some put such statements down to Owen's undoubted intellectual insecurity. However, it was not mere talk. Owen took various practical initiatives in relation to the New Lanark workforce. For example, at that time it was common practice for employers to pay wages at least in part in the form of tokens exchangeable only at the company shop where prices were kept artificially high and quality low. But Owen's New Lanark shop sold high quality goods at little more than cost and he passed on the savings from bulk purchases to the workers, which idea later formed the basis of the co-operative movement. Under Owen the New Lanark village was much the same as under Dale except that there were some new public initiatives, such as the school and playground as well as the company shop. Alcohol was limited in supply with neighbouring sources progressively closed down, and higher standards of hygiene were generally enforced.

---

5   Owen, R., (1857), *Life of Robert Owen Written by Himself*, London edition to which page numbers refer, p. 42.

Owen's most notable innovation was in worker education, especially of the young, and he established the company school to provide free education for employees and their children.

In the preamble to his articles which comprised *A New View of Society* Owen wrote:

> *'To the superintendents of manufactories, and to those individuals generally, who, by giving employment to an aggregated population, may easily adopt the means to form the sentiments and manners of such a population.*
>
> *Like you, I am a manufacturer for pecuniary profit, but having for many years acted on principles the reverse in many respects of those in which you have been instructed, and having found my procedure beneficial to others and to myself, even in a pecuniary point of view, I am anxious to explain such valuable principles, that you and those under your influence may equally partake of their advantages.'*

Owen was motivated to make a profit by fair means. He was not driven by any religious conviction which he energetically rejected. The principles he referred to were based on the idea that a person's character is formed by the effects of environment. Education was therefore central to the formation of a rational and benign human being. The educator should therefore provide a benevolent environment, in which a child could develop; corporal punishment was prohibited and child labour limited.

Owen's management approach was shaped 150 years before McGregor's Theory Y assertion that:

> *'the limits on human collaboration in the organizational setting are not limits of human nature but of management's ingenuity in discovering how to realize the potential represented by its human resources.'*[6]

He was successful at New Lanark. Clearly the mills had to be viable as businesses in a competitive world, but he demonstrated that management, which was enlightened from the point of view of workers, could also be successful from a business point of view. The way the company shop operated

---

6   McGregor, D., (1960), *The Human Side of Enterprise*, Tokyo: McGraw Hill Kogakusha, International Student Edition, p. 48.

helped to raise real wages. And the infant school enabled mothers to return to work when their children reached the age of one year. The operation created its own self-perpetuating momentum.

But he was not a life-time manager. His report to the County of Lanark, though informed by his experience at the industrial village, was focused on social development rather than management and industry.

His 'new view of society' was in effect an attempt to recreate the imagined old English rural society of supposedly contented interdependence, which he took some steps to recreate in the modern industrial society at New Lanark. His subsequent experiments, such as New Harmony, Indiana, were failures.

Many other enlightened employers in the nineteenth century were motivated by religious scruple stirred by the obvious and extreme inequality created by industrialization. Notable among these were many Quakers, successful in starting and developing various businesses, notably in chocolate manufacture, soap, metal industries and retailing. Their approach to management was similar, both in their underlying sympathy and in practical implementation, to Owen's New Lanark model. Many of these were highly successful businesses for many generations, some surviving through to the twenty-first century.

The wealth unleashed by industrialization was orders of magnitude greater than had ever been seen previously and in the main it came into the hands of the entrepreneurs and new industrialists. When Arkwright set up his first large-scale mill it was possible for him to do it without money of his own. For a generation, new factories were established and managed by people without prior wealth. Owen had no money of his own when he set out on his mill management career, yet he was able to make substantial investment in New Lanark and in due course become a relatively wealthy man before retiring as a practitioner.

By the mid-nineteenth century such entrepreneurial innovation and achievement were becoming more difficult. The scale of viable manufacturing operations had grown so that the required investment was beyond the scope of individuals with no funding of their own. By the end of the century, such enterprises were being run by professional managers reporting on their stewardship through an annual general meeting to their increasingly diffuse owners: the shareholders.

Financing industrialization was fundamental to its birth and survival. The land and buildings, tools and equipment and the raw materials and wages all had to be paid for before the customer paid for the goods they had received. Raising finance as well as its investment and subsequent control were management responsibilities that had to be well understood by the early industrialists.

Responsibility for all these areas of decision were management's, neither as worker nor as owner, but mediated between the two, ensuring at least some minimum level of justice and equity without frustrating the process of economic growth. Perhaps it was inevitable when management's role became explicit, that it be seen by workers merely as the tools of owners, and by owners as individuals interested only in feathering their own nests at the owners' expense. Such suspicion, and denial even of the possibility of higher motives, spring naturally from the ingestion of classical economic theory.

4

The Developing Economic and Political Context

Since the eighteenth century, economic theory has shaped the development of industry and its management, both directly and through its pervasive influence on the industrial–political context. Though it has undoubtedly been effective in promoting economic growth, it has been criticized for its concomitant unfairness and from time to time it has appeared to be dangerously unstable.

Defenders of the system recognized its unfairness, but rather than seeking to interfere with its simple logic, their approach was to attempt its justification on various grounds. This defence included some surprising contributions from those whose primary concern was moral and ethical rather than purely economic.

Marx acknowledged the economic effectiveness of the system but regarded its exploitation of labour as indefensible. Moreover, he predicted the capitalist system would destroy itself when it culminated in monopolistic markets dominated by a small number of super-rich capitalists brazenly exploiting the labouring masses. In this, he significantly contributed to the legislation and regulation which moderated the basic system and limited its worst excesses.

Simultaneously with the moderating industrial legislation, capital ownership was becoming less concentrated in the hands of individual owners and more diffuse among many small shareholders; this diffusion also saw the recognized emergence of management as an autonomous and potentially enlightened category.

Defence of Classical Theory

The exercise of classical economics produced both pleasure and pain. A fundamental question was whether the one could justify the other.

The keystones of the theory, established by Smith and his immediate successors, were 'economic man', open competition and free markets with minimal government regulation or interference. Under these circumstances the engagement of business people, acting purely out of amoral self-interest, competing against each other, would, through the operation of free market forces, reduce prices of products and increase the quantities produced so that the population as a whole would benefit. Moreover this beneficial system was stabilized around the natural wage rate for labour which was at the level of its subsistence. The unequal distribution of the surplus generated was acknowledged but not addressed other than through Smith's proposal for a more than proportionate redistributive system of taxation of income and wealth

Capital accumulation by the few and dispossession of the many, protected by law that had been shaped and implemented by the few, was acknowledged and explained with attempts made for its justification rather than its rectification. Malthus had argued that it was inevitable: the working classes, should they ever escape poverty's clutches, would always breed themselves back to the bread line.

Smith had himself speculated as to why 'the great body of the people' should tolerate such inequalities. One possibility appeared to be that though inequality increased, the absolute standard of living of all sectors, including that of the workers, also increased. That may have been a plausible explanation so long as the unemployed underclass, Marx's 'industrial reserve army', was excluded from consideration.

However, inequality and injustice were not simply matters of economics, but also of morality. Bentham, writing not much more than a decade after publication of *The Wealth of Nations*, advocated a utilitarian approach to assessing the morality of a situation and developing legislation accordingly. He opened chapter one of his *Introduction to the Principles of Morals and Legislation* as follows:

> *'Nature has placed mankind under the governance of two sovereign masters, pleasure and pain ... The principle of utility recognises this subjection and ... approves or disapproves of every action whatsoever according to the tendency which it appears to have to augment or diminish the happiness of the party whose interest is in question.'*[1]

---

1   Bentham, J., (1789), *Introduction to the Principles of Morals and Legislation*, Oxford: Clarendon Press.

To apply this principle, 'the party whose interest is in question' had first to be identified. From the point of view of the accumulator of capital, the utility of the system might have appeared to be high; from the perspective of the worker, it might not. The two Mills, James and his son John Stuart, expressed the utilitarian approach as:

> *'the creed which accepts as the foundation of morals, utility, or the Greatest Happiness Principle, (which) holds that actions are right in proportion as they tend to produce happiness, wrong as they tend to produce the reverse of happiness. By happiness is intended pleasure and the absence of pain; by unhappiness, pain, and the privation of pleasure.'*[2]

J.S. Mill accepted Malthus' argument regarding the fecundity of the working class, and added in his *Principles of Political Economy* the immutable idea of diminishing returns to labour as their numbers increased. Their poverty, even if not morally justified, therefore seemed inescapable.

The principle of the greatest happiness for the greatest number was widely accepted as a way of assessing the moral justification for actions through the nineteenth century till the practical difficulties were confronted in measuring happiness or pain and pleasure. J. S. Mill, philosopher and economist, had no difficulty measuring happiness in terms of economic consumption. So he identified as good the reducing prices and more ready availability of products for the general population made possible by industrialization. And that 'happiness' for the great number who benefited, outweighed the pain being born by those labouring in its production. Thus the inequality and unfairness caused by industrialization were morally justified!

The conflation of economics and moral philosophy achieved a curious but significant principle. By equating utility with consumption, utility became simply measurable in monetary terms, the value of money being fixed and not dependent on whose money was being considered. Orthodox theory therefore established that the marginal utility of money was fixed, unlike the marginal utility of other commodities which declined as supply increased. This device therefore denied the obvious, common-sense fact that the utility of an additional pound, i.e. the marginal pound, was much greater for the poor than it was for the rich. Theory's necessary assumption that the marginal utility of money was

---

2   Mill, J.S., (1861), *Utilitarianism*, Chapter 2, paragraph 2, quoted in Warnock, G., (1967), *Contemporary Moral Philosophy*, London: Macmillan.

fixed worked as yet another justification for the inequities of the free market economy.

Moreover, Mill argued that outcomes would become progressively more benign over time. Working conditions would improve; work would become easier; standards of living would rise; even employers would become more enlightened. To some extent, these were already happening as Mill himself observed in his employment with the East India Company. But improvement was by no means universal. Nevertheless the utilitarians did lend the inequities resulting from classical theory a cloak of moral respectability.

Much of the happiness, as well as the pain, arising from the workings of the classical model resulted from unregulated competition. Smith acknowledged that employers such as the butcher and baker would, given half a chance, conspire against the public to fix prices so as to increase their profit. Such challenge to the working of classical theory was real enough. However, Smith could not envisage that laws would ever be passed to prevent such conspiracy.

His suspicions that business people would incline to avoid competition where possible and otherwise minimize its effects, may have proved broadly correct. But his doubts as to the possibility of legislation against such anti-competitive actions were less well founded. But it was not till the monopolistic enterprises became over-powerful that anti-trust law was made effective. The potential weakness in the classical system was recognized and governments were sensitized to the need for vigilance which eventually produced anti-trust and competition legislation to limit the natural outcomes of unregulated markets without destroying the effectiveness of free market forces.

A further justification of the inequities caused by free market economics was provided by the social Darwinist argument of Herbert Spencer: the survival of the fittest – Spencer's term rather than Darwin's – made it respectable, even desirable, to resist both taxes and charity; poverty and insecurity were necessary, if regrettable, in liberal systems. Though Spencer was British, his approach was more readily accepted and influential in the United States than at home.

With these defences, despite all its shortcomings, classical theory remained the dominant explanation of how the economic world worked. And the industrialization process it reflected, and helped to shape, was hugely successful in terms of economic growth and wealth generation. Among its limitations, in this brief history of management it is apt to repeat the model's explicit omission of management as a valid and significant autonomous actor. The theory denied management's role as a separate entity within the industrial process, with responsibility for managing both capital and labour and with the opportunity to do so in a way which was fair and equitable as well as effective. Instead, classical theory saw the process as simply pitting capital against labour, accepting that power rested with capital and that it would therefore necessarily always win.

Marx's Assault

A fundamental difference between classical theory and Marx's economics was their opposing views as to the economic system being stable around an equilibrium position. Marx rejected equilibrium, recognizing that economic forces were in continuous flux with no necessary stability or equilibrium state. He predicted that the 'capitalist' system defined by classical theory contained within it the seeds of its own extinction, which process he and Engels had prophesied in 1848 with *The Communist Manifesto*, which famously opened:

> *'A spectre is haunting Europe – the spectre of communism. All the powers of old Europe have entered into a holy alliance to exorcise this spectre: Pope and Tsar, Metternich and Guizot, French Radicals and German police-spies.'*

The manifesto advocated a broad programme of political initiatives such as the progressive abolition of private property, heavily progressive income tax, abolition of inheritance rights, centralization of banking, communications media and transport, the central control of industry and agriculture, provision of free education for all and the abolition of child labour in industry. Marx's aim was for a laissez-faire system far in excess of Ricardo's, for government was required primarily to protect private property. Under Marx's communism there would be need for intrusive government; the acquisition of wealth would no longer need policing, so the state could progressively wither away. But first had to come the revolution which would initially see the proletarians taking over from the capitalist bourgeoisie, but with a classless society being the longer-term aim.

Marx's 'Capital', published 20 years later, contained the more reasoned critique of the then orthodox economic theory. He accepted that the 'capitalistic' system worked well in terms of productivity and wealth generation, it having

> *'created more massive and more colossal productive forces than have all preceding generations together.'*[3]

He was primarily motivated by its extreme lack of equity which he recognized as an essential underpinning of the system:

> *'Accumulation of wealth at one pole is therefore at the same time an accumulation of misery, agony, of toil, slavery, ignorance, brutality and mental degradation at the opposite pole.'*[4]

Marx rejected Ricardo's argument that the working class would inevitably be locked into poverty because of their fecundity. Instead he held that poverty was the result of the wage negotiation which was not a bargain between equals: employer and labourer. Labour was:

> *'no "free agent" ... the vampire will not loose its hold on him "so long as there is a muscle, a nerve, a drop of blood to be exploited". For "protection" against "the serpent of their agonies" the labourers must put their heads together, and, as a class, compel the passing of a law, ... that shall prevent the very workers from selling ... themselves and their families into slavery and death.'*[5]

He identified the negotiation between the employer/'capitalist', who he personalized as 'Mr Moneybags', and the possessor of labour power, as the critical stage in capital accumulation, the actual act of theft of surplus value. He introduced it with heavy irony and then went on to refer to the unequal wage negotiation on completion of which:

> *'He, who before was the money-owner, now strides in front as capitalist; the possessor of labour power follows as his labourer. The one with an air of importance, smirking, intent on business; the other, timid and*

---

3   Marx, K. and Engels, F., (1847), *The Communist Manifesto*, republished in 1964 by New York: Modern Reader Paperbacks, p. 10.

4   Marx, K., (1867), *Capital*, Volume 1, Chapter 25, Section 4, an abridged edition published in 1995 by Oxford World's Classics, an imprint of Oxford University Press, p. 362. In references from *Capital* page numbers are quoted from this Oxford edition unless stated otherwise.

5   Ibid, p. 181.

holding back, like one who is bringing his own hide to market and has nothing to expect but – a hiding.'[6]

Marx gave the analysis a historical foundation going back to feudal, aristocratic and landowning classes which had largely been displaced by the industrial 'capitalist'. He would probably be surprised that the old hierarchies, even in some cases extending to monarchy, were still tolerated 150 years after 'Capital'.

Marx had total confidence in the moral rightness of his critique. He also offered some detailed analysis of classical theory as well as an empirical review of its effects. His explanation of the production and accumulation of capital was a mixture of obscure Ricardian theory of value plus overt anger at the injustice of the workers' treatment within the 'capitalist' system. Theory seems to have been the necessary justification of the anger which was itself essential to the implementation of a solution.

The accumulation of capital was only achieved by the 'capitalist', 'Mr Moneybags', expropriating the surplus value produced by the worker, which Marx discussed at length in terms of use value and exchange value. Marx's 'Mr Moneybags' accumulated the surplus value as further capital which he reinvested in:

> *'the technical necessities of Modern Industry …(which) … dispels all fixity and security in the situation of the labourer.' (The consequent) 'antagonism vents its rage in the creation of that monstrosity, an industrial reserve army, kept in misery in order to be always at the disposal of capital; in the incessant human sacrifices from among the working class, in the most reckless squandering of labour-power; and in the devastation caused by a social anarchy which turns every economic progress into a social calamity.'*[7]

Marx foresaw the fundamental paradox in the free-market 'capitalist' system: the natural consequence of an unregulated competitive market being a monopoly. In any market, the most successful competitor will in the end defeat the rest. This process would lead to the extinction of the middle class and the concentration of capital in the hands of a very small number confronting the massed and growing ranks of workers and their comrades in the 'industrial

---

6   Ibid, p. 113–4.
7   Ibid, p. 292.

reserve army'. This concentration has been acknowledged in standard text books: as industries mature, the number of competitors declines and oligopoly emerges as the natural state of industry in advanced economies.

For Marx, the dichotomy between the few capitalists and the massed ranks of labour excludes consideration of any autonomous role for management, it being merely the officer rank reporting direct to 'Mr Moneybags'. Having seen the early development of publicly owned companies and predicted the development of monopolistic corporations Marx might also have recognized the role of management had his agenda not been focused elsewhere:

> *'This despotism takes form peculiar to itself. Just as at first the capitalist is relieved from actual labour so soon as his capital has reached that minimum amount with which capitalist production, as such, begins, so now, he hands over the work of direct and constant supervision of the individual workmen, and groups of workmen, to a special kind of wage-labourer. An industrial army of workmen, under the command of the capitalist, requires, like a real army, officers (managers), and sergeants (foremen, overlookers), who, while the work is being done, command in the name of the capitalist ... It is not because he is a leader of industry that a man is a capitalist; on the contrary, he is a leader of industry because he is a capitalist. The leadership of industry is an attribute of capital. Just as in feudal times the functions of general and judge, were attributes of landed property.'[8]*

Marx's critique was about the unequal distribution of power and income and the 'capitalist' crisis of depression and unemployment which he predicted, in straight denial of Say's Law which held that production would always create its own demand. Say's Law is now consigned to history, so in this at least Marx was right, as he was also right that the natural outcome of unregulated competition is monopoly. Possibly he was right about much else as well, though the demise of 'capitalism' has been a long time coming. Marx mistakenly accepted classical theory's denial of the role of management independent of ownership. But perhaps his main miscalculation in this area was his underestimation of the power of the law which not only limited the extent of monopoly market power and led to ownership being dispersed beyond the control of 'Mr Moneybags', but also in many different ways limited the worst effects of industrialization.

---

8   Ibid, p. 203.

Mitigating Legislation

A Marxist revolution was probably avoided in most of Europe because the great injustices done to working people were recognized and attempts made to limit those wrongs. Laws were passed in England relating to working conditions and hours of work, to public health and to the rights of workers to combine in unions.

Disease and ill health had been rife in the early cotton mills and mill towns of Lancashire and had resulted in a series of Factory Acts and other associated legislation to improve the worker's lot.

The first of these, in 1802, laid down that no parish apprentice (i.e. pauper child) employed in cotton or woollen mills should work for more than 12 hours a day, and night working was forbidden. Ventilation was enforced, sanitation improved and apprentices were to be provided with proper sleeping accommodation and adequately clothed. Some provision was also to be made for apprentice education and a system of inspection and enforcement was instituted. The terms of the Act serve as a reminder of the working arrangements and conditions then existing. It had little practical impact and was widely ignored. Nevertheless it was a first step. Other Acts followed, in 1819, 1825 and 1831. These fixed a twelve-hour maximum day for 'free' children and minimum working age as nine, but there was no mechanism for their enforcement. Substantive progress was not really made till the 1833 Act which followed publication of a Commission of enquiry report earlier that year which:

> 'disclosed a frightful state of affairs. The worst of the population had been gathered from all parts of the country and collected in the north country towns. A factory type had grown up, often weak and even deformed, often with hereditary diseases, deficient in mind, and doubtful as to morals. In the early years of the century the term "factory hand" was almost one of disgrace. ... England no longer depended on its yeomanry, but upon pauper workers.'[9]

The 1833 Act outlawed the employment of children under nine, those under 13 being limited to a working week of 48 hours maximum and their working day to a maximum of nine hours. In addition, the first factory inspectors were appointed. Initially, the factory inspectors were viewed with suspicion by

---

9   Briggs, M. and Jordan, P., (1967), *Economic History of England*, sixth edition, Foxton: University Tutorial Press Ltd, p. 539.

workers and employers alike, but they nevertheless dedicated themselves to the task of:

> 'correcting the great moral evils that had taken root and extensively spread in … industry.'[10]

Further Acts in 1844 and 1847 set the maximum working week at 60 hours for women and children working in the textile industry, with further limitations enacted in the 1860s and 1870s. From 1880 onwards legislation established workers' rights to compensation for injury or fatality at work, levels of compensation being set as weekly amounts for injury and lump sum payments to dependants in the case of death. Previously an employer could escape liability if the cause could be shown to arise from the victim's own negligence or that of a fellow worker. These loopholes were closed and most employers took out insurance against such liabilities though it was not obligatory.

These legal limitations had been hard fought and won against vehement opposition from hardline employers and their parliamentary representatives. The battle for social justice was initially focused on efforts to establish the right to form a combination or trades union.

Smith had noted the disparity of treatment between employers and employed on the question of combinations:

> 'We rarely hear, it has been said, of the combinations of masters, though frequently of those of workmen. But whoever imagines, upon this account, that masters rarely combine, is as ignorant of the world as of the subject. Masters are always and everywhere in a sort of tacit, but constant and uniform combination, not to raise the wages of labour above their actual rate … Such combinations, however are frequently resisted by a contrary defensive combination of the workmen, who … are desperate, and act with the folly and extravagance of desperate men, … The masters upon these occasions are just as clamorous … and never cease to call aloud for the assistance of the civil magistrate, and the rigorous execution of those laws which have been enacted with so much severity against the combinations of servants, labourers, and journeymen.'[11]

---

10   Briggs, A., (1983), *A Social History of England*, London: Weidenfeld and Nicolson, p. 280.
11   Smith, A., (1776), *Wealth of Nations*, Book I, Chapter 10, Part 2, p. 129.

Legislation outlawing worker combination and representation were difficult to make effective and were finally repealed in 1824, making trade unions no longer illegal. Joining them and becoming active nevertheless remained perilous. In 1832 the 'Tolpuddle martyrs' formed the Friendly Society of Agricultural Labourers to protest against a one-third reduction of their wages. Legal action was brought against them under an Act of 1797 normally used against the holding of seditious meetings and they were found guilty and transported, but the public outcry was such that the rights of trade unionism and collective bargaining were accepted thereafter.

The ongoing struggle for social justice contributed to the politicization of labour, which from time to time was expressed as open rebellion as in the Luddite riots of 1812 and the Chartist rebellions of 1839 and 1842. And in due course, it led to the formation of the Labour Party and the realignment of the Tory landowning interest with the new rich free-market Whig radicals to form the twentieth century left/right political divide.

Some of the fire was undoubtedly taken out of industrial relations by the improving working hours and conditions, the more permissive legislation regarding unions, and the ability for workers to make their voice heard. At the same time, the prediction was not fulfilled that free-market 'capitalism' would destroy itself by its monopolistic tendency. Again, legislation mitigated the otherwise probable monopolistic outcomes, even though the laws to limit monopoly were slow in being enacted. And even when they were enacted their real effect on competition was uncertain, though the existence of anti-trust law, together with the means of it being vigorously implemented, no doubt provided some protection against 'conspiracy' to fix prices or otherwise limit competition.

Further pressure was released from Marxist revolutionary fervour by the rising standards of living, provided by industrialization. And where Marx's reserve industrial army of unemployed might have been expected to suffer continued poverty, its worst effects were offset by public expenditure on various nascent components of a 'welfare state' being first established in the late 1880s in Germany and subsequently in Britain. These components served to reduce the anger and violence which Marx had anticipated would be unleashed by the failure of the 'capitalist' system.

By the time 'Capital' was published, it was clear that Marx's 'spectre' of revolution had already lost some of its potency in the industrialized economies.

But reducing hardship was not the only reason Marx's predictions did not work out in Europe. He had been most exercised over the iniquities of 'Mr Moneybags', the personal beneficiary of capitalist monopoly power. But 'Mr Moneybags'' position was radically changed by the company formation law in the mid-nineteenth century. Ownership of large-scale enterprise was becoming less the charge of a wealthy individual and more the aggregate of many smaller shareholders.

Ownership and Management

The first shareholders in business enterprise were those who invested in overseas trading expeditions. Originally, each expedition had been financed separately. Investors put up the money to pay for an expedition and waited, powerless but committed, for news of their particular expedition's progress. They were necessarily locked in to their investment till their ship came safely home and the contents of its holds be unloaded and sold. Only then were the investors rewarded with a share of the proceeds which, if the expedition was successful, might be substantial.

However, ownership of such stock was not without risk, liability being without limit. An expedition might simply not be as profitable as hoped so the returns might be meagre. Or the ship might not return at all, being lost with all hands, when the shareholder might not only lose the value of their initial investment but be required also to provide some compensation as well. Moreover, investors were not able to reverse their investment or dispose of it, there being no open market for such stocks.

Ownership had become separated from management in such enterprises. The ship's master had total control while the ship was away from its home port; and with that control went the legal right and duty to act as the company's agent in all matters affecting the expedition.

The trading companies which organized these expeditions gradually accumulated permanent capital. So the 'terminable stocks' – shares relating to individual expeditions – became inappropriate. By the mid-seventeenth century the practice of dividing the capital, as apart from profits, among shareholders was ended and from then on the companies traded as single units with a permanent indivisible capital fund which incorporated the interests of many shareholders in the formation of a joint stock company.

This was the organizational form, protected by a royal charter granting monopoly rights, which Adam Smith had in mind when he suggested it was not to be expected that managers *'of other people's money'* would *'watch over it with the same anxious vigilance'* as if it were their own. He was not referring to the expeditionary seamen, but the permanent staff at the administrative headquarters. He was certainly right to make the distinction between those 'managers' and shareholders who took the financial risk.

Joint stock organization without limited liability was then also adopted for the major infrastructural projects such as canals and turnpikes. Shareholders in these enormous projects remained responsible for the whole of a company's debts, just as they would as partners. And there was still no ready market for the purchase and sale of shares, so they remained effectively committed to their original investment and shared the risks involved in the enterprise, which usually took several years before commencing to earn any sort of return.

The formation of such joint stock companies remained both expensive and cumbersome until the Joint Stock Companies Act of 1844 greatly simplified company formation as independent legal entities. The Act brought to an end the costly and hazardous method of seeking incorporation by royal charter, letters patent or special Act of Parliament, replacing it with a relatively simple registration process.[12]

Limited liability had been long debated in the British parliament and was finally accepted in the Act of 1855. This brought company ownership to a wider section of the public, applying as it did to companies with more than 25 shareholders. By that time the small owner-managed workshops and factories such as Adam Smith's pin factory, were still in aggregate the major employers, but the successful enterprises which Marx envisaged as the developing monopolies, were joint stock companies with an increasingly widespread share ownership. The personalization of the capitalist as 'Mr Moneybags' had already become an inappropriate metaphor.

The entrepreneur owner-manager was nevertheless depicted as the ideal type. Smith had dismissed the concept of hired management and classical theory fully endorsed that dismissal in idealizing the owner-manager entrepreneur who latterly became famous for quick decision-taking and lack of bureaucracy, being flexible, innovative and risk-accepting. The entrepreneur set the very best example. As an owner, the entrepreneur was locked in and personally took

---

12   Levy, A.B., (1950), *Private Corporations and Their Control*, London: Routledge & Kegan Paul Ltd.

all the financial risks. As a manager, the entrepreneur's first aim was simply to survive, and could, according to economic theory, be relied on to act in his own self-interest.

The rewards for successful entrepreneurship could be considerable, though the prospects for success for new start-up businesses have never been much more than a one-in-ten chance of surviving the first five years. The rewards were not necessarily restricted to maximized self-interest expressed solely in monetary terms. They might also include the intrinsic satisfaction of creating a prosperous and lasting enterprise that supplied some valued new product or service, which also provided employment which could be made congenial, as well as playing a valued role in the wider economy. The model entrepreneur would be motivated more by the possibility of that creative achievement than by the chance of making quick money.

Divergent Economics

Classical economic theory attracted critics from the start, notably because of its careless treatment of industrialized workers who it appeared content to exploit without restraint. It survived more or less without serious challenge so long as it worked. And that it appeared to do, generating great wealth, some of which was deployed to offset and compensate its worst effects on the underprivileged.

But classical theory contained some curiosities: the elaborate and unreal assumptions required to breathe life into its model of a competitive market; the illusory nature of competitive equilibrium; the fact that real markets were neither purely competitive nor monopolistic, but were at some intermediate oligopolistic state where the classical model lost precision; that agriculture was the nearest thing to a real competitive market, but in that market above all others it appeared to be necessary for governments to intervene and regulate prices and quotas. And there was also Say's law, which gave the curious assurance that production created its own demand and that therefore the whole economic system was stable. This failed to explain the boom and bust reality which persisted throughout the nineteenth century and beyond, and was anything but a stable equilibrium. Each such curiosity was received by theoreticians as a challenge to provide an explanation which preserved classical theory more or less intact.

But the theoreticians themselves were less than convincing as to the theory's validity. Malthus and Ricardo both argued that in a progressive society, by which they meant one with a growing population, the beneficiaries of economic growth would be the small number of wealth owners. The economic position of all other members of society would merely remain the same or could even worsen. Malthus' argument that only 'moral restraint', by which he meant marriage later in life, could rescue the working class from poverty was widely accepted, and Malthus himself recognized that the likelihood of 'moral restraint' was slight.

J.S. Mill recognized the problems of the classical approach and having justified them with the utilitarian argument, proposed the taxation of rent, the limitation of inheritance and the development of what he referred to as 'co-operative production'. His final contributions were those of an Owenite socialist, a form of idealism lacking somewhat in practicality and without great hope of enactment.

Since the start of industrialization economies were subject to the periodic production of more commodities than were demanded. The consequent cutback in production created large-scale unemployment, which reduced the amount of money available to buy commodities. Thus demand for commodities was further reduced. Such a vicious cycle of events was clearly unstable.

Despite this, the classical theorists developed their defensive theories to explain the booms and slumps of business cycles. For some people speculation was the problem, for others the cause was sun-spot activity, while others cited waves of technological innovation. Whatever the cause, it was clear that Say might be wrong: production did not appear to create its own demand.

Alfred Marshal in his 1890 *Principles of Economics* emphasized continuity from the classical tradition of Smith and Ricardo. Though a mathematician, he was concerned with the moral contribution of economic theory, for example, in resolving the long-term problem of poverty and the inequitable distribution of economic benefits. His contemporary, the Austrian economist Carl Menger, also a mathematician, focused on mathematical modelling, describing relationships between economic phenomena in terms of simultaneous equations. With Jevons and Walras, Menger developed the mathematical expression of classical theory, which became labelled as 'neo-classical'. It opened up a rich new seam of quantitative theoretical analysis which became a primary focus of academic interest for itself, rather than its practical application to real-world situations.

Marshall's concept of marginal analysis was a significant step in theory development. Using this idea, it was asserted that the value of a commodity was equal to the utility provided by the last incremental unit in its supply, i.e. the marginal unit. This marginal utility approach was generalized across economic analysis and effectively disposed of Ricardo's labour theory of value which had been subsequently adopted by Marx.

Marshall was concerned with the practical relevance and effect of theory. He recognized that different circumstances presenting in different industries at different times required different solutions. For him there was no one best way applicable to the economy as a whole and readily expressible by a mathematical formula. This more empirical approach led him to analysis in terms of partial equilibrium, with each industry having its own distinctive situation regarding resources, technology, geography and economy. Were the general equilibrium model applicable to the whole economy at a particular point in time it would merely be a happy coincidence of many partial equilibria.

Additionally Marshall acknowledged the time dependence of economic theory: in the short run very little could be changed whereas in the long run most things were changeable and problems, such as poverty and inequity, could be open to solution. However, neo-classical theory's mathematical analysis was unable convincingly to accommodate time dependence.

Marshall's partial equilibrium approach disposed of Say's law in theory, but it was not until the great depression of the 1930s that it was finally ditched in practice. In the interim, it was the workers who were forced to shoulder the main burden of economic slumps and recessions. This energized early manifestations of the British socialist movement. Trade unions, Fabianism, Guild Socialism, the co-operative movement and the British brand of Marxist communism, were all firmly aligned with the lot of the industrial worker and correcting the inequitable divide of the gains from industrial activity.

These various initiatives added pressure on government to ameliorate the workers' lot and led in due course to the establishment of various components of what became known as the welfare state. The first elements of welfarism involved the payment by the state of a benefit for the unemployed. This not only relieved its recipients of the worst effects of economic deprivation but at a macro level assisted the general economic recovery. Similarly, investment in public works, primarily of economic infrastructure such as transportation and communication systems, also served to initiate economic recovery.

Such initiatives, which were widely adopted before the First World War in most European economies, including Britain, were largely the result of pragmatic common sense rather than economic theory. The theory did not come till 1936 with the publication of Keynes' *General Theory of Employment, Interest and Money*. Keynes himself was influential on both sides of the Atlantic but the model of the state-managed economy promulgated by his followers was never accepted with much enthusiasm in the United States while in Britain and Europe it became the new orthodoxy.

During the nineteenth century, the United States' higher growth rate insulated it from the very worst effects of the booms and slumps of business cycles. Its dedication to classical theory was not therefore challenged to the same degree as in Europe. That remained the case until the great depression of the 1930s, when government intervention in markets was found to be essential to the economy's survival and, ironically, to preserving the capitalist system intact.

By then the United States had achieved world leadership in economic and business affairs. Initially it did not develop any uniquely American explanations of economic and business development which differed significantly from the old European models. Yet the United States' situation, with practically infinite resources, especially land, and the rapid economic expansion this facilitated, was quite different from that of the Old World. And in due course the development of theory followed practice across the Atlantic.

PART II
The Rise of Professional Management

Management, though clearly apparent as a practice, was not formally recognized till around a century after Arkwright's first cotton-spinning mill and Smith's *Wealth of Nations*. By then the size of companies had grown substantially and their ownership was becoming more fragmented among large numbers of shareholders. The hired managers, so distrusted by Smith as not having the 'anxious vigilance' of owners to prevent 'negligence and profusion', were becoming powerful, hugely effective and largely autonomous.

During the mid-nineteenth century the centre of gravity of management, practice and theory, started to move across the Atlantic to the United States. There the world's biggest and most successful corporations prospered in the freely competitive domestic markets which were much bigger than any in the old world. Not only did they enjoy substantial economies of scale, but more importantly from the business perspective, the United States markets were growing more rapidly than those of the old world. The greater scale and more rapid growth of markets justified substantially greater investment in new capacities, technologies and methods. So the United States became the world's leading industrial producer, creator of what was referred to as the 'mass production society'.

The big business which developed in the United States required new functions and roles to be undertaken by management and these were consolidated into a body of professional expertise, specific to different tasks but coalescing into a consistent management approach. Researches into industrial organization, particularly the management of people, were adopted as general systems of management, each successive system adding new knowledge and understanding.

The United States management advance was not restricted simply to industrial practice. It also led the old world in terms of education and in particular the development of a management curriculum capable of being taught in specialist colleges. Management education programmes developed in American universities around the turn of the twentieth century, long before their equivalents elsewhere, and United States business schools and their MBA degrees, became the ubiquitous standard of management professionalism.

Over the 80 years or so up to the late 1960s, professional management saw business and industry grow and prosper and become more enlightened in its understanding and treatment of its people. This was the period of management's rise. Theories of management emerged from academic studies of practice, and practice benefited from the lessons learned.

By the end of the 1960s, management, though it had become the dominant industrial actor nurtured by governments, was being seriously challenged by organized labour which had prospered in the more benign environment which followed the 1930s depression. Industrial ownership had over that same period become fragmented and weakened both within companies and in its relationship with governments. Management was distinctive in being a major power group not founded on the traditional base of private property. Nevertheless theirs was, as Chandler expressed it in 1977, the key role in twentieth-century wealth creation.

This second part looks at the development of management in the new United States context of big business, the division of its labour, its practices and responsibilities as an autonomous category addressing the opportunities and problems presented by mass industrialization. And the development of theories of management, again predominantly shaped from observation of big business practices.

Initially management had been promulgated as a putative profession and early United States educators had sought to invest it with the social and public ideals of the older professions. But management could not operate a closed shop; its ranks comprised those with professional credentials and those without, those with appropriate training and those with none. So professional progress was far from even.

Classical free-market economic theory which failed to foresee and deal with the great depression was modified by Keynes who targeted the achievement and maintenance of full employment. The new economics, led by Keynes with modifications by Harrod, became the new dominant orthodoxy, briefly in the

United States, but through western Europe lasting till the late 1970s. By that time the combination of inflation and slow economic growth seemed to have defeated government interventions and the embittered divisions between employer and employed warranted a political solution.

That is when this part of the story ends, before the adoption by Anglo-Saxon governments of the more fundamentalist, explicitly amoral version of free-market economics zealously promulgated by Nobel laureate, Professor Milton Friedman.

New World, Big Business and Educating Management

5

The American colonies declared their independence from Britain in the same decade as Arkwright opened the first cotton mill and Smith published *Wealth of Nations*. Within around 60 years the United States population at over 17 million had overtaken Britain's. Over the following 25 years it almost doubled, and doubled again in the following three decades. By 1880 the United States gross national product was already one and a half times that of Britain. By 1900, it was double Britain's and by 1920, three times.

Such economic success may have been a sufficient defence of classical economic theory which had been accepted with only minor modification. American capital accumulation and investment produced inequalities just as it had in Europe, but in the United States the workers enjoyed a more comfortable and continually improving standard of living and the unemployed 'reserve army' was a smaller proportion of the population.

The inequalities inherent in the classical system were nevertheless defended, as they were in Europe, with the added weight of Herbert Spencer's social Darwinism which could be used to justify even slavery, the greatest inequality of all, which the economy of the south was based on till the end of the civil war in 1865.

The greatest differences between the American economy and those in the old industrialized world were those of scale and growth. By 1890, the domestic United States market was substantially bigger than any in the Old World, encouraging ever larger-scale businesses to become established with the clear threat of monopolization. It was only then that the Sherman Act was passed in the United States stating that:

> *'Every contract, combination in the form of trust or otherwise, or conspiracy, in restraint of trade or commerce among the several States, or with foreign nations, is declared to be illegal.'*

The size of the domestic markets and their urgent and continuous growth enabled profitable investment in industrial operations of a scale never before contemplated. The earlier British experience of Lombe, Arkwright and others, individuals with no capital but able to pioneer completely new industrial activities, was repeated in the United States.

A generation of such entrepreneurial individuals emerged to lead the railroad, steel, ship building, shipping, real estate, oil and finance industries in the United States during the growth phases of their development.

Many such 'captains of industry', sometimes referred to as 'robber barons' because of their amoral, exploitative business methods, subsequently became notable philanthropists, funding among other things the establishment of management education. The United States culture in which they prospered depended distinctively less on public welfare and more on self-help.

As American industries matured and their growth slowed down, there was generally a period of 'shake out' and concentration. Some competitors ceased business while others joined forces through mergers and acquisitions to form even more massive organizations which required a new form of administration to achieve the necessary effectiveness and efficiency of operations. Such administration exercised control quite separately from any questions of ownership. And the education and training required for this new form of administration was pioneered in the United States to create a new category in society: professional management.

The Affluent Economy

H. C. Carey, America's leading economist of the 1830s and 1840s, pointed out the United States difference from Europe was one of fundamental abundance. He noted that Ricardo:

> *'had never seen from his window the progress of a new settlement; had he done so he would have had a different view of the prospects for mankind ... with the passage of time, men were not forced as Ricardo claimed to poorer and poorer land with ever lower return to their labour and, for any land that was better than the worst, ever higher rents to the landlords. On the contrary they first cultivated the thin but unencumbered soil on the top of the hills. Then at a later period they*

tackled the thick vegetation in the valleys; having cleared away the trees they proceeded to work this richer alluvial soil. The returns to their toils were not less but more.'[1]

The United States was then still largely agricultural with farms being worked by their owners, quite differently from Britain where landlords and tenant farmers employed waged labour. There being no shortage of undeveloped land in the United States, holdings were vast by European standards, later confirmed by The Homestead Acts which set out 160 acres as enough to support a family. In such circumstances, every man was able to earn a rich living from his own industry. The same land advantage applied in the south where the more labour intensive cotton industry prospered on the back of the slave system.

Slavery apart, the United States experience was of growth and rapidly improving standards of living, which included the working class. The Old World's experience on the other hand was of rising affluence for the owners of capital but continuing misery and insecurity for the working people and unemployed. The classical economic ideas may not have been appropriate for the United States and while Carey argued strongly for domestic *laissez-faire* on the grounds that interference by government could only stifle initiative, he was a staunch tariff protector of foreign trade.

The early United States economic idea was simply to develop industry in line with agriculture and for infant industries to be tariff protected from European competition in the north with the south to enjoy free trade with Europe so as to expand exports of cotton and in return import cheap European manufactured goods.

By around the middle of the nineteenth century, America had become the world's most dynamic economy. The economic infrastructure in communications and transportation was being developed to open up ever more territory adding further to the size of domestic markets. Economic progress in the United States, though not completely continuous, far exceeded the European achievement. Nevertheless, great inequalities resulted and in a land strongly espousing Christian values, these had to be justified. The Malthusian argument that the workers would always breed themselves back to poverty, should they ever escape it, was clearly untrue in the United States. The utilitarian argument that the greatest good for the greatest number could justify the misery of some was deployed in defence of classical theory's unequal outcome.

---

1   Galbraith, J.K., (1958), *The Affluent Society*, London: Hamish Hamilton, p. 49.

Moreover, the generally positive economic opportunities in the United States would have made it easier to accept that anyone who failed did so because of their own shortcomings. Clearly, in Britain, such failure was the result of any number of causes which may have had nothing to do with the individual concerned. Social Darwinism, promulgated by the Englishman Herbert Spencer, did not therefore attract much support in the Old World, but it was influential in the United States. Spencer's 'survival of the fittest' argument not only justified not supporting the weakest members of society, but actually their 'weeding out'. For Spencer and his followers, the process of natural selection was inevitable and unavoidable. Thus any governmental intervention or charitable works intended to reverse the process could only result in prolonging the agony of the 'unfittest'. Moreover, at the other end of the social scale, as one of his supporters put it:

> 'the millionaires are a product of natural selection ... the naturally selected agents of society for certain work. They get high wages and live in luxury, but the bargain is a good one for society.'[2]

John D Rockefeller of the Standard Oil Company which was subsequently broken up as a result of anti-trust law offered this further explanation:

> 'The growth of a large business is merely the survival of the fittest ... The American Beauty rose can be produced in splendour and fragrance which bring cheer to its beholder only by sacrificing the early buds which grow around it. ... This is not an evil tendency in business. It is merely the working-out of a law of nature and a law of God.'[3]

Thus the affluent need not feel guilty over the hardships and inequalities suffered by those less fortunate. In addition, the same arguments were used to enable, with the same guilt-free conscience, the hereditary passage of riches down the generations, such hereditary advantage being a matter of genes from which the species gained.

Such a curiously elaborate argument promulgated by some fascist dictator might have been roundly condemned as evil, but social Darwinism

---

2   Sumner, W.G., (1914), *The Challenge of Facts and Other Essays*, (ed.) A.G.Keller, New Haven: Yale University Press, p. 90, quoted in Galbraith, J.K., *A History of Economics*, London: Hamish Hamilton, p. 123.
3   Hofstadter, R.A., (1959), *Social Darwinism in American Thought*, New York: Braziller, p. 45.

held considerable sway in the United States through the second half of the nineteenth century.

An alternative American perspective on the inequalities produced by the accumulation and investment of capital was provided by Thorstein Veblen who held up to considerable amusement the 'conspicuous consumption' and 'conspicuous waste' of the 'leisure class'.

> *'No one finds difficulty in assenting to the commonplace that the greatest part of the expenditure incurred by all classes for apparel is incurred for the sake of a respectable appearance rather than for the protection of the person. And probably at no other point is the shabbiness so keenly felt as it is if we fall short of the standard set by social usage in this matter of dress. ... people will undergo a very considerable degree of privation in the comforts or the necessaries of life in order to afford what is considered a decent amount of wasteful consumption; so ... it is by no means ... uncommon ... in an inclement climate, for people to go ill clad in order to appear well dressed.'*[4]

> *'The ostentation, waste, idleness, and immorality of the rich were all purposeful: they were advertisements of success in the pecuniary culture. Work by contrast, was merely a caste mark of inferiority.'*[5]

The point was serious: 'conspicuous consumption' and 'conspicuous waste', had already become a significant part of aggregate demand when Veblen was writing more than a hundred years ago. And so they remain, provoked by corporate marketing and promotion.

Galbraith pointed out that conventional economic wisdom was developed in and for a world of poverty where the emphasis was wholly on production because it was through production that wealth was created and the standard of living of everyone was raised. But in an affluent economy, the production of goods was not so important as the employment it provided. The goods themselves might be, as Veblen pointed out, utterly frivolous, but the work involved in their production and sale as well as its remuneration, was necessary for the maintenance of a stable economy. Therefore it would make sense to engage people in more useful employment. Rather than in the production of

---

4   Veblen, T., (1899), *The Theory of the Leisure Class: An Economic Study in the Evolution of Institutions*, New York: The Macmillan Company, p. 167–8.

5   Galbraith, J.K., (1958), *The Affluent Society*, London: Hamish Hamilton, p. 53.

goods for which there was no need and no natural want unless energetically promoted, they should be employed in the production of goods for which there was a general desire, such as:

> *'better schools, hospitals ... urban development, sanitation, ... police and a thousand other things ... The economy is geared to the least urgent set of human wants. It would be far more secure if it were based on the whole range of need.'*[6]

That debate continued, but the argument had to assume that private production of goods was profitable and therefore paid the taxes to provide the public employments to which Galbraith referred. But first, firms must continue to be competitive if they were to survive and make profits. And this was what United States business achieved supremely well.

Birth of Big Business

Chandler's account of the railroads, which he described as 'the nation's first big business', identified their role in the development of management practice capable of controlling and developing a scale of business hitherto not experienced.

The United States had followed Britain in establishing a transportation infrastructure, first with canals and subsequently railroads. Major canal building projects started with the construction of the Erie Canal which connected the Hudson River with Lake Erie and which was completed in 1825. By 1890, the United States had built around 4,000 miles of canal, almost twice the length of the British system. Furthermore, the American builders had to contend with more mountainous terrain, more severe weather conditions and sparser population as well as far greater distances over which to manage the manual labour force. The potential profitability of the American canals was less apparent than the British though the benefits to states in opening up territory were real enough. Consequently public funding played an important role in American canal building, the Erie Canal, for example, being funded by New York State.

The initial reduction in costs achieved by canal transport, as compared with wagon haulage, was decisive in establishing trade between the east and west

---

6   Ibid, p. 249

and opening up the United States interior. However, their economic life span was short before they were overtaken by railroad transportation.

Railroads were not new. In Britain, a 'wagon way' carrying coal from Newcastle to the river Tyne had been used since the mid-1500s. In 1767 iron rails were adopted at Coalbrookdale on its 'wagon way' carrying iron ore and coal. An early but unsuccessful steam engine devised by Trescothick was used to replace horses pulling coal at Merthyr Tydfil in 1804. More successful coal moving attempts were made at Leeds in 1811 and Newcastle in 1813. Stephenson built his first steam engine in 1814, got authorization for the 26-mile long Stockton and Darlington Railway in 1821 and four years later the railway opened with the immediate result that the price of coal at Darlington dropped from 18 shillings a ton to 8 shillings, some measure of the economic impact of fairly short distance railway transport in a system already served by canals.

Following the success of these lines, major British railway developments got under way, only briefly interrupted by a financial crisis in 1847 caused by wildly speculative and disastrous investments in rail projects. By 1850, there were 6,600 miles of railway line in Britain. By 1860, there were 10,000 miles and by 1870 15,000 miles, after which further development slowed.

The United States railroad building started a little later than the British system but quickly overtook it in terms of miles of track, having around 9,000 miles laid by 1850. Ten years later, this had grown to over 30,000 miles and continued to expand rapidly till by 1890 there were over 166,000 miles of track laid, far in excess of any other country. It had a massive impact on the American economy. One contemporary commentator described the opening up of the West by the railways as follows:

> *'The pioneer, as he moves forward over the prairie of the west, carries with him the railway – as necessary to his life as are the axe and the plough. The railway keeps pace with the frontier line of settlement; so that the crop of this year of a frontier farm, in the great march of civilization, has only to be held to the next, to be sent whizzing to the Eastern market at a speed of thirty miles to the hour.'*[7]

Railroads quickly opened up the new agricultural areas of Illinois, Indiana and Wisconsin to the markets of the Eastern seaboard. Moreover, concurrent

---

7   Chandler, A.D., (1965), *The Railroads: The Nation's First Big Business*, NY: Harcourt, Brace & World Inc (The Forces in American Economic Growth Series), p. 21–22.

with the new railroads, developments in shipping, the iron hull and steam driven screw propulsion, increased the scale, speed and efficiency of overseas transportation thus opening up European markets to United States produce. American registered steam shipping tonnage grew from 5,631 in 1847 to 97,296 in 1860.[8] Cunard's transatlantic steam packet line from New York to Liverpool began in 1848, quickly followed by others, cutting the crossing time from an average of 35 days to less than two weeks.

The carrying capacity of ships and railways to both domestic and export markets grew continuously. But their impact was not restricted simply to opening up new markets for the 'frontier farm'. The new means of distribution for manufactured goods to all parts of the new United States market made it feasible to produce on a large scale. Previously, only in textiles had factories employing more than 200 been viable; other manufacturing had been accomplished through small workshops and a system of subcontracting work. Now, large-scale production units became the norm, manufacturing such things as *'shoes, clothing, clocks, watches, sewing machines, agricultural implements, machine tools, and small arms for the civilian market as well as such basic materials as iron and brass.'*[9] All these began to be mass-produced.

Both the impact and the scale of the United States railroad development were without precedent. By the 1850s, American railroads had become the biggest market in the world for coal, wood, machinery, felt, glass, rubber and brass. The requirement for capital investment caused a revolution in banking and the scale of employment of workers and managers caused a revolution in the practice and theory of management.

Unlike the canals, most of the investment in railroads was obtained from non-public sources. Initially individuals at termini towns or along the route of a proposed railroad would invest as they stood to gain from its development. But these investments were insufficient to meet the needs of the railroad companies. So further investment was sought from Eastern cities or even from Europe, such investors' sole interests being in the returns they stood to gain from their stock, given the risks involved. These distant investors often were attracted to bonds and preference stock rather than full risk-bearing shares and their need for professional advice led to the formation of many investment banks for this purpose. This in turn led to the New York stock exchange becoming the dominant national exchange, gaining precedence over Boston and Philadelphia

---

8   Ibid, p. 7.
9   Ibid, p. 9.

largely because of its commercial port and communications with the capital exporting countries of Europe. As Wall Street was the main exchange for railroad securities its position as the nation's leading stock exchange was further consolidated after the 1850s.

Railroad managements were of course concerned not just with the raising of finance. Running the railroads was as expensive as building them. In the 1850s, the largest United States manufacturer, the textile mills of the Pepperell Manufacturing Company, had operating costs of around $300,000 and employed around 800 people. The New York and Erie Railroad cost almost $3m per annum to run in 1855 and employed over 4,000. The Pennsylvania railroad cost well over $2m to run in 1855 and by 1862 costs were almost $5.5m.

But the scale of the railroad operations was only part of their management problem. Unlike manufacturing operations, their activities were spread over hundreds of miles and included rail tracks, telegraph lines, rolling stock, workshops, terminals, stations, warehouses, offices, bridges etc. Management had responsibility not only for the overall profitability of operations but for the safety and time-keeping of their customers and the safety and condition of freight. Routinely decisions had to be taken as to the numbers of cars to be scheduled to meet constantly changing requirements and the determination of charges and prices. Management had also to be concerned with the longer-term decisions as to expansion, maintenance and/or replacement of tracks, terminals, cars and freight wagons, equipment and other facilities and how to finance such developments.

These decisions, being confronted on a scale of operation that had not previously been faced, required new methods of corporate management. Management of the Baltimore and Ohio Railroad were the first to separate accounting and finance from those of the railroad operations. The accounting department kept track of all the company's financial transactions and the treasurer's section was concerned with raising finance and controlling the allocation of funds to maintenance and replacement of assets. Management of the Erie and the Pennsylvania railroads initiated the setting down of line management responsibilities and what became known as the chains of command and communication. The Pennsylvania also pioneered the setting up of a separate traffic management function responsible for obtaining and processing freight and passengers.

By the 1870s, the focus of railroad management had ceased to be on expansion and was more on competition which was destroying profitability and becoming a consequent concern with costs and pricing. This focus led to federations between railroad companies and consolidation by mergers and acquisitions into a smaller number of integrated railroad systems. New York's financiers played a leading role in this rationalization process, not just arranging finance but importantly being involved in the achievement of greater efficiency and effectiveness.

Some managements of these newly created complex organizations introduced a decentralized structure with regional managements being responsible for the profitable operation of their regional system. This sort of structure foreshadowed the famous decentralization of manufacturing led by General Motors some fifty years later.

Clearly, railroad management was not an optional addition to the costs of running a railroad; they were an unavoidable part of the organization and one which pioneered effective and efficient ways of doing things without which the railroads, and subsequent large-scale business organizations, could not have prospered.

The precedent set by the railroads was the big business model. There was no question of the small workshop building and operating an entrepreneurial railroad. To build and operate a railroad from New York to Chicago was a large-scale operation from the beginning; it clearly couldn't achieve the necessary scale by organic growth. The management of such an enterprise was forced to pioneer new ways of doing things. Equally, the financing of such a project could not be achieved by the progressive accumulation of capital and its incremental investment in further track extension; it had to be financed from the outset as a whole entity. As in Britain, financing was achieved by selling the stock of a limited liability company, but in the United States the scale of such projects meant the stock ownership was substantially more fragmented and complex.

For such projects, management and ownership were necessarily separated. It was not an option; there was no other way such projects could have been planned and executed. The days when an Arkwright could arrange the financing of a whole new factory business among a small number of individuals were over.

Control Without Ownership

The separation of ownership from control of the large American railroad companies was followed by similar separation of big business manufacturers and distributors.

Such separation was widely held to be more democratic than the tyranny of owner control and was achieved among the vast majority of big United States businesses, Ford being one of the few exceptions. While Henry Ford retained ownership and management control of his motor company and was initially pioneering and successful, his retention of personal control resulted in the near disastrous collapse in company fortunes which was only rectified by his grandson establishing a professional management regime to run the company.

The separation of ownership and control was effective in enabling large business to be financed and it was successful in permitting such large-scale businesses to be run effectively and efficiently. It was widely regarded as preferable to the ownership and control being in the hands of a single individual such as had been envisaged by Marx with 'Mr Moneybags'. But it was controversial. Western democratic government and the legal system it had developed were largely based around the notion of protecting private property rights and classical economic theory had identified the divergence of interest between company owners and its hired managers.

Though the interests of enterprise and owner might coincide in the entrepreneur role, it was not necessarily true for businesses which had developed beyond the entrepreneurial stage. For such business, the distinction between management and ownership was fundamental. Whatever form its ownership took, business decisions which had direct profit implications were taken by those in control of the business, its management. But economic theory taught that management without ownership would result in managers seeking to maximize their own self-interest. Smith had suggested they simply wouldn't be vigilant while later theoreticians held that they would develop what they referred to as 'slack' which they would deploy for their own personal benefit. Separation therefore involved not only a distinction between management and ownership, but also a direct conflict of interest.

Berle and Means studied this divergence of interest as it had developed in the late nineteenth century through to the late 1920s. They identified three distinct functions: 'business ownership', 'business control' and 'participation in action on behalf of the business'. They noted that in the nineteenth century the owners fulfilled the first two and hired managers fulfilled the third:

> *'the owners ... **were in a position** (their emphasis) both to manage an enterprise or delegate its management and to receive any profits or benefits which might accrue. The managers on the other hand ... operated an enterprise, presumably in the interests of the owners.'*[10]

With the growth of big business towards the end of the nineteenth century they noted that the position of owners had been reduced and management advanced. For Berle and Means, owners had three main interests:

> *'first that the company should be made to earn maximum profit compatible with a reasonable degree of risk; second that as large a proportion of these profits should be distributed as the best interests of the business permit ...; and, finally, that his stock should remain freely marketable at a fair price.'*[11]

These interests were couched in measured terms. There was no simplistic assertion that the company should just maximize profit or dividend payments, or therefore, shareholder wealth. Nor was there any explicit assertion of the interests of management though they did conjecture about their possible interest in personal profit, or in prestige or power or perhaps in the gratification of 'professional zeal'.

The theory's assertion that company management might exercise their natural desire to maximize their own self-interest by usurping profit for their personal use, comes close to a suspicion of management criminality. Company law in the United States and Britain specified the duties of directors. While non-conformance might be difficult to identify and prove, it was nevertheless binding on management to conform. The British Companies Act of 1844 provided the first legal identification of a company director's responsibilities as 'the direction, conduct, management, or superintendence' of the company's affairs. This was important as it specified the directors' duty as being to the company itself, which was established as an independent legal entity, rather than to its shareholders, or indeed allowing self-interest to pervert that prime duty.

---

10 Berle, A.A. and Means, G.C., (1932), *The Modern Corporation and Private Property,* NY: Macmillan, p. 119.
11 Ibid, p. 121.

The shareholders had a separate contract with the company, based on their purchase of share certificates which entitled them to a potential receipt of dividends and benefit of capital growth, both of which carried a risk. Beyond that shareholders were established with the right to appoint directors (or confirm their previous appointment, or not, at a company general meeting) and were able to vote for resolutions raised at company general meetings. The shareholders owed no duty to the company or its employees, having discharged it in full when they paid for their shares. Thereafter the relationship between the shareholders and the company is one of risk and reward.

Management's responsibility to the company as a separate legal entity, rather than its shareholders, was explicit from 1844 on. Management had no statutory contract with shareholders, despite Smith's enthusiasm for 'co-partneries' and suspicion of hired managers.

Nevertheless, management had a clear responsibility for providing shareholders with a return in terms of dividends and the prospect of capital growth which would be sufficient to ensure the company's survival and long-term prosperity.

The separation of ownership from management may have first occurred with the creation of limited liability and the ready transferability of shares in stock markets which enabled the establishment of big business. But it is repeated for successful enterprises going through the metamorphosis from business start-up to publicly quoted corporation. The change may be more real than apparent. From a start-up the typical successful business goes through a stage of entrepreneur management, then a family business, family managed with wider ownership, and finally publicly quoted company. At each such stage of development, management becomes further remote from ownership, though retaining all control and responsibility.[12]

Management Education and Neo-Classical Theory

United States pioneering large-scale business and the consequent necessity for competent management led it to establish suitable training and education for those specialists.

---

12 Pearson, G., (1995), *Integrity in Organizations: An Alternative Business Ethic*, Maidenhead: McGraw Hill Book Co.

By 1895 there were around 130,000 business colleges established in the United States teaching skills such as book-keeping, typing, clerical and secretarial work.[13] Professional engineering education had been provided at the US Military Academy at West Point since its founding in 1802. The University of Michigan offered courses in engineering from 1854, to be followed by others. But there was no provision of management training or education, though the increasing numbers of university graduates going into business did not go unnoticed.

The president of Harvard University reported that even in his year of graduation, 1853, more graduates were going into business than any other calling and that by 1900 the figure had grown to more than half. The need for Harvard to provide suitable education had become pressing. He noted that:

> 'thorough mental training must give a man an advantage in any business which requires strong mental work.'[14]

However, the precise nature of that 'mental training' remained unclear. A relevant debate had been raging in England following publication in 1854 of Newman's 'The idea of a University'. Newman supported the idea of liberal education being 'a training of the mind' which would fit a person for any purpose:

> 'This process of training, by which the intellect, instead of being formed or sacrificed to some particular or accidental purpose, some specific trade or profession, or study or science, is disciplined for its own sake, for the perception of its own proper object, and for its own highest culture, is called Liberal Education.'[15]

John Locke's rejoinder, quoted below from Newman's text, makes the case for more specific practical training:

> 'Tis a matter of astonishment ...that men of quality and parts should suffer themselves to be so far misled by custom and implicit faith. Reason, if consulted with, would advise, that their children's time

---

13 Khurana, R., (2007), *From Higher Aims to Hired Hands: The Social Transformation of American Business Schools and the Unfulfilled Promise of Management as a Profession*, Princeton NJ: Princeton University Press.

14 Ibid, p. 46.

15 Newman, J.H., (1854), *The Idea of a University: Discourse 7. Knowledge Viewed in Relation to Professional Skill*, Newhaven, CT: Yale University Press.

should be spent in acquiring what might be useful to them, when they come to be men, rather than that their heads should be stuffed with a deal of trash, a great part whereof they usually never do ('tis certain they never need to) think on again as long as they live; and so much of it as does stick by them they are only the worse for.'

This argument still surrounds the management education curriculum, part of which is undoubtedly mental training, liberal education with the specific management focus being secondary, while other parts cover particular technical aspects of the management responsibility.

The first business schools at Pennsylvania, Dartmouth and Harvard pioneered education for the new big business management, instilling them with a sense of social obligation, typical of the accepted professions of the day. This may well have been in reaction against the worst excesses of the 'robber barons' who had grown up with their new industries, as exploitative of their workers as the worst kind of mill owners recorded by Engels had ever been, no matter that a few of them later turned into major philanthropists financing, among other things, private business school education.

The leading university academics and the industrialists who provided much of the funding, shared a view as to the values which they thought industry should espouse. They included a belief in scientific rationality, an acceptance of the puritan work ethic, a politically liberal perspective, a view of education as formative of character as well as technical competence, and an avowed commitment to meritocracy.

Professional education had been pioneered at Harvard, with its Medical School being established as early as 1782 and its Law School in 1817, long before those professions were themselves firmly established. The American Medical Association (AMA) was joined in 1847 and the legal profession founded with the American Bar Association in 1878. Previously practitioners had been trained under a system of articles or apprenticeship with no nationally recognized standards of competence or codes of practice and no national association or organization to act as gatekeeper to the professions.

The AMA was established at the Academy of Natural Sciences in Philadelphia and one of its first tasks was to appoint a committee on medical education. They established standards for preliminary medical education for the degree of MD and also published their code of medical ethics. Article 1 of

Chapter 1 of the code encapsulated some of the essence of what distinguished a profession from other callings:

> *'A Physician should not only be ever ready to obey the calls of the sick, but his mind ought also to be imbued with the greatness of his mission, and the responsibility he habitually incurs in its discharge. Those obligations are the more deep and enduring, because there is no tribunal other than his own conscience, to adjudge penalties for carelessness or neglect. Physicians should therefore, minister to the sick with due impressions of the importance of their office; reflecting that the ease, the health, and the lives of those committed to their charge, depend on their skill, attention and fidelity. They should study, also, in their deportment, so to unite tenderness with firmness, and condescension with authority, as to inspire the minds of their patients with gratitude, respect and confidence.'*

This emphasis on the ever ready willingness to provide competent and diligent service to their clients, in that case patients, totally without regard to pecuniary reward, required the professional person to be a different sort of human being from the economic man assumed by classical economists to inhabit all other walks of life.

The professions were becoming established at the turn of the century with the number of professional schools increasing rapidly and including dentistry, pharmacy and veterinary medicine all recognized as professions by 1910.

The distinguishing characteristics of the professions included professional knowledge and credentialed expertise combined with an altruistic ideal reflected in the espousal of values and codes of practice protected by a central national association acting as gatekeeper.

As the United States research university became more important and influential it became the natural home for the education of the professions. Research university growth was therefore accompanied by the establishment of an increasing number of professional schools which won support not only from public sources but increasingly from private donors such as the Carnegie, Stanford and Ford foundations. The conviction grew that professional managers not only could, but should, be trained in universities as professional practitioners.

The problem for management education was firstly that it was clearly not a profession. There could be no central gatekeeper to management jobs demanding specific professional qualifications since a substantial number of successful managers might have emerged, as did many captains of industry / robber barons / great philanthropists, from entrepreneurial or purely practical backgrounds. That being the case there could be no universally recognized management body equivalent to the American Medical Association. Nor could there be an ethical code of practice to which all recognized managers *must* subscribe. And there could be no universally held management ideal relating the job to its positive contribution to the greater good of society.

Anyone could become a manager with no particular knowledge, training or qualification. The eighteenth and nineteenth century industrial entrepreneurs were blazing completely new trails. There were no rules telling them what they should do. It was within them that they created something new, worthwhile and lasting from which others could benefit either directly or indirectly.

So the aim of the early business school academics and their industrial sponsors, to establish management as a profession, was frustrated. Moreover, the question of a coherent management curriculum was not satisfactorily resolved. It was not so much a single subject in itself but a composite of fragments of professional training such as finance, accounting and law, plus other accepted academic disciplines such as applied mathematics and statistics, social psychology and, most critical of all, economics. From this assortment of subjects with the addition of new learning methods such as the case study, a management curriculum did emerge and form the core of most business school degrees.

By 1914, there were 25 United States business schools and by then they were teaching what was referred to as the science of management, which was to be distinguished both from scientific management and management science. The science of management was an approach which purported to make use of the scientific method, was analytical, avowedly objective and, where possible, quantitative. The quantitative approach also informed the revised version of economic theory, the neo-classical, which became dominant in most American research universities and business schools.

The application of mathematics in neo-classical theory added a further layer of justification to that body of orthodox wisdom. Its significance was not that it changed theory in any substantive way but that it confirmed the rightness of the theory from this more 'scientific' perspective.

The application of calculus enabled theoreticians to create models of the economic world which appeared to deliver the truth with quantitative precision, defining how firm managements decided such critical issues as the prices of products and the amounts to produce in both competitive and monopolistic markets. For these models to work according to their own logic, they required various assumptions to be made about markets, products and competitors. The basic assumption was that businesses sought always to maximize profits. The model considered the immediate profit effects of particular pricing and quantity of output decisions. It was not sensitive to the difference between short and long term effects of those decisions. The concept of long term profit maximization had no operational meaning within the theoretical model.

To make such a crude and simple model operative it was necessary to assume that the market was clearly defined with its boundaries unambiguous, that all products in the market were identical, that all producers had exactly the same costs, and all producers were unable to influence the market price for products, that suppliers and buyers in a market all had total information as to products and prices, that there were no barriers to entry to and exit from the market and so on. With these assumptions in place, and feeding cost and price information into the model, the producer would, according to the theory, supply that quantity of product which would result in its marginal cost being equal to the market price. One item more might raise costs by requiring expense to increase capacity, while one item less might increase costs by resulting in underutilized facilities; thus either more or less would result in a reduction in profit. Such was the curious nature of economic theory of the firm in a competitive market.

No assertion was made that the model reflected reality. Clearly it did not. But if it was not a model of reality, of what was it a model? The instrumentalist argument, borrowed from natural science though with spurious logic in its application to the uncertain world of a social science, was raised in its defence: that the model should not be assessed as to whether it depicted reality, but by how effective it was at predicting phenomena. Many argued that it failed in this as well. What it did was offer a mathematical version of the classical theory, which might serve some academic purpose, but which if it explained anything, only appeared to explain the practical limitations of the theory itself. However, the instrumentalist argument was accepted by theoreticians even though it was never truly tested. Nor indeed was it capable of being put to the test in the way that natural science models were. There was a general broad truth in the classical theory, but not a precise one.

The theory identified both competitive markets and monopolies, competitive markets operating for the common good, monopolies for the benefit of the monopolist against the common good. In a perfectly competitive market, it might be proposed that one participant managed to achieve some innovative progress which either allowed a cost reduction and therefore reduction in price or a product enhancement at no additional cost. Then according to all the remaining arcane assumptions about competitive markets, that innovator would be able to sell whatever quantity they wanted. In due course, they would become a more powerful supplier, able to influence or even dictate market prices and in the end such dominant supplier would, so long as there was no external constraint, achieve a monopoly position. The almost inevitable paradoxical result of an unregulated perfectly competitive market would therefore be a monopoly.

The only alternative to the monopolistic outcome of competitive markets would be that the market was controlled and regulated so as to prevent a monopoly being established, which was what became regarded as necessary in the real world, though abhorred by theoretical purists.

The general prediction of neo-classical theory, for example, that competition drives prices down and that reduction usually increases demand, required no mathematical modelling. The precise predictions (elaborated by calculus), were more or less spurious, not just in the obvious way, that outputs and prices were not set on the basis of marginal costs etc, but in its simplistic modelling of both competition and monopoly which betrayed little understanding of the conditions governing actual management decisions in an industrialized world.

Nevertheless, this was the economic theory which was the theoretical foundation of much that was taught and learned in the business schools and management departments of research universities. It was to have a dominant influence on the conduct of business and its relations with government through much of the twentieth century and beyond. The unreality of neo-classical theory and the curiosities it contained, referred to in the previous chapter, were to come under direct challenge, with its failure to foresee, avoid and reverse the great depression of the 1930s.

Economics of Depression

The depression was signalled by Wall Street share values almost halving during the autumn of 1929. A 25 per cent drop was recorded in just two days' trading on 28 and 29 October. Shares had lost almost 90 per cent of their value by July of 1932 when industrial production was at its lowest ebb and United States unemployment was reaching 25 per cent. The economy remained at this disastrously low ebb through the following summer after which it commenced a slow recovery, interrupted by a recession in 1937–9, but finally completed after the United States entered the Second World War.

The causes of this depression have been put down to a careless expansion of the money supply through the 1920s leading to a reckless credit-driven boom that inevitably bust in the shape of the Wall St crash, the effect of which in the real economy was magnified by the initially strict contraction of the money supply by federal authorities which sparked off numerous bank failures and industrial bankruptcies.

It was not just an American affair. It was experienced through all industrialized economies, the brunt of its worst effects being experienced by industrial workers across the world. Responses to the depression led to changes of government in the United States with the inauguration of F. D. Roosevelt as President and in Britain with the collapse of the first Labour government and its replacement with a Conservative-dominated coalition. The question was what governments should do to revive the economies when market forces failed to do the job.

The solution that appeared to work was a mixture of pragmatic economic action from Roosevelt apparently motivated more by a desire to achieve some social justice rather than following the promptings of any economic theory. This produced short-term benefits. In the longer term such initiatives had to be given some explanation and rationale if they were to have lasting effect and this was provided by one of Marshall's students, J.M. Keynes, whose *The General Theory of Employment, Interest and Money* was published in 1936. Keynes provided the justification and support for initiatives taken under Roosevelt's New Deal, some of which were still operative more than seven decades on.

The New Deal saw massive government investment in the economy intended both to ameliorate hardships by creating employment to stimulate economic growth and also to prevent the economy falling victim to future depression. It established a system of universal retirement pensions, unemployment insurance, and welfare benefits for poor families and the handicapped, all paid for by a payroll tax.

In terms of job creation the New Deal included a public works administration set up to instigate large public projects providing mass employment; a civil works administration offering temporary jobs to millions of unemployed; a works progress administration to employ more millions across the country, mainly in rural and western mountain regions; and a civilian conservation corps created to employ young men doing unskilled work in rural areas under army supervision.

Roosevelt took particular interest in farming, believing agriculture to be a litmus test for the whole economy. The Agricultural Adjustment Act raised farm prices both by cutting total farm output of major crops and livestock and also by providing a system of subsidies.

On the financial front legislation was passed to insure bank deposits, the aim being to restore confidence in the banking system. The Securities and Exchange Commission was established in 1933 to establish and control stock exchange operations including for example the requirement for transparency regarding investment risk. Also, the gold standard was abandoned so bullion reserves were no longer required to support the currency.

There were also several initiatives aimed at protecting the interests of labour. The National Labor Relations Board was established to supervize labour–management relations, protecting the rights and interests of trade unionists. A maximum normal working week of 40 hours and a minimum wage were established and most forms of child labour were outlawed.

Though the main aim of the New Deal was to address the short-term problems of the depression, various of its components were of a permanent nature. This dichotomy between short and long term was present in the theory as well as practice.

For Keynes an economic slump was a short-run problem of a lack of demand. If the normal action of market forces did not stimulate the required increase in demand then government should be prepared to spend – investing in public works to create employment or by reducing taxes to add to spending power – in order to boost demand and to do this by running a budget deficit in the short term. When the economy recovered, as surely it would, then normal market forces would resume and the government could reduce its spending and pay off the debts accumulated during the recessionary times. Keynes proposed a balanced budget in the medium term. But not in the short run. As he famously pointed out in regard to the long term: 'In the long run we're all dead.'

Keynes' main criticism of classical theory was its *'failure to provide for full employment and its arbitrary and inequitable distribution of wealth and incomes.'*[16] In addition to improving the short-term problem of unemployment the New Deal also went some considerable way to solving Keynes' long-term problem of inequitable distribution of wealth and incomes.

During the twentieth century, he noted, significant progress had been made, especially in Britain, *'towards the removal of very great disparities of wealth and income ... through the instrument of income tax, surtax and death duties'* and he suggested that the accumulation of capital on which an industrialized economy depended would not be restricted if those forms of taxation were increased. Keynes argued that more progressive taxation would assist the accumulation of capital since redistribution to the less well off would have the beneficial effect of increasing aggregate demand and thus economic growth.

Keynes was no revolutionary. He thought of classical economic theory as merely a special case of his general theory, which applied only at times of full employment. Others would argue that Keynes' theory was but a special case of the classical model valid only in times of depression. The essential point was that the two models were not wholly incompatible.

As Keynes himself pointed out:

> *'Our criticism of the accepted classical theory of economics has consisted not so much in finding logical flaws in its analysis as in pointing out that its tacit assumptions are seldom or never satisfied, with the result that it cannot solve the economic problems of the actual world. But if our central controls succeed in establishing an aggregate volume of output corresponding to full employment as nearly as is practicable, the classical theory comes into its own again from this point onwards.'*[17]

During the years up to the Second World War, the Keynesian focus on full employment became the new orthodoxy, justifying the New Deal initiatives.

---

16 Keynes, J.M., (1936), *The General Theory of Employment, Interest and Money*, London: Macmillan & Co, p. 372.
17 Ibid, p. 378.

They were only partially successful, it being the Second World War which finally eliminated the last vestiges of depression. Federal expenditure rose from its 1929 level of 3 per cent of GNP to over 40 per cent by 1944. With the American military employing around 12 million men, unemployment was ended and employers found great difficulty recruiting sufficient workers. Wages rose sharply reducing the inequitable gap between rich and poor, with food rationing and price controls ensuring a healthy diet at reasonable cost for everyone.

Today it is often overlooked that Keynes' focus on the achievement of full employment did not make him an enthusiast for government intervention in any other circumstance than an economic slump causing unemployment. He in fact argued that:

> *'the important thing for government is not to do things which individuals are doing already ... but to do those things which at present are not done at all.'* [18]

He was certainly not advocating extensive ongoing government intervention in the economy. The only government department he ever proposed new duties for was the British Treasury, a department which had an administrative staff, amazing though it may seem now, of just over twenty when he joined it during the First World War. [19]

Keynes died in 1946 and what became known as 'Keynesian economics' was something which the man himself would almost certainly have disowned. R.F. Harrod had provided a mathematical demonstration of the intrinsic instability of economic growth and consequently concluded, in agreement with Keynes, that there was no natural tendency for an economy to establish a stable equilibrium with full employment. Harrod's conclusion was that government intervention would be necessary on an ongoing basis to manage the level of economic output rather than simply to intervene to correct economic downturns. This ongoing intervention is the approach now associated with the term 'Keynesian', a long-run model of government intervention to achieve a self-sustaining economic growth at an acceptable level of inflation.

---

18   Skidelsky, R., (1977), 'The Political Meaning of the Keynesian Revolution', in *The End of the Keynesian Era*, (ed.) R. Skidelsky, London: Macmillan, p. 34.
19   Cairncross, A., (1978), 'Keynes and the Planned Economy', in *Keynes and Laissez-Faire*, (ed.) A.P. Thirlwell, London: Macmillan Press, p. 36.

For clarity here, that approach is referred to as Harrod–Keynesian to distinguish it from that of Keynes himself who argued for government intervention only to overcome recession and unemployment. The Harrod–Keynes approach dominated post-war university departments and business schools and was adopted wholeheartedly in Britain and briefly, and with less enthusiasm, in the United States.

In the United States there was some disagreement over the New Deal reforms as to whether they were intended solely to achieve short-term recovery, as Keynes proposed, or whether they were aimed at permanent reforms as the Harrod–Keynesian disciples would have intended. In the event, after the war, the United States chose to reassert its rugged individualist commitment to private enterprise by reversing many of the New Deal initiatives with the Taft–Hartley Act of 1947. In Britain, the Harrod–Keynesians were joined by a genuinely democratic socialist government establishing a truly mixed economy, which was a substantial step beyond anything Keynes himself would have supported. Thus the United States and Britain provided substantially different industrial contexts for post-war management, though management itself was essentially the same in both the United States and Britain, the division of its labour being the subject of the next chapter.

6

Division of Management Labour

A sociological approach to understanding the role of management might be to view it, without prior conception, as a class of individuals. They have no democratically won authority, being merely appointees. Yet within their own organization, they appear to have more or less absolute power. Their authority is not legitimated by any obvious means. Weber identified three categories of leadership: charismatic, hereditary and bureaucratic, the latter meaning through the acceptance of the rational–legal rules and procedures of bureaucracy.[1] Drucker pointed out the three most charismatic leaders of the twentieth century were Stalin, Hitler and Chairman Mao, concluding 'God preserve us from charismatic leaders!' Nor are managers for the most part appointed as a result of an agreed hereditary succession or any other traditional process, and the legitimacy of those that are so appointed is dubious.

Management authority appears to lack a moral justification, yet they exercise moral discretion over all manner of significant decisions affecting not only those employed in their company but on a much wider front, for example, including their suppliers, customers, local community and the world at large. They decide, on whatever grounds they choose, how the surplus their company generates will be distributed. They are all-powerful but with arguably limited claims to legitimacy.

Such an analysis might raise interesting questions about management. But industrial management itself has not been much concerned with making claims for its own legitimacy. Management was drawn into existence by sheer necessity. The most obvious fact about management was that it cost money. While it did not itself make anything, or sell anything, it nevertheless had to be paid a salary and provided with a space in which to work. Such additional cost, without apparent profit, would not be attractive to 'the butcher, the brewer

---

1   Weber, M., (2001). *The Protestant Ethic and The Spirit of Capitalism,* London: Routledge Classics. First published in 1904.

or the baker' and would not have been incurred if it could have been avoided. But it could not. And the surprising thing was that management, once it was established, proved an effective contributor to productivity, profitability and growth in what has been referred to as 'the management revolution'.

Management matters but its precise nature often remains obscure. Academic theorists have generally shrunk from any detailed explanation. Smith seemed to think that in a company run by hired managers as opposed to owners, the managers should spend their time looking after 'other people's money' with 'anxious vigilance'.

Marx, writing 90 years after Smith, thought of managers as the equivalent of an army's officers, responsible for the 'direct and constant supervision' of 'foremen and overlookers'. He may have been right in the sense that they were responsible for the 'esprit de corps' of the organization, to use Fayol's terminology. However, the army officer analogy captures only the people management part of the role. The aims and tasks of an army are determined for it, war being 'simply the continuation of policy by other means.'[2] The officer ranks are not therefore engaged with formulating policy, whereas managers of an industrial company are responsible for every aspect, strategic and operational, of their autonomous competing organization.

Business historian Chandler referred to managers as 'administrative coordinators', which might mean whatever is wanted for it to mean, without shedding much light on what they actually did. Management practitioners themselves have not generally been very good at explaining their role. Most have focused on prescriptions for what they believe in any circumstance will be most effective, but without offering much descriptive analysis of management practice. More thoughtful practitioners, such as Alfred Sloan, Geoffrey Vickers, Chester Barnard, Wilfred Brown and a small number of others, have provided invaluable insights into aspects of the management process, but their main aim has not been descriptive.

Clearly, the management task is not simply that of the bureaucrat, operating according to a prepared set of rules which cover all known eventualities, as might have been the case, for example, in a government department. Their

---

2   Von Clausevitz, C., (1830), *On War*, currently available in the Wordsworth Classics of World Literature series, based on the translation by J.J. Graham, revised by F.N. Maude, abridged and with an introduction by Louise Willmot. The quotation is from Book 1, Chapter 1, section 24.

responsibility was, and is, to deal with variety and the unexpected, and ultimately to create variety and innovation.

Perhaps Galbraith was right when he claimed that what he referred to as 'businessmen' found it difficult to explain what they actually did. The term 'businessmen' was then in common usage, especially among economists and sociologists who had little understanding of, or sympathy for, those who held the management responsibility. Mintzberg's PhD study of managerial work was more enlightening about the allocation of management time to different types of work rather than describing the work itself. The essential characteristic was one of fragmentation and discontinuity, confirmed by Parker referring to management work in the very different setting of a research university.[3] But it is important to know what management work is and to distinguish between the version of management appropriate for the baker, butcher or pin maker, and the management that developed as large scale business grew up in the United States.

Adam Smith suggested that every form of labour, so widely defined as to include even philosophers, would be subject to specialization. The labour of management was certainly no exception. Chandler indicated some of the management specializations achieved by the American railroad companies. As businesses grew in scale, it was imperative for the management process to be so divided.

The process came to full fruition in the big manufacturing businesses of the late nineteenth century such as the United States Steel Corporation which was not just a steel producer but also manufactured a wide variety of steel end-products. The division of management labour was repeated in every kind of business organization. And it continues to be repeated today as every successful start-up business progresses towards robust viability. Its aim is for ever increasing efficiency and effectiveness.

The division of management must have started, as it still starts today, when the successful founding entrepreneur, the sole proprietor of the business, found that he or she was no longer able to manage everything themselves. Some portion of their workload had to be delegated to another if the business was to survive and grow. That first division of responsibility carried certain unavoidable consequences with it. It was, and is, a big decision.

---

3   Parker, M., (2004), 'Becoming Manager', *Management Learning*, Vol. 35, No. 1, pp. 45–59

Firstly, it immediately increased the cost base of the business and necessitated a significant increment in gross profit if the business were to remain viable. Secondly, the owner manager would be concerned to ensure that the first appointment would not adversely affect the way business was conducted. The established focus on, for example, standards of service and customer relations must not be compromised. And as the business continued to grow and further new appointments were made, it would be important to maintain the internal climate and culture of the organization so as to preserve and develop its reputation with customers, suppliers and others, critically including potential employees.

Manufacturing, even pin making, remains a useful context for considering the division of management labour as it includes the production process as well as selling and administration. Typically, responsibilities for internal operations and those for marketing and sales are the first to be separated, while in the early stages at least, responsibility for finance is likely to be held by an external professional on a consultative or part-time basis. At the same time a back office administrative role has to be established keeping track of orders being processed as well as basic book-keeping and preparation of accounts. This is the basic division of management discussed in the following sections which occurred when management first emerged and which is still, in broad principle, repeated today.

The division of management labour demonstrates the possibility that management without ownership can be professionally focused on avoiding 'negligence and profusion' and that 'anxious vigilance' would be an inadequate substitute for professional expertise in any business which has grown more complex than *'the baker, the brewer or the butcher'*.

The division of management is a variable but continuing process. The division that was appropriate in the eighteenth century was not apt in later times. What was appropriate in textiles may not have been in automobiles or internet firms. Furthermore, with each increment in growth the management of a business is forced to consider the possibility of further division, the potential for application of more detailed expertise or newer technology, or simply the division of existing processes among a greater number of hands.

There is no universal truth about the division of management labour. The following is an approximation intended to give some flavour of the potential complexity and sophistication of management specialisms which goes beyond the simplifications offered by economic models.

Operations Management

The manufacturing process can be accomplished in various ways. Some organizational decisions will depend on whether the items being manufactured are standard products sold on a continuous basis through normal distribution chains, or are items designed and made specifically to the specifications of an individual customer and manufactured and despatched to them in one or more discrete batches. Perhaps the most interesting manufacturing organization would combine both continuous and batch production. That combination has clear implications for all aspects of manufacture from the receipt and acceptance of raw materials, their storage and control, issue to the manufacturing unit, shop floor operations, production control, the management of quality throughout the whole process and final despatch of finished product.

There is no need here to review any of these different jobs in detail but a summary might indicate the nature of management responsibility. The business process is a continuous cycle but for the present purpose it can be assumed that it commences with the receipt of a purchase order from a customer. Clearly, the order has resulted from some prior process which for the moment can be disregarded. The order will require the acquisition of materials necessary for its completion, so the real work starts with the purchase of those materials.

Procurement is one of the critical management support functions. The purchase decision depends on a mix of criteria including price, quality, delivery performance and reliability in all these categories. Moreover, the purchase decision is not simply a one-off, but part of a continuing series of such decisions which may be taken on a purely open market basis, or a longer-term agreement may be reached whereby both supplier and buyer accept a degree of interdependence in which the supplier is given a contract which excludes other suppliers in return for reliable deliveries which enables the purchaser to minimize their holdings of material stocks. The aim of purchasing management is to minimize the long-term costs which arise not only from the prices paid and stock levels needing to be carried but also the reliability of continuous supply and the quality of materials.

When the relevant materials are delivered and their quality assessed and approved they will be accepted into store. Materials control is a basic management responsibility, the aim of which is to ensure that sufficient materials are always available so that the factory is never held up for their lack, but on the other hand that there is no more money tied up in stocks than is necessary to assure the sufficiency. Clearly, the treatment of materials for standard products in continuous manufacture and for products ordered and made in discrete batches is quite different. For standard products, materials will be ordered and received on a regular basis, the most economic order quantities being agreed with suppliers. It may be that each delivery of such items would comprise a four-week supply, with deliveries being made four- weekly and a safety stock amounting to, say, two weeks' supply, being permanently held in store. The safety stock would be held to cover for any interruptions to supply so as to ensure the factory is never stopped awaiting supplies. Such a traditional system of materials control is little different from the modern just-in-time system which operates with more frequent deliveries and without safety stocks.

This summary account of purchasing and materials control is intended only to indicate that there are techniques and procedures which are important to the effectiveness of the company's operations, for which management is responsible and which have no relevance to, or relationship with, matters of the company's ownership. The middle managers carrying these responsibilities are employed to work for the company's good and their performance in that is typically open to regular review.

Similar disciplines apply to the rather more complex processes of production scheduling and control, whose responsibility is to advise the customer of a date for delivery of the finished product and to issue the materials and making instructions onto the shop floor at the appropriate time and to monitor progress through its various work stations to completion. Production scheduling aims not only to satisfy customer delivery requirements but also to minimize the amount of work in progress on the shop floor and consequently the amount of money tied up, at the same time ensuring there is sufficient work available so that no workstation runs out of work and is kept waiting. A key part of the production control function is the maintenance of information as to the stage of the process achieved for all customer orders.

Quality management works hand in glove with the above control systems, in the early days presiding over systems of inspection which were not infrequently in conflict with production management over the required standard of quality to be achieved. Such issues were often heightened by the methods of payment of production workers who may not have been paid for substandard work. The American quality gurus responsible for radically improving quality standards in post-Second World War Japan, Deming and Juran, changed the practice of quality management. Quality standards were defined precisely in terms of conformance to customer requirements, statistical process control techniques were applied to ensure that variations from those standards were identified before production went out of tolerance limits, and methods were adopted which aimed to build quality into products rather than inspecting it out, as was previously the practice with final inspection systems. Quality standards could be achieved at very little if any cost by eliminating scrap and the necessity for reworking. But as with the other areas of operations management, there was a balance to be struck: achieving the customer's requirements could be done efficiently but aiming to achieve quality standards in excess of what the customer required, or was prepared to pay for, may simply have been wasteful.

Although the above account is much oversimplified, it nevertheless indicates that Smith's suspicion of hired managers, on the grounds that they can't be trusted to be vigilant since they are looking after other people's money, is simply misplaced. It is not to deny that his basic contention, especially around a baker's or butcher's shop, might not have some truth, but that it is simply not relevant to the operations on a larger scale.

It might be asked how the above account of operations management lines up with economic theory, for example, that quantities of output are set at the level where marginal cost is equal to market price in order to maximize profit. Economic theory does not appear to contribute anything of worth. The relevance of economic theory may be more aptly considered in relation to the whole management project rather than in relation to a particular functional area.

Marketing Management

Whilst the functional expertise in marketing is quite different from that of operations, the management concerns to achieve efficiency and effectiveness, avoiding waste and achieving an ever improved competitive position, are just the same. Most businesses start with a product or service for which there appears to be some customer demand and they are initially oriented around that product and the definition of its particular characteristics. As businesses progress they develop their focus more into the processes of production as previously described with the aim of reducing costs and improving quality and performance.

In terms of the division of management labour it is often the sales responsibility which is the specialism that is first identified and the business becomes sales oriented. But it is quickly recognized that responsibility for sales is not simply a matter of selling, but of marketing. As Levitt pointed out:

> 'The difference between marketing and selling is more than semantic. Selling focuses on the needs of the seller, marketing on the needs of the buyer. Selling is preoccupied with the seller's need to convert the product into cash, marketing with the idea of satisfying the needs of the customer by means of the product and the whole cluster of things associated with creating, delivering, and, finally, consuming it.'[4]

The American Marketing Association (AMA) defines marketing as:

> 'the activity, set of institutions, and processes for creating, communicating, delivering, and exchanging offerings that have value for customers, clients, partners, and society at large',[5]

a definition approved by the AMA's board of directors in October 2007 and which bears the certain hallmarks of definition by committee. Kotler more succinctly defined it as:

> 'the science and art of finding, keeping and growing profitable customers',[6]

a definition that is so general as to be a little short on specific meaning. Levitt suggested that a business:

> 'must learn to think of itself not in terms of producing goods and services but as **buying customers**, as doing the things that will make people **want** to do business with it'[7] (original emphasis in bold italics).

Drucker suggested the job of business was to create a customer.

4   Levitt, T., (1960), 'Marketing Myopia', *Harvard Business Review,* July/August, p. 7. Now accessible as Best of HBR series reprint R0407L at http://www.dallascap.com/pdfs/MarketingMyopia. pdf
5   http://www.marketingpower.com/AboutAMA/Pages/DefinitionofMarketing.aspx
6   Kotler, P., (1999), *Kotler on Marketing,* New York: The Free Press, p. 36.
7   Levitt, T., (1960), 'Marketing Myopia', *Harvard Business Review,* July/August, p. 13.

The tools at marketing management's disposal include firstly marketing research, which involves whatever techniques and methods are required to identify details of existing and potential customers and markets, and technologies. Such research is conducted partly on an ongoing basis so that the company is aware of critical changes, if possible before they occur and at least as and when they occur; and partly on a one-off basis when specific researches are designed and executed to find answers to particular questions which may be critical to the further development of the business.

Other mechanisms for which marketing management are generally held responsible, referred to as the marketing mix, are product, price, promotion (of which selling is one element) and distribution, sometimes referred to as placement, or place, in order to comprise '4 Ps'. Each of these variables is controlled by management and none of them is as straightforward as they might first appear.

The concept of the product (or service) is multi-dimensional. According to standard definitions it comprises a core benefit or service for which the customer has a need or want. It has a physical existence which is manifest in its price and quality, its performance, specification, design, reliability and longevity. Beyond that, there is the question of the service that is involved with the product, such things as its warranty, delivery, after-sales service and promotional support. And even beyond that, there are psychological characteristics such as the product image and brand and corporate images which are perceived by existing and potential customers.[8] Product analysis goes beyond this level of detail. For example, Garvin suggested that quality be defined by such additional characteristics as conformance, durability, serviceability, aesthetics and perceived quality.[9]

Marketing management's responsibility is to ensure that the product which is delivered, defined in terms of its various attributes as above, is the product which the customers need and want and believe they are getting when they purchase. Moreover, it is marketing's responsibility to ensure they understand which attributes are most important to the customer and to ensure that the company does not incur cost delivering levels of attribute the customer does not need or want.

---

8   Pearson, G., (1999), *Strategy in Action,* Harlow: FT Prentice Hall, p. 59.
9   Garvin, D.A., (1987), 'Competing on the Eight Dimensions of Quality', *Harvard Business Review,* November/December.

Price is one important attribute of the product and it is interesting to compare how marketers are taught to treat pricing with how economic theory suggests prices should be set. Many different approaches to the pricing decision have been proposed by marketers: premium, penetration, economy, price skimming, psychological pricing, product line pricing, optional pricing, captive product pricing, product bundle pricing, promotional pricing, geographical pricing and value pricing.[10] To this list might be added simple cost plus pricing or even marginal cost pricing. Whatever approach is adopted, the pricing element is clearly only one of many product attributes which need to be complementary rather than contradictory if the product is to present itself as a coherent whole.

Promotion can involve any or all of advertising, internet promotion, personal selling, sales promotion, public relations, direct mail, trade fairs, exhibitions and sponsorship. The management decisions on promotion involve selecting the methods and media to be used based on their efficiency and effectiveness and critically including their compatibility with the other product attributes and existing and potential customer and market characteristics.

Finally, among the marketing mix is distribution, a management decision which is easy to overlook since the most appropriate distribution channels might appear obvious. Distribution could be direct, such as via mail order, internet or telephone sales. Or it could be through an agent who sells on behalf of the producer, or via a wholesaler who sells to retailers, or it could be direct to the retailer who sells to end-customers. Innovative distribution decisions could be critical to the success of a particular business.

As with all management decisions those on the marketing mix have to be planned and executed and their effectiveness monitored and adjustments to the original decisions considered. These issues may appear more remote from the business of processing customers' orders than is operations management. But their effectiveness and efficiency are clearly crucial to the company's survival and prosperity. The degree to which the company has absorbed the marketing philosophy is widely seen as a mark of its stage of development.

Economic theory is largely silent regarding any of this. It simply does not engage with the concept of marketing management. It is concerned with what it refers to as commodities whereas marketing is concerned with differentiated products, identifying their uniqueness to differentiate them further from

---

10 Marketing Teacher at http://marketingteacher.com/Lessons/lesson_pricing.htm

competing products in ways which customers find appealing. Economic theory is concerned with market prices whereas marketing management is concerned with differentiating their product by all means including price in order that it is perceived as more desirable than competing products. Economic theory suggests that corporate ownership is essential to those in control if they are to be 'vigilant' but ownership is utterly irrelevant to professional marketing management. It is competition, rather than ownership which drives management to efficiency and effectiveness.

Financial Management

The third primary division in the work of management is the finance responsibility. While often headed up by a professionally qualified accountant, it is a management responsibility. Accounting is a distinct sub-division of financial management.

Accounting is concerned with recording management stewardship over past periods and is a tool of management control. It involves the accurate recording of all monetary transactions and the preparation, at the end of each accounting period, of reporting schedules such as the balance sheet, the profit and loss account and cash flow statement. As well as these formal documents, accounting is also concerned with recording and preparing management accounts such as budgets, actual results and reports of variations between the two and the likely import of such variance. Accounting is intended to assist in the effective and efficient internal control of day to day business.

Financial management is a more strategic responsibility, ensuring the business has adequate, but not excessive, funding to survive and prosper, that it makes effective and full use of its assets and does not retain underutilized assets and that it invests effectively in its future security and development.

The planning of adequate funding requires detailed knowledge and understanding of the funds, actual and potential, generated and consumed by business operations and the funds required for the planned business future. This requires an ability to control short-term cash conservation and generation from the business, so that sufficient cash is available to fund raw material purchases, employee wages and all the costs of producing goods plus the provision of credit to customers till they pay for the goods they receive, as well as any other short-term needs such as tax payments. Nothing is quite so strategic as running out of cash. Management is concerned first and foremost with avoiding waste and financial management is responsible for waste incurred by lax control of working capital, or by payment of more taxation and dividend than necessary.

Financial management involves responsibility for generating funds from external sources, usually including shareholders, purchasers of loan stock and banks who might provide short and medium-term loans. The mix of such sources of finance is critical to the future viability of the business. While bank loans may be satisfactory for the short and medium-term liquidity requirements of the business, its long-term structure depends on: a) the mix of shareholders' funding which is rewarded by dividends and the possibility of capital growth as the share price rises; and b) the long-term debt component which is rewarded by interest payments to holders of bonds and loan stock.

Dividends are paid out of profits on which taxes have been paid, whereas interest is treated as a business cost prior to payment of tax. Consequently interest-bearing loan stock is generally a substantially less costly form of externally funded capital. Financial management therefore has a fine judgment to make regarding the mix of the equity and debt it issues to generate funds. If the proportion of debt is too low, the company will be paying more for its funding than is necessary. If the proportion of debt is too high, the company may be perceived as too risky and the share price may be damaged, thus raising the cost of future increments in external funding. Minimizing the cost of the company's capital, (calculating it as the average cost of its different sources, weighted by their proportions in the total capital mix) reduces the return the company has to make on future investments if they are to be profitable. Thus the lower the weighted average cost of a company's capital the more the investment it can afford to make in its future.

The quantification of debt and equity capital and their remuneration has generally been recorded on a company's balance sheet and has therefore traditionally embodied a degree of objectivity, or at least, transparency. However, in more recent years the nature of a company's assets has changed making it more difficult to record their true value on the balance sheet. And at the same time there has also been an incentive for accounts to deliberately mislead by taking real liabilities off the balance sheet, thereby reducing the apparent scale of risk involved and enabling companies to take on more debt than would otherwise be thought prudent. The truth and fairness of a company's published accounts has therefore been allowed to be compromised.

Associated with decisions regarding the capital structure of the business are the more routine decisions as to the level of dividend payments. Dividends impact on the stock market performance of the company's shares, but it is only one such influence. The company's shares, traded in the freely competitive stock market, may be regarded as a 'product' competing with other 'products', and dividends are just one of the product's attributes. Financial management has responsibility for marketing the company's shares using all the marketing tools available to it, not simply relying on the one lever, dividends.

Financial management's task is not to maximize the share price on the stock market but to ensure it performs sufficiently to ensure the company's autonomous survival. Distributing more dividends than necessary to achieve this would be just as wasteful as giving the customer levels of quality, or any other characteristic, for which they are not prepared to pay.

This requires the general stock market to be aware of the company's true position and to have that reflected in the current share price as accurately as possible. Given that the market itself is subject not merely to factual analysis but to sentiment, not to mention hysteria and panic, the accuracy is fairly limited, but this only makes it more important that the share price and the company's underlying value do not get too disconnected. If they do the company's autonomy will be threatened because such misleading valuations will almost certainly become apparent at some point.

Financial management is also responsible for ensuring that investment decisions are taken on the basis of rational financial grounds. Non-financial criteria, for example, related to the appropriateness of the strategic direction of the investment, may be critical, but properly conducted financial assessment is also necessary to try to ensure the future viability of new investment. These may include the setting of an appropriate interest rate which new investments might be required to return if they were to proceed, the hurdle rate being set by reference to the weighted average cost of the company's capital.

This brief summary of aspects of the financial management responsibility is sufficient for the present purpose. Clearly, the many and various financial decisions would normally be taken guided solely by the best interests of the company. That is no different from all other management decisions such as those in operations and marketing already considered. However, were financial management to be persuaded that their responsibility was to act solely in the best interests of shareholders, capital structuring and the distribution of dividends might be decided quite differently, subordinating the long- term interests of the company to the immediate or short-term interests of its shareholders.

Technical Management

The three primary divisions of management labour appear to be generally applicable in any industrial activity. But the industry-specific technical management responsibility is likely to be just as important as the others and may in some circumstances be paramount. Technical management has always been an important management responsibility, right from the beginning of industrialization. The famous names associated with the first canal, road and rail systems were the engineers such as Brindley, Macadam, Stephenson and Watt. The same is true of manufacturing industries of the initial industrialization: Arkwright, Crompton, Darby, Kay, Hargreaves and others, are all known for their industry-specific technological contributions.

The distinction between the technologists and the mere 'businessmen' was made by Thorstein Veblen.[11] He contrasted the engineers and scientists, *'professionals of great skill and productive potential'* with the *'profit oriented businessmen'*.[12] This appreciation of the technical role, which economists make no attempt to model, adds to the denigration of the 'businessman' which economists from Smith onwards have claimed to account for. But the 'businessman', synonymous with the capitalist 'Mr Moneybags', is not management, while the professional technical role is part of the management responsibility.

Technical management requires knowledge and expertise, relevant to the specific industry, which is nowadays normally obtained through graduate education in the particular science or technology. It requires continuous updating as technology advances, so that the company's use of technology remains competitive. It oversees the research and development activity which aims to take the company ahead of competition in terms of its use of technology.

The vast majority of inventions and innovations emanate from research and development groups operating within large-scale business organizations.[13] The

11   Veblen, T., (1904), *The Theory of Business Enterprise*, New York: Macmillan.
12   Galbraith, J.K., (1987), *A History of Economics*, London: Hamish Hamilton p. 172.
13   Schmiemann M., 'The Link Between R&D, Inventions and Innovations in Europe', *World Patent Information*, Volume 21, Number 1, March 1999 , pp. 43–45(3).

commonplace assertion that big businesses cannot be innovative is patently untrue. But the organizational characteristics which permit organizations to be efficient in their day to day operations can tend to frustrate and inhibit the effective operation of research and development. Protecting the ability to be creative, within a large and efficiency and effectiveness focused organization, is one of the responsibilities of technical management.

There has always been some disagreement as to the role of technical management in the initiation of innovations. Marketers can argue that their role is prime, there being no point in producing an innovative new product for which there is no market. The opposing argument holds that constraining research and development to projects approved by marketing effectively rules out the possibility for fundamental step-change innovations for which there is no existing sale and no market experience. The truth is that either markets or technology can initiate innovations, but successful developments will need to satisfy the requirements of both.

The industry specific nature of technical management means that further generalization on the division of its labour would be problematic, save to note that it may be the most important managerial role in some industrial situations and is excluded from the economic model.

The Management Mindset

The division of management labour may continue indefinitely as organizations grow. The tendency to create bureaucracy as organizations grow and mature is understood and appropriate countermeasures have been prescribed.[14] Mintzberg was quoted as saying he could offer an account of problems an organization had experienced by reference to the titles of head office departments, many having been created to solve specific issues. Some functions, which might be thought of as management, actually are the providers of administrative support rather than being themselves management responsibilities.

People management is a good example of Mintzberg's analysis. The personnel or human resource management function was traditionally a responsibility of line management, an implicit and important part of the role of any manager. The staff function merely provided administrative support on such matters as pay and occasionally being asked to provide arbitration when

---

14   Pearson, G., (1999), *Strategy in Action*, Harlow: FT Prentice Hall, pp. 223–248.

line management and workers were in dispute. The role gained importance in situations where industrial relations were contentious, and sometimes, in fulfilment of Mintzberg's contention, separate departments of industrial relations were established. But managing people is so much an intrinsic part of management that many, including Drucker, have been doubtful whether there should be such a separate function operating continuously as intermediary between line managers and workers. Such a function might well be indicative of an organization's personnel problems, and its existence dependent on continuation of those problems.

No matter how management labour is divided there are consistencies of approach amounting ultimately to a management mindset which drives decisions in all such specialist areas. Adam Smith's assertion that it was from the producer's self-interest that 'we' – Smith makes it clear he was referring to 'we' as customers – benefit, rather than their 'humanity'. The customers' benefit arises from the fact that producers compete with each other to offer customers a better deal; it does not derive from any aspect of ownership. The need to avoid losses, or to survive in the face of competition, is what drives management, not the narrow self-interest of ownership.

Smith denied the possibility of business improvement by management without ownership and in this he was demonstrably wrong. Management without ownership has achieved massive improvement. Chandler referred to it as 'the managerial revolution in American business'; Drucker referred to it as the 'productivity revolution' which had more dramatic impacts on the general population than did the first industrial revolution. The division of management labour demonstrates the means by which this was achieved. It is a technical, professional process rather than simply being based on the subsequently ubiquitous 'greed is good' caricature of Smith's approach.

Management labour may start as described previously or it may take a different route depending on the nature of the business and possibly the personal strengths of its founding entrepreneur. It does not necessarily imply any particular organizational structure. Perhaps the only generalization that can be made is that while the business is successful and continues to grow, so the division of management labour will also proceed.

Operations management may spawn an industrial engineering function whose job it is to continually improve production methods, ensuring the company maintains its position in available technology. Technical management may set up a separate research and development unit to initiate the development of new products or completely new technologies, such a department being quite separate from the main business so that different cultural rules might apply to this essentially creative work. Marketing may initiate a separate research department devoted to identifying new markets or new applications or new customer wants or needs. Finance may establish a separate treasury function whose job it is to ensure that any short-term cash balances the company might accrue are deployed in the most lucrative ways commensurate with their ready accessibility. They may also develop specialist tax expertise whose job it is to ensure the company does not miss any opportunities to reduce its tax payments. Similarly, of support systems, accounting may establish a specialist credit control function to ensure invoiced payments are received on time.

The division of management labour is continuous while ever the business grows, and it can contribute substantially to its success.

The management responsibility is for the survival and future prosperity of the organization and as it grows to find ever better ways of dividing that work so as improve the methods of manufacture (i.e. to reduce costs, improve yields or improve quality of production), or to improve the products (i.e. by either lowering their cost, improving their quality or performance or adding more features).

Eliminating waste is invariably the first and simplest way of improving the way things are done. This applies to all the various functional areas of management which have been briefly reviewed in this chapter. The preoccupation is, as Drucker emphasized, with avoiding losses, i.e. surviving, rather than maximizing profit:

> 'Nothing shows more clearly how deeply we are still entrapped in pre-industrial thinking than our pre-occupation with "profit". The central fact of industrial economics is not "profit" but "loss" – not the expectation of ending up with a surplus, its justification, and the legitimacy of the claims to a share in it; but the inevitable and real risk of ending up with an impoverishing deficit, and the need, the absolute need, to avoid this loss by providing against the risks.'[15]

Drucker's concept of management, largely shared by Barnard, Brown and others, is of a continuously innovative process of improvement, introducing

---

15 Drucker, P.F., (1950), *The New Society*, New York: Harper & Brothers, p. 52.

the new, eliminating waste, reducing costs, improving quality, and so giving the customer a better deal than competitors do. This is the management mindset which drives management across all its responsibilities in operations, marketing, finance and technical management, focusing on ever better use of resources so as to ensure the company's survival and its ability to win in its chosen markets.

The complaint that commercial management seeks to avoid paying, for example, more tax than is absolutely necessary, is based on a misunderstanding of the management project. Of course, it will seek to minimize its tax payments, just as it does any other expense. It is up to government to set the tax rules without ambiguity. It is not up to management to pay additional unnecessary tax motivated by generosity or patriotism.

It is a paradox of classical economic theory that while it claims to be an objective study, it is based on the concept of the amoral, self-interested individual seeking only to maximize his own utility. Smith knew nothing of large-scale industry and its management. His models were the butcher, the brewer, the baker and the pin-making workshop. For all his insights, these were the foundation of his theory, which held that hired managers could not be expected to work in the long-term interests of the company they managed, but only in their own rather shorter-term self-interest. Like much economic theory it may have been appropriate in its own time, but its relevance was not permanent.

7

Theories of Management

The practice of management had been established for the best part of a century before theoretical approaches were developed which might offer guidance to practitioners and short circuit their learning how to make their labour more effective. Curiously the first systematic general management text was not Anglo-Saxon. Henri Fayol's *Administration Industrielle et Générale* was based on his experience working for a French coal mining company. It was published in French in 1916 and not translated into English till 1949 by which time Taylor's 'scientific management' and much of the subsequent 'human relations' work had already been completed. But whereas they focused primarily on the employer–employee relationship, Fayol's aim was more general.

He provided an approach to the structuring of organizations with certain detached guidance on worker relations which he intended should be applicable in all organizational settings as indicated in his preface:

> *'Management plays a very important part in the government of undertakings, large or small, industrial, commercial, political, religious or any other.'*[1]

Concurrent with Fayol's mining management experience, management education and training were being established in the United States. The first business school, the Wharton School, was named after its entrepreneur founder, Joseph Wharton. He had achieved his considerable wealth through the American Nickel Company and Bethlehem Steel Corporation, which coincidentally was home to Taylor's study of the science of handling pig iron. Wharton School was established in 1881 at the University of Pennsylvania with the avowed aim of establishing management as a profession, Wharton's vision

1   Fayol, H., (1949), *General and Industrial Management,* translation by Constance Storrs, London: Pitman Publishing Company, p. 3.

being that the school would produce graduates who would become *'pillars of the state, whether in private or in public life.'*[2]

Successive theoretical approaches focused to a considerable extent on how to motivate people at work. The concept of motivation may now be seen as problematic: is the word motivate a euphemism for manipulate, or even exploit? Is it more the intent to deal with people simply so as to maximize profit? Or is it to make working life more congenial and help people develop themselves further? And if the latter – naïve thought though that may be regarded by some – is it in order to increase the productivity of a healthy, happy workforce or is it for the benefit of the workforce with no thought to extract any advantage from them?

In the case of Arkwright it may have been to create a contented workforce with which to combat the Luddite machine breakers as well as to increase productivity. In the case of Owen it was his social idealism, demonstrated repeatedly in his subsequent career, which drove the process of improving the worker's lot, albeit for a profit. Marx included Owen among those he labelled 'utopian idealists', implying they were well intentioned but ineffective. The purposes of management aside, later managers provided a more satisfactory working environment simultaneously with a sufficient return to the employer.

The employer–employee relationship was always an important part of management's responsibility. The potential for the strong employer to exploit the weak worker was apparent from the start of industrialization. Marx's reference to the 'negotiation' between the labourer and 'Mr Moneybags', after which the latter was 'smirking' his satisfaction at the outcome, was theoretical rather than based on personal experience. It did not include any report on the actual negotiation, the act of stealing the surplus earned by the worker. Fred Taylor had no such qualms. His account was based on personal participation.

Scientific Management

The application of 'science' to management was timely as it coincided with the blossoming of various branches of natural science and scientific discovery and

---

2   Quote is from the Wharton School website: http://www.wharton.upenn.edu/whartonfacts/history

it was attractive since it appeared to depersonalize the potentially explosive employer–employee relationship. Taylor, a devoted Quaker, was focused on how to bring management and labour together in productive partnership from which both should gain.

Kanigel's biography of Taylor describes him as:

> '... the first efficiency expert, the original time-and-motion man. To organized labour, he was the soulless slave driver, out to destroy the workingman's health and rob him of his manhood. To the bosses, he was an eccentric and a radical, raising the wages of common labourers by a third, paying college boys to click stopwatches. To him and his friends, he was a misunderstood visionary, possessor of the one best way that, under the banner of science, would confer prosperity on worker and boss alike, abolishing the ancient class hatreds.'[3]

Taylorism, or scientific management, was concerned first and foremost with how business could survive, rather than with how to divide the spoils of industry. Taylor himself claimed that resolving the power struggle was the end to which efficiency was the means, not the other way round.

The following is Taylor's own account of the scientific management process, including his famous 'negotiation' with Schmidt, as told to a House of Representatives Special Committee investigating his methods. It was subsequently included in *Scientific Management*, published in 1910:

> 'Our first step was to find the proper workman to begin with. We therefore carefully watched and studied these 75 men for three or four days, at the end of which time we had picked out four men who appeared to be physically able to handle pig iron at the rate of 47 tons [as opposed to the customary 12½ tons] per day. A careful study was then made of each of these men. We looked up their history as far back as practicable and thorough inquiries were made as to the character, habits, and the ambition of each of them. Finally we selected one from among the four as the most likely man to start with. He was a little Pennsylvania Dutchman who had been observed to trot back home for a mile or so after his work in the evening about as fresh as he was when he came trolling down to work in the morning. We found that upon wages of

3   Kanigel, R., (1997), *The One Best Way: Frederick Winslow Taylor and the Enigma of Efficiency*, London: Little, Brown & Company, p. 1.

$1.15 a day he had succeeded in buying a small plot of ground, and that he was engaged in putting up the walls of a little house for himself in the morning before starting to work and at night after leaving. He also had the reputation of being exceedingly 'close', that is, of placing a very high value on a dollar. As one man whom we talked to about him said, "A penny looks about the size of a cart-wheel to him." This man we will call Schmidt.

The task before us, then, narrowed itself down to getting Schmidt to handle 47 tons of pig iron per day and making him glad to do it. This was done as follows. Schmidt was called out from among the gang of pig-iron handlers and talked to somewhat in this way:

"Schmidt, are you a high-priced man?"

"Vell, I don't know vat you mean."

"Oh yes, you do. What I want to know is whether you are a high-priced man or not."

"Vell, I don't know vat you mean."

"Oh, come now, you answer my questions. What I want to find out is whether you are a high-priced man or one of these cheap fellows here. What I want to find out is whether you want to earn $1.85 a day or whether you are satisfied with $1.15, just the same as all those cheap fellows are getting."

"Did I vant $1.85 a day? Vas dot a high-priced man? Vell, yes, I vas a high-priced man."

"Oh, you're aggravating me. Of course you want $1.85 a day – every one wants it! You know perfectly well that that has very little to do with your being a high-priced man. For goodness' sake answer my questions, and don't waste any more of my time. Now come over here. You see that pile of pig iron?"

"Yes."

"You see that car?"

"Yes."

"Well, if you are a high-priced man, you will load that pig iron on that car to-morrow for $1.85. Now do wake up and answer my question. Tell me whether you are a high-priced man or not."

"Vell – did I got $1.85 for loading dot pig iron on dot car to-morrow?"

"Yes, of course you do, and you get $1.85 for loading a pile like that every day right through the year. That is what a high-priced man does, and you know it just as well as I do."

"Vell, dot's all right. I could load dot pig iron on the car to-morrow for $1.85, and I get it every day, don't I?"

"Certainly you do – certainly you do."

" Vell, den, I vas a high-priced man."

"Now, hold on, hold on. You know just as well as I do that a high-priced man has to do exactly as he's told from morning till night. You have seen this man here before, haven't you?"

"No, I never saw him."

"Well, if you are a high-priced man, you will do exactly as this man tells you to-morrow, from morning till night. When he tells you to pick up a pig and walk, you pick it up and you walk, and when he tells you to sit down and rest, you do that right straight through the day. And what's more, no back talk. Now a high-priced man does just what he's told to do, and no back talk. Do you understand that? When this man tells you to walk, you walk; when he tells you to sit down, you sit down, and you don't talk back at him. Now you come on to work here to-morrow morning And I'll know before night whether you are really a high-priced man or not."

... Schmidt started to work, and all day long, and at regular intervals, was told by the man who stood over him with a watch, "Now pick up a pig and walk. Now sit down and rest. Now walk – now rest," etc. He worked when he was told to work, and rested when he was told

to rest, and at half-past five in the afternoon had his 47 tons loaded on the car. And he practically never failed to work at this pace and do the task that was set him during the three years that the writer was at Bethlehem. And throughout this time he averaged a little more than $1.85 per day, whereas before he had never received over $1.15 per day, which was the ruling rate of wages at that time in Bethlehem. That is, he received 60 percent higher wages than were paid to other men who were not working on task work. One man after another was picked out and trained to handle pig iron at the rate of 47 tons per day until all of the pig iron was handled at this rate, and the men were receiving 60 percent more wages than other workmen around them.

... The writer trusts, however, that before leaving this illustration the reader will be thoroughly convinced that there is a science of handling pig iron, and further that this science amounts to so much that the man who is suited to handle pig iron cannot possibly understand it, nor even work in accordance with the laws of this science, without the help of those who are over him.'[4]

Taylor's treatment of Schmidt was delivered in a world which no longer exists, but the simple outcome was that Schmidt, by following the prescribed methods of working, achieved a 276 per cent increase in output and a 60 per cent increase in his wage. It may be difficult, a hundred years later, to interpret the 'negotiation' and assess its fairness. A contemporary trade unionist, George Preston, General Secretary and Treasurer of the International Association of Machinists expressed his view as follows:

'As one who has devoted the best years of his life to the labor movement I was pleased to have the opportunity of reading in the March issue American the article by F W Taylor, the founder of "Scientific Management".

Any theory of elimination of waste of resources, supplies of labor, from the standpoint of the business world — yes, from the standpoint of society as a whole — is not only worthy of consideration, but should receive the support of all right minded men, irrespective of the class to which they belong. There should be no difference of opinion between

---

4   Taylor, F., (1910), *The Principles of Scientific Management,* this extract available from Northern Illinois University's website at http://www3.niu.edu/~td0raf1/labor/Story%20of%20Schmidt. htm

us as to the advisability of increasing the output for a given amount of labor especially when that increase is the result of new machinery or of the institution of new methods. It is only by increased efficiency in production that we, the Trade Unionists, can hope to reduce our hours of labor and thereby gain for ourselves a reasonable amount of leisure which is so necessary for our mental, physical and moral wellbeing.

The foregoing systems are beautiful in theory but have been found by those employed under them to be oppressive and often impractical. These so called efficiency systems are not introduced for the purpose of distributing larger earnings among the employees but to more successfully exploit them.

Take his pig iron illustration where one man "who merely happened to be of the type of an ox" and Mr Taylor assures us seriously that "he was no rare specimen" – had by his system been able to move forty-seven tons of pig iron in the same time formerly required to move twelve and one-half tons. Not by the old "rule of thumb method". Oh no. Such men "of the type of an ox" "are not sufficiently intelligent to properly grasp even the necessity of their obtaining high wages". Therefore it was necessary to have a high priced college student "to train him" or what would be more to the point to watch him work and keep him at it.

The more we reflect, the more we are amazed at the possibilities of "Scientific Management". What grand opportunities for employing whole ship loads of "Schmidts" and then consider the avenues of advancement that are opened up for college students.

The fact is the system does not count for so much as does judicious management. The highest efficiency can only be reached and made permanent where a fair average day's work has been ascertained under improved methods and a reasonable compensation is given to the employees in recognition of merit so that individual incentive may be stimulated and a true spirit of co-operation between employer and employee may be preserved and fostered, the employee receiving his just compensation and the employer his maximum output and in addition such suggestions from time to time from the employee as will tend to lessen the labor cost in the reproduction of the goods manufactured.[5]

---

5 The Letter is archived by the Samuel C Williams library of the Stevens Institute of Technology, Hoboken, New Jersey, and can be seen in full at http://stevens.cdmhost.com/cdm4/document.php?CISOROOT=/p4100coll1&CISOPTR=442&REC=1

The 'science' of pig iron handling, and of shovelling, studied by Taylor as well as Frank Gilbreth's later study of the 'science' of bricklaying, produced massive improvements in productivity. Their system of studying work and work methods was applied to all kinds of manual work and later to clerical work also, as well as feeding into such matters as the layout of factories and the design of mass production lines etc. The aims were twofold. Firstly, to improve both the efficiency and the effectiveness of work by eliminating unnecessary actions and activities, improving methods and building in suitable relaxation breaks. Secondly, to share the resulting benefit between employer and employee and so remove the distrust between workers and management which had resulted in 'soldiering' or slow working and restricting output intended by the workers to safeguard jobs. Scientific management became a major influence on the management process for decades, in effect raising the factory system to new heights of efficiency, but paying less regard to its dehumanizing effects on workers.

The Ford mass production line is the most often cited exemplar of scientific management. Henry Ford's insight was to realize the possibility of a mass market for automobiles if they could only be sold cheaply enough. The black Model T and the mass production lines based on the total standardization of product and production, according to scientific management principles, was the means to the market end. 'Any color as long as it's black' became the symbolic expression of this mass production standard. Ford is widely cited as the scientific management example because it demonstrated not only the success of the system, but also its ultimate failure. By 1920 the Model T had over 60 per cent of the domestic United States market, while General Motors with eight different models had 12 per cent. Five years later Ford, still committed to the basic Model T, had been overtaken by GM and ten years further saw Ford's share at around 20 per cent and their survival much in doubt. Scientific management and standardization clearly had limitations.

Scientific management's foundation was time and motion study which involved the detailed study of work and the assessment of what a normal competent worker would achieve working at normal speed for a given time. The 'science' clearly accommodated some subjective judgment. This was the basis of many and various incentive payment systems which were applied across much of manufacturing industry and which became the symbolic focus of industrial disputes through the first half of the twentieth century.

The idea of scientific management spread wider than its origins in the study of work. It became almost a philosophy which coloured the whole of subsequent management practice as well as theory. The idea was to be rational, objective, analytical and 'scientific' in terms of methodology. It led naturally to a more quantitative approach making extensive use of statistical analysis to produce optimal solutions to specific problems. Management science, otherwise known as operations research, descended directly from scientific management, the titles referring alternately either to the application of mathematical methods or more broadly to a quantitative curriculum for management education which included the social sciences of psychology and sociology as well as quantitative methods of financial and market analysis plus economic analysis and econometrics.

The approach begged the simple question as to whether management was an art or a science. For some, the hard quantitative solutions were the essence, while for others, the key to management was understanding the irrationalities and inconsistencies of people.

There may still be some debate as to the rights and wrongs of scientific management. It undoubtedly contributed substantially in its day to the productivity of industrial organizations. But equally it did substantial damage to the possibility of a 'true spirit of co-operation between employer and employee'.

Looking back to scientific management it is easy to overlook how different the world of work was in Taylor's time from our own. The Ford production lines were not congenial places to work, but no doubt they were preferable to the French coal mines of a few years earlier where Henri Fayol developed his structural approach to management.[6]

Structural Approach

Both Taylor and Fayol were professionally qualified engineers, Taylor a mechanical engineer and Fayol a mining engineer. But while Taylor was essentially a management consultant, perhaps the first ever, Fayol was a manager, serving as Chief Executive of the French mining company, *Compagnie de Commentry-Fourchambeau-Decazeville*, for 30 years from 1888. Not surprisingly, their perspectives on management were quite different. While Taylor studied work at the bottom of the organization, Fayol's view was essentially from the top down with a certain detachment from the shop-floor work itself. Nevertheless, it was the nature of that work which defined his approach to the management task.

---

6   Fayol, H., (1949), *General and Industrial Management*, translation by Constance Storrs, London: Pitman Publishing Company.

Zola's 'Germinal' [1885] provides a vivid picture of the people, the work and the working conditions that Fayol managed in the French coal industry:

> *'The four pikemen had spread themselves one above the other over the whole face of the cutting. Separated by planks, hooked on to retain the fallen coal, they each occupied about four metres of the seam, and this seam was so thin, scarcely more than fifty centimetres thick at this spot, that they seemed to be flattened between the roof and the wall, dragging themselves along by their knees and elbows, and unable to turn without crushing their shoulders. In order to attack the coal, they had to lie on their sides with their necks twisted and arms raised, brandishing, in a sloping direction, their short-handled picks.*
>
> *Below there was, first, Zacharie; Levaque and Chaval were on the stages above, and at the very top was Maheu. Each worked at the slaty bed, which he dug out with blows of the pick; then he made two vertical cuttings in the bed and detached the block by burying an iron wedge in its upper part. The coal was rich; the block broke and rolled in fragments along their bellies and thighs. When these fragments, retained by the plank, had collected round them, the pikemen disappeared, buried in the narrow cleft.*
>
> *Maheu suffered most. At the top the temperature rose to thirty-five degrees, and the air was stagnant, so that in the long run it became lethal. In order to see, he had been obliged to fix his lamp to a nail near his head, and this lamp, close to his skull, still further heated his blood. But his torment was especially aggravated by the moisture. The rock above him, a few centimetres from his face, streamed with water, which fell in large continuous rapid drops with a sort of obstinate rhythm, always at the same spot. It was vain for him to twist his head or bend back his neck. They fell on his face, dropping unceasingly. In a quarter of an hour he was soaked, and at the same time covered with sweat, smoking as with the hot steam of a laundry. This morning a drop beating upon his eye made him swear. He would not leave his picking, he dealt great strokes which shook him violently between the two rocks, like a fly caught between two leaves of a book and in danger of being completely flattened.'[7]*

Maybe Zola exercised some poetic licence, but this was in essence the work situation Fayol was managing. For him the basic problem was how to get large

---

7   Zola, E., (1885), *Germinal*, Penguin Classics, (2004) translated by Roger Pearson. The quote is from the opening of Chapter 4.

numbers of unskilled and mostly ill-educated people to do fundamentally unpleasant and dangerous work and do it efficiently in return for wages set low enough for the company to make a sufficient profit to survive and prosper. This was the problem of the nineteenth and early twentieth century, and was not much different from the early years of industrialization.

Fayol identified various immutable rules that managers should follow if they were to be successful. He referred to these as 'principles of management' and they related to the structure of an organization as well as what we might now call its strategy and the treatment of its people.

In terms of structure, Fayol prescribed the centralization of management decision-making from the top, a formal chain of command running from top to bottom of the organization, with management having authority to give orders and have them obeyed, and with each employee having only one boss. Operationally the system was focused on the division of labour and the consequent improvement in skills and working methods and the maintenance of order throughout the organization.

The focus on strategy was limited but pertinent, emphasizing the need for a unity of direction, devised and planned at the top but with all members of the organization actively engaged in its implementation.

The focus on employee relations was mainly that equity and justice should prevail in terms of pay and general working conditions and treatment. Fayol emphasized the need for loyalty to 'good' workers, advocating lifetime employment where possible. At the same time, he demanded discipline with workers being obedient, focusing solely on the interests of the organization while at work, and being loyal to the organization. Finally, he held that it was management's responsibility to establish an 'esprit de corps' among all employees.

In summary, these principles prescribed a fair but strict management attitude and a hierarchical and rather rigid structure for organization. This was probably appropriate for Fayol's situation, though certainly not as generally applicable as he had intended. The principles were to guide management in what he regarded as their five prime functions:

1. *Prévoyance* – literally foresight but often translated as examining the future and drawing up a plan of action.

2.   *Organization* – building up the structure, material and human, of the undertaking.

3.   *Command* – maintaining activity among the personnel.

4.   *Coordination* – binding together, unifying and harmonizing all activity and effort.

5.   *Control* – seeing that everything occurs in conformity with established rule and express command.

Frequently referred to by theoreticians as a 'theory', it was more accurately described as an approach to management, as it had evolved entirely from practice. It was labelled alternatively as the 'classical' or 'structural' theory of organization. It was commonly characterized as the 'command and control' model, implying top-down management, the top being assumed to have the knowledge, understanding, foresight and wisdom so to organize the various organizational components as to achieve the best result. It was a system to which most early industrialists would have subscribed. Even the enlightened Owen had a clearly hierarchical concept of how organizations worked. Fayol also recognized the necessity to plan for the future and get everyone contributing to the fulfilment of those plans.

The structural approach omitted significant reference to the crucial management responsibility of raising and managing capital to finance the organization and its development.

There were several other contributions which became embedded in the structural literature. Mary Follett was widely regarded as a key contributor. In publication terms, she was a near contemporary of Fayol's, long before he became known to the English-speaking world. Her main thrust was to explicate the notion of hierarchy, emphasizing joint responsibilities among partners rather than responsibility and power emanating solely from the top. Like Fayol, she believed principles of management were applicable to all spheres of organization. Her collected writing was published under the title *Dynamic Administration* which, though it sounds rather like an oxymoron today, probably contributed the title of the postgraduate management degree, the MBA.

Urwick and Breck, management consultants and writers, developed Fayol's structural principles further, adding the distinction between line and staff management, the staff being professional specialists without line responsibilities acting only for and on behalf of their line boss. They also added the principle that authority should only be commensurate with responsibility and that managers were wholly responsible for the work of their subordinates. Further, they added what they referred to as the principle of definition which led to the formal specification of jobs, their duties, responsibilities and authority which should be made transparent to all.

Despite Follett's citing of *dynamic* administration, the structural approach appears to define a rather rigid, rational–legal bureaucratic form. As the scale of businesses grew, the structural principles were applied widely, though unevenly, across all industries. Some confirmation of this was provided by a major empirical study conducted by the Aston Group assessing the degree to which organizations exhibited characteristics of bureaucracy. These included the specialization of functions, standardization of procedures, formalization of documentation, centralization of authority and the configuration of role structures, for example, with a published organization chart.[8] The study found that the larger the organization, the more it tended to some form of bureaucratic organization, various other forms being identified with only the small personal or family owned organizations not conforming to bureaucratic norms.

Other contributions to the structural approach came mainly from practitioners, Drucker being the exception. Though he was not himself a practising manager, Drucker's contribution to practitioner literature was immense, though his tendency to let incisive prose occasionally take precedence over fact damaged his reputation among academics. Despite this, he contributed to many areas of management practice, not least to the structural approach with his advocacy of decentralization as conducted at General Motors under the leadership of the then CEO, Alfred Sloan.

Recognizing the dangers of rigid hierarchy and bureaucracy Drucker also advocated the use, throughout a business, of a system he referred to as 'management by objectives'. In this individuals were engaged in Follett-like partnership with their line boss, in identifying the three or four key purposes of their job, setting themselves target levels of performance in those three or four main areas and subsequently appraising that level of performance achieved together with their line boss at the end of the relevant time period and agreeing action to facilitate future improvement.

---

8   Pugh, D.S., Hickson, D.J., Hinings, C.R. and Turner, C., (1968), 'Dimensions of Organisation Structure', *Administrative Science* Quarterly, Vol. 13, pp. 65–105.

'MbO' (management by objectives) became one of the first popular acronyms of modern management, its intention being to cement co-operation between employer and employee though more often abused as a top-down tool of control. It was the possibility of this co-operation which was the focus of the various studies which came to be known as the human relations school. The human relations approach was to be more or less entirely benign in its impact on working conditions, but was nevertheless subject to interpretation as to its aims, which depended largely on the prior position of the interpreter. Was it all part of the conspiracy to exploit labour? Or was it an initiative which was genuinely motivated to achieve an improvement of the workers' lot as well as the company's? The involvement of labour's own representatives in many of the empirical studies went some way to ensure they were genuine researches, observing and learning from the workplace and seeking better ways of doing things, better in that they might combine improved economic result with its distribution being fair and just.

Human Relations

While the structural approach of Fayol and others propounded a general system of management, the human relations school exclusively focused on management's relationship with people at work. Barnard suggested that:

> 'understanding in the field of human relations ... is of first importance
> to the executive; for human relations are the essence of managerial,
> employee, public and political relations.'[9]

The dehumanization of work on the shop floor, where the imperatives of working with machines had tended to dominate the work of people, had become more evident as mechanization and automation proceeded, threatening jobs which depended on continually increasing markets.

Elton Mayo and colleagues began their observation of work at Western Electric's Hawthorne Works in 1929 with the aim of identifying any link between working conditions and worker productivity. Their observations were at the time surprising. The so called 'Hawthorne effect' was observed when there were short-term increases in productivity in response to experimental changes in working conditions no matter what the changes were. The

---

9   Barnard, C., (1948), *Organization and Management*, Cambridge, Mass: Harvard University Press, p. 199.

productivity increases were generally ascribed to the interest and attention being given to the workers by the researchers when working conditions were changed. The Hawthorne Studies served to emphasize the importance of social and psychological factors in the working environment and the recognition of informal organization structures at work, in contrast to the assumptions of scientific management that motivation was simply a matter of payment by results.

The experiments suggested that workers were motivated by a 'logic of sentiment' and a major task of management was to organize 'spontaneous co-operation' in the workplace.[10] This was a direct challenge to the neoclassical orthodoxy, with which scientific management had concurred, that motivation was necessarily based around money as the sole measure of self-interest and its maximization being the human aim. A theory of management which included sentiment and cooperation was clearly inconsistent with the competitive greed of economic theory.

Mayo concluded that the Hawthorne programme:

> '... has come to a clear specification of the relation of working groups to management as one of the fundamentals of large scale industry. It was indeed this study that first enabled us to assert the third major preoccupation of management must be that of organizing teamwork, that is to say, of developing and sustaining cooperation.'[11]

[Mayo had defined the other two preoccupations of management as *'The application of science or technical skill to some material good or product'*, and *'The systematic ordering of operations.'*]

Not surprisingly, for the first thoroughgoing experimental social science study of industrial work, the Hawthorne Studies' conduct, and the conclusions drawn therefrom, have over the years attracted a substantial critique. But, whatever their shortcomings, they opened up a new avenue for study and the possibility of new understanding of how best to manage work. As always, the question of what motivated the studies was never far below the surface. Was it an attempt to find new ways of exploiting the workers, or was it a genuine attempt to find ways to improve both their lots?

---

10 Mayo, E., (1933), *The Human Problems of an Industrial Civilization*, New York: Macmillan.
11 Mayo, E., (1949), *The Social Problems of an Industrial Civilization*, London: Routledge, quoted in *Organization Theory*, London: Penguin p. 357.

There is no universal answer. The difference is one of management philosophy, of attitude to people. McGregor expressed the dichotomy as two approaches, Theory X and Theory Y, which made assumptions about people at work. Theory X assumed:

1. *The average human being has an inherent dislike of work and will avoid it if he can.*

2. *Because of this human characteristic of dislike of work, most people must be coerced, controlled, directed, threatened with punishment to get them to put forth adequate effort toward the achievement of organizational objectives.*

3. *The average human being prefers to be directed, wishes to avoid responsibility, has relatively little ambition, wants security above all.*[12]

McGregor referred to this assumption as the 'mediocrity of the masses' and pointed out that while a good deal of lip service was given to people being the most important asset, nevertheless:

> *'a great many managers will give private support to this* (Theory X) *assumption, and it is easy to see it reflected in policy and practice.'*

McGregor used Maslow's expression of the hierarchy of intrinsic human needs in evaluating Theory X, pointing out that though by 1960 employees' physiological needs were largely satisfied, safety needs could be threatened by arbitrary management actions which revealed *'favouritism or discrimination'* which might threaten the employment relationship. Similarly, inept management might inhibit the satisfaction of workers' social needs fearing that the development of a 'tightly knit, cohesive work group' might oppose the achievement of the organization's objectives. Self-esteem needs and self-actualization would similarly be frustrated by a Theory X style of management which was, however, perfectly compatible with the economic man assumptions of classical economic theory.

The alternative Theory Y set of assumptions were as follows:

1. *The expenditure of physical and mental effort in work is as natural as play or rest.*

---

12 McGregor, D., (1960), *The Human Side of Enterprise,* New York: McGraw Hill, pp. 33–34.

2.   *External control and the threat of punishment are not the only means of bringing about effort toward organizational objectives.*

3.   *Commitment to objectives is a function of the rewards associated with their achievement.*

4.   *The average human being learns, under proper conditions, not only to accept but to seek responsibility.*

5.   *The capacity to exercise a relatively high degree of imagination, ingenuity, and creativity in the solution of organizational problems is widely, not narrowly, distributed in the population.*

6.   *Under the conditions of modern industrial life, the intellectual potentialities of the average human being are only partially utilized.*[13]

If people behaved in a way which was consistent with Theory X, McGregor argued, it was because of their experience at work. It was management's responsibility to organize work so that people could achieve their own personal goals by directing their efforts towards organizational aims. Both approaches were to a great extent self-fulfilling.

Theory Y was not a soft option. It required consistent care and understanding if it was to be successfully implemented. It was sometimes naively followed by human relations devotees believing that management was simply a question of being nice to people and that they would respond in kind. But that didn't work. It was not a management style that could be adopted as and when it appeared appropriate; it was a fundamental set of beliefs about people to which managements were either committed or not.

Herzberg's motivation-hygiene theory[14] provided some insights as to what actually motivated people at work and in so doing explicitly denied the 'economic man' thesis. He identified factors which led to dissatisfaction at work if they were unsatisfactory, but which would not be positively motivational. These 'hygiene factors' were extrinsic to the job and included such things as relations with the supervisor, working conditions, company policy and pay. The motivators were intrinsic items such as responsibility, achievement,

---

13   Ibid, pp. 47–48.
14   Herzberg, F., Mausner, B. and Snyderman, B.B., (1959), *The Motivation to Work,* New York: Wiley.

advancement and recognition, factors which would tend to be naturally addressed by a Theory Y committed management.

Drucker agreed that the human relations approach:

> '*freed management from the domination of viciously wrong ideas; but it did not succeed in substituting new concepts.*'[15]

It focused on individual psychology and interpersonal relations with fellow workers that determined worker behaviour and effectiveness. For Drucker therefore management of human relations readily degenerated into a device to 'sell' whatever management was peddling:

> '*it is no accident that there is so much talk in human relations about 'giving workers a sense of responsibility' and so little about their responsibility, so much emphasis on 'their feeling of importance' and so little on making them and their work important.*'[16]

The human relations approach suggested a distinct break with the former scientific management, but it was not achieved. The divide continued between traditional and progressive management, between exploitative and enlightened management, between systems focusing purely on economic rewards and those that tried to take account of the whole human being. That dichotomy continues to this day.

The human relations approach provided many new insights into effective people management during the four decades of its investigation and diffusion. It resulted in the dismantling of many scientific management based structures which had in their time improved productivity but damaged employee–management relations. Human relations was focused on that one aspect of management to the exclusion of all others. Wilfred Brown took a broader view:

> '*Effective organisation is a function of the work to be done and the resources and techniques available to do it. Thus changes in methods of production bring about changes in the number of work roles, in the distribution of work between roles and in their relationship one to the other. Failure to make explicit acknowledgement of this relationship between work and organisation gives rise to non-valid assumptions,*

---

15   Beatty, J., (1998), *The World According to Drucker*, London: Orion Publishing, p. 116.
16   Ibid, p. 117.

e.g, that optimum organisation is a function of the personalities involved, that it is a matter connected with the personal style and arbitrary decision of the chief executive, that there are choices between centralised and decentralised organisation etc.'[17]

Brown presided over one of the best documented experiments in breaking down a fully operational traditional system and replacing it with a more progressive approach. This was at the Glacier Metal Co where he was chief executive for over 20 years from 1939, during which time he employed social psychologist Elliott Jaques of the Tavistock Institute of Human Relations to study the psychological and social forces affecting the group life, morale and productivity of the Glacier people.

Glacier was a traditionally managed engineering company employing around 5,000 people. The paraphernalia of scientific management was still in place in 1945. Workers 'clocked on' when they arrived at work and 'clocked off' again when they left. They were paid strictly by piecework, i.e. for each item produced. Brown and Jacques oversaw the abandonment of piecework payment systems and the clocking-on control procedures.

Despite widespread fears of disaster, the results were largely as predicted by Theory Y. Brown concluded his case against wage incentive systems such as piecework and clocking systems:

> *'I am convinced that instead of optimising production and individual satisfaction in work, they are hindering both. ... operators, supervisors and managers in our Company ... shun the idea of reintroducing a wage incentive system.'*[18]

He added that other companies which had taken the same route – he referred to Vauxhall Motors, Lever Bros and F Perkins of Peterborough – were all of the same view.

Systems Approach

Writing before and after the Second World War Chester Barnard, one-time president of the New Jersey Bell Telephone Company and substantial

---

17 Brown, W., (1960), *Exploration in Management*, London: Heinemann, p. 42.
18 Brown, W., (1962), *Piecework Abandoned*, London: Heinemann, p. 93.

contributor to the structural theory of organization, was the first to conceive of the organization as including those external stakeholders with which it directly interacts:

> *'an integrated aggregate of actions and interactions having a continuity in time ... (including) the actions of investors, suppliers and customers or clients.'*[19]

This significant advance in the concept of organization was perhaps influenced by the ideas then emanating from systems theorists whose work in biology was beginning to be generalized to social and other non-biological systems and was later taken up by Elliott Jacques and colleagues at Tavistock studying how social and technical systems interacted under conditions of change.

Underlying all these approaches to organization and management was an assumption as to the key issues involved. For Taylor it was the productivity of manual and clerical labour, for structuralists it was how the organization should be organized, for human relations it was what motivated people. For systems, it was how to understand the organization in its wider setting.

Systems theory focused on overall system properties and characteristics which appeared to apply generally to all living systems from a simple biological cell to a complex social organization such as a business. These critical system properties appeared capable of providing an overall explanation of system behaviour and this was used in the analysis of industries' chronological development as well as product life cycles.

A very simple explanation of a system was given by Koehler using a candle's life cycle as his example.[20] At first when a light is put to its wick the candle may spit and sputter and possibly go out several times before the wax achieves the temperature for ignition and is successfully lighted. This birth, introduction or infancy stage is characterized in many systems by volatility and high rates of infant mortality whether we are considering lighted candles, human babies, electronic components, business start-ups or new products.

---

19 Barnard, C., (1948), *Organization and Management,* Cambridge, Mass: Harvard University Press, p. 112.
20 Koehler, W., (1938), *Closed and Open Systems,* included in *Systems Thinking,* F.E. Emery (ed.), Harmondsworth: Penguin Books, Penguin Modern Management Readings.

If the candle successfully lights then the flame quickly burns up to its full size. This adolescent or growth stage is again typical of many systems in the speed and continuity of its growth up to a certain ceiling level characteristic of its mature phase.

As the candle reaches this ceiling it again exhibits a generally applicable characteristic of volatility before settling down to a mature-phase steady state. The candle's volatility is manifested in a short period of flickering; adolescent human beings exhibit extraordinary volatility as any parent will vouch; the volatility of businesses and products as they move from growth to maturity is also remarkable, for example, as growth predictions have to be permanently downgraded, forcing management's attention on to a different set of problems.

In its mature-phase steady state, the candle exhibits the general systems characteristic of maximum strength and efficiency. In the case of the candle, this is the phase when it burns the wax fastest and gives off the greatest light. It will maintain this maximum energy conversion steady state as determined by its inputs of wick, wax and oxygen and its system characteristics of size and composition of wick and diameter and length of candle. Human beings exhibit similar characteristics, in their maturity being at their strongest and physically most efficient stage. Businesses also appear to be at their most efficient and intrinsically most profitable, cash generating stage.

The steady state will only end when one of the determining factors changes. For example, the wax is used up to the extent that there is no longer a full quantity available for burning. At this stage, the system goes into a decline, but again the change from the mature phase to decline is marked by further volatility as the candle flickers and putters and frequently goes out prematurely, i.e. before it has used up all its wax.

One of the intriguing characteristics of this general model is the apparent breadth of its applicability. All manner of systems appear to share these general characteristics and be subject to parallel pressures and influences at the different stages.

A start-up business, for example, is likely to be dominated initially by the need to survive. If it survives this first phase, it will be able to turn its attention to growth and the development of competitive strength. As it progresses through adolescence it is quick, flexible, opportunistic and focused on satisfying customers' needs. It carries no spare weight, no passengers. It is lean and fit, quick on its feet and builds its strength through constant striving and exercise.

This phase sees the business change from being the creature of the founding entrepreneur with a simple structure, to employing an increasing number of professional specialists concerned with either the firm's technological development or the development of its various management functions.

In a growing market, the adolescent business has to run fast in order simply to maintain its market share. If it fails to do this, it will probably not survive the first shake out when market growth starts to falter. In a static market, there is not the same necessity to grow. Many businesses stay small, providing relatively stable employment for small numbers of people. Nevertheless, other businesses are more ambitious and grow rapidly in order to achieve the critical mass at which the new specialists can be profitably supported. Growth in static markets can only be achieved by increasing market share or by moving into new markets, both of which may be problematic in highly competitive situations.

To achieve maturity is the goal of all systems. In the case of a business, maturity is the phase when wealth creation is maximized, when the most surplus cash is generated, when the business achieves its position of greatest power and influence, and when the business should be able to focus, with the least inhibition and interruption, on the achievement of its long-term objectives.

Maturity is the result of successful infancy and adolescence. The success is usually based on doing the right things right and the business progressively becoming more expert. It learns successful ways of doing things. It finds out what its customers like and gets good at delivering those things. It develops its technological expertise. It uses recipes which work and it becomes efficient. And it becomes effective. All this happens as a result of deliberate management initiatives – it is by no means automatic.

It is difficult, however, for a successful business to make a fundamental change in what has established its leading position. This is especially the case with technology when a successful mature business is likely to have major investments sunk in the old technology. Getting into something new may mean writing off huge capital assets which will weaken the balance sheet and in the short term wreak havoc with profitability. Also, there are psychological investments in the old technology. One of the fruits of maturity is the ability to pay top salaries and thus attract top calibre people. Many of these highly qualified professionals may have built their entire careers on the old technology and their very natural response to such a change is likely to be defensive and reactive. Nor is it at all certain that leadership in the new technology will necessarily follow being a leader in the old; giving up a leading position should certainly not be done lightly.

A successful mature business, as the systems model suggests, is likely to generate substantial surplus funds which are not required in order to maintain the status quo. How these funds get invested depends very much on the circumstances of the individual business.

Diversification not only adds complexity and confuses strategic direction, but it also creates an alternative focus for future development and an ongoing demand for investment which may in the end result in the starvation of the once successful mature business. Thus diversification leads naturally to the mature business which has lost its direction and failed to keep up investment in its key technologies.

In terms of goal orientation, the mature business, like many other systems, seeks to control its environment in order to ensure its own future well-being. The one thing the mature business, with all its heavy investments sunk in the status quo, seeks to avoid is change and instability. It will find it advantageous to invest heavily in preserving the current state of affairs. First of all, it will seek to control its own industry, if possible through the achievement of a monopolistic position. In this way, it can hope to control prices at a level which ensures its own profitability, and can control the level of business to set limits on the competitive activity which would be profitable for any other business to embark on.

For similar reasons it may well seek to achieve control over its inputs whether sources of raw material or possibly core technologies, if they are in any way insecure. It may seek to achieve this through the exercise of its purchasing muscle in tying up long-term arrangements or by acquiring key suppliers.

The systems approach offers a way of understanding business organizations. It is quite different from the other three approaches considered here, but like the other approaches adds to the knowledge and understanding of management. Organizations and particular organizational situations can be analyzed in terms of the various interacting systems they comprise. These may be both social and technological.

Members of the Tavistock Institute of Human Relations studied the structure and functioning of organizations at the interface of their social and technological systems under conditions of change. They revealed, for example, the dramatic and previously unremarked social and psychological consequences of technological changes in British coal mining[21] and also the substantial impacts on productivity of changes in social structural arrangements in an Indian textile factory.[22] The work of the Tavistock Institute showed the systems approach could provide invaluable insights into management of people in conditions of rapid technological change as well as the formation of organizational strategy and associated systems of management.

Based on this work, Emery[23] proposed ways in which systems, notably business organizations, could be managed over their long term. This included setting and maintaining organizational direction as prerequisites to survival and prosperity; similarly, establishing a goal which was demanding but achievable. Management's strategic task was to control the boundary conditions between the organization and its various environments rather than to exercise rigid control within the organization. Management's internal responsibility seemed to be more to do with communication with all members of the organization, and the establishment of agreements and commitments with them regarding the organization's direction and progress.

The systems approach to understanding organization and its management added new insights not provided by scientific management, the structural approach or human relations. But one of its more significant contributions to understanding was that there was no one best way of managing, that the most effective course of action was largely dependent on the particular system conditions and circumstances which applied. This was the contingency approach.

Contingency

Contingency, usually suffixed with the word 'theory' presumably to give it more significance, is the simple idea that 'there is no one best way; it all

21 Trist, E.A. and Bamforth, K.W., (1951), 'Some Social and Psychological Consequences of the Longwall Method of Coal-getting', *Human Relations*, Vol. 4, No 1, pp. 6–38.
22 Miller, E.J. and Rice, A.K., (1967), *Systems of Organization: Task and Sentient Systems and Their Boundary Control*, London: Tavistock Publications.
23 Emery, F.E., (1969), *Systems Thinking: Penguin Modern mManagement Readings*, Harmondsworth: Penguin Books Ltd.

depends'. Many theorists contributed to the development of 'contingency' recognizing for example that approaches that might be effective in large mass production factories may be completely inappropriate in small professional offices or jobbing shops. Some researchers demonstrated how organizational structure, for example, depended on such contingent issues as the production technology[24] or the demands of the firm's environment in terms of its degree of uncertainty and diversity[25] or the level and pace of technological change.[26]

Tom Burns and George Stalker studied the attempts to implant the fledgling electronics industry in parts of Scotland which had only previously experienced the old heavy industries of coal, steel and ship-building. These industries were dying and it was hoped to take up some of the inevitable unemployment with the new high-growth high-technology industry.

In carrying out their research, they identified two types of organization which have since found their way into fairly common currency: mechanistic and organismic (or organic) organizations.

The mechanistic organization was suited to stable conditions. In it, the job of management was broken down into specialist functions, each with its precisely defined task. There was a clear hierarchy of control, with the reins firmly held at the top. Communications flowed down the line and occasionally back up, but rarely across the organization. There was an emphasis on loyalty to the company and obedience to one's superior. The result of this bureaucratic system was that individuals in the organization were not committed to its fundamental business aims, only to obeying the rules and fulfilling their (strictly limited) employment contract and enjoying whatever perks such a regime might offer. Mechanistic organizations were found to be ill-suited to handling innovation.

Croome described mechanistic organizations as demanding that everyone shall have one job, clearly defined and delimited, with responsibility running up to a recognized limit and stopping there. The employee was not isolated, but was part of the organizational machine. In so far as he had to think at all about his relations with other parts of the machine, he saw them as outside 'his' job. They were necessary to the job only as tools are necessary.

---

24 Woodward, J., (1965), *Industrial Organisation: Theory and Practice,* Oxford: Oxford University Press.

25 Lawrence, P.R., and Lorsch, J.W., (1967), *Organization and Environment,* Harvard: Harvard University Press.

26 Burns, T. and Stalker, G.M., (1961), *The Management of Innovation,* Oxford: Oxford University Press.

'For some data needs he can appeal to the slide rule, for others he may appeal to another individual; some tasks can be performed by a tool, others by an order to a subordinate.'[27]

The clear definition of 'the job' and the simple set of outside relationships, broke down when conditions changed. New situations did not exactly match the traditional frontiers of responsibility. The individual no longer knew just what instructions were needed or where to seek them; he had to consult with, rather than merely give orders to, his subordinates.

The organic organization lacked rigid structure, lived by a process of continual adaptation, often involving the redefinition of individual tasks. Communications occurred in any direction as was required at any particular time, and the commitment of employees was open ended and generally dedicated to the achievement of organizational aims. As one might expect, organic systems were well suited to handling the new and unfamiliar: they were highly effective innovators.

According to Burns and Stalker, the work of the manager under the organic system was much more exacting:

'The shift from mechanistic to organic procedures, therefore, makes considerable demands on individual members of an organization. In general terms, they are required to surrender the safe determinacy of a contractual relationship with the firm for one in which their obligations are far less limited, to replace a view of the firm as an impersonal, immutable boss by one which regards it as something kept in being by the sustained creative activity of themselves and other members, to cease being "nine to fivers" and turn "professionals".'[28]

Burns and Stalker did not suggest that there was 'one best way' of organizing. If the mechanistic system was adequate, then so much the better because it was the most efficient. However, as Croome suggested, when the firm was tackling new tasks, whether commercial or technical, this system of differentiated responsibilities must be 'elastically shared'. Every effort must be made to encourage the sense of the business as a whole with objectives and

27 Croome, H., (1960), *Human Problems of Innovation*, Department of Scientific and Industrial Research pamphlet, Problems of Progress in Industry, No 5.

28 Burns, T. and Stalker, G.M., (1961), *The Management of Innovation*, third edition (1994), Oxford: Oxford University Press, p. 234.

goals common to all its members, rather than a complex of 'separate jobs'. The stronger this sense, the more there would be resource to lateral consultation. This should be recognized and facilitated, and not regarded as a mere semi-legitimate supplement to vertical channels of command.

Organismic and mechanistic were opposite ends of a continuum. Neither was likely to be met in its full glory, but most companies exhibited tendencies to be closer to one or the other. The more organismic a business organization was, the better suited it was likely to be to handle innovation and change. This was the basis of the orthodoxy that flexible systems with high levels of participation and open communications were essential for handling change, while rigid, mechanistic, bureaucratic systems were most efficient for handling routine and stable situations.

Thus the contingency approach suggests that any theory of organization is inevitably complex and contradictory because of the variety of organizations and organizational situations. What works in one circumstance may not be appropriate in another. The most appropriate approach is contingent on the circumstances of the particular situation.

Heavy industry, iron and steel, shipbuilding and other traditional manufactures such as textiles, gradually migrated from the developed to the newly industrializing economies. These were the large scale organizations which used rigid, hierarchical organization structures, formal decision processes and static bureaucratic ways of operating. New electronic and IT-based technologies which replaced the old smoke stack firms, had more flexible structures with fast decision making and increased responsiveness to environmental change.

Incomplete though these various theoretical approaches to management undoubtedly were, they nevertheless provided managers insights into, and understanding of, issues that they might well confront in their practical lives. Even though they might only be encountered as part of an academic management syllabus they could contribute additional knowledge and understanding to support the practical job of management.

8

Management in Practice

The development of large-scale multi-business corporations, initially in the United States and subsequently through the rest of the industrialized world, achieved massive economies of scale but required competent 'administrative co-ordination', to use business historian Chandler's term for management, in order to achieve productivity and profitability. In those terms the resulting management was highly successful.

Chandler propounded the view that business management replaced market forces in *'coordinating the activities of the economy and allocating its resources'*[1] and so became *'the key role in twentieth-century wealth creation'*. If it were true that management had usurped the role of market forces it would invalidate classical theory, founded as it was on primacy of market forces and the almost total exclusion of management from its account of the economic system. The truth was less clear cut. A major part of marketing management was the research of 'market forces' so that a business might accommodate to them rather than engage in a vain attempt to defy them. In practice the invisible hand had remained a powerful influence.

However, management's role was not restricted to concerns with the market. Technical, operations and financial roles were of equal importance in 'creating wealth'. General managers, standing at the apex of the management hierarchy, were responsible for the performance of their companies through the post Second World War period of unprecedented technological change.

The contrast in scale of American and European production and management practice was highlighted during the Second World War when British industry in particular was required to expand armaments production beyond its capacity.

---

1   Chandler, A.D., (1977), *The Visible Hand*, Cambridge Mass: Belknap Press of Harvard University Press, p. 1.

This was well illustrated by the single common wartime production project of the Rolls Royce designed Merlin aero engine for the Spitfire fighter aircraft.

> 'British craftsmen "cut out the pieces and fitted them ..., milling them here, machining them there, and piecing them together, until a superb engine materialised." The Packard Company, which took over the Rolls Royce contract, could not build engines this way. The sketchy British blueprints befuddled the American engineers. To put the Merlin into production, they had to tear an engine down and copy it part by part, in some cases redesigning components for mass production. The result was a product which, if no better than the original, could be produced faster, cheaper, and in far greater numbers.'[2]

The Rolls Royce craft approach, without the engineering finesse of Rolls Royce, was no doubt apparent in other British industries which consequently declined after the war, in the face of competition not just from the United States but also from the resurgent German and Japanese industries which had to rebuild themselves almost from scratch. The British management which presided over at least the start of this manufacturing decline was still to some extent class based and amateur, drawn from the public schools and from Oxbridge which disdained to provide management education till 50 years after the war.

Traditional industries were migrating from the developed economies to the third world where labour was cheap and where the industrialization process, for good and ill, could be repeated, though apparently with few lessons learned from the earlier experiences of industrializing the advanced economies.

New technologies, developed and applied mainly in the United States, Europe and Japan, created new industrial problems requiring new solutions, new structures and new ways of managing business organizations.

Management had evolved from command and control through scientific management to a primary concern for the human relations within organizations and customer relations without. The new conditions led to a concern with shaping the culture of organization in order to influence the way all people in an organization behaved. The obvious ambiguity inherent in culture management focused attention on the necessity for integrity in managerial behaviour. And

---

2   Nelson, D.M., (1946), *Arsenal of Democracy: The Story of American War Production*, New York: Harcourt Brace & Co., p. 226.

it was the responsibility of general management to provide that integrity and to shape the organization's culture. These were roles which were necessarily learned on the ground in practice.

Management Recruitment and Development

As industry developed in the more meritocratic era following the Second World War, individuals holding general management posts might be expected to have won their initial appointment on merit in competitive circumstances. However, there being no professional gatekeeper controlling entry to management ranks, heredity and the unbalanced influence of the Ivy League in America and public school Oxbridge in Britain, continued to frustrate meritocratic selection.

Nevertheless, by whichever means individuals gained initial selection, the management training programmes provided by most large companies were themselves prolonged selection processes. Typically, in-company management trainee schemes would last for at least one year and often more than two, during which individuals would be given immediate though brief experience in most of the specialist areas outlined in Chapter 6 and more extended experience in one or more of them. They would be subjected to at least some advanced management education and training and not infrequently secondment to a business school advanced management or degree course where they would be acquainted with, among much else, economic theory and various management approaches such as those outlined in Chapter 7.

They could expect during their trainee period to be under continuous observation and assessment and could be removed from their traineeship should their performance not meet expectations. They would most probably be enabled to develop as general managers with their spheres of initial control being limited to relatively small scale operations, subsidiary companies or divisions of larger organizations where their mistakes would not be life threatening. Whilst granted substantial autonomy in these limited operations, they would be coached and nurtured as they gained their experience and learned from their successes, as well as mistakes. They would gain practice in key areas of decision making, under conditions of real uncertainty and risk, to make effective use of the resources under their control, notably including their people.

The assertion that large companies inevitably became bureaucratic, frustrating the ambitions and talents of young managers was not necessarily true. Drucker noted in his study of the decentralization of General Motors:

> *'With the big company safety net beneath them they could display their entrepreneurial talents. And given real authority, they weren't likely to retire on the job or quit out of boredom and frustrated ambition.'*[3]

Thus equipped such trainees might in due course, in the organization that originally employed them, emerge as senior general managers with responsibility for both the business's day to day operational viability and also its longer-term survival and development as well as responsibility for effectively balancing those short and long term concerns. In addition they would be responsible for the work and results of all their subordinates, and thus for all the work and results of those specialisms into which management labour is divided.

This general management first came to full fruition in the large–scale, often diversified, businesses of the twentieth-century United States. As these firms established a presence internationally, their approach to management development was adopted more widely. In *The Practice of Management*, Drucker revealed that in the 1940s he could only find two such management development programmes: Sears Roebuck in America and Marks and Spencer in Britain, and only three universities, all American, offering advanced management courses. Ten years later there were over 3,000 company trainee schemes and scores of American university programmes. Thereafter the numbers of company schemes and university programmes grew rapidly in both the United States and Britain. In Britain, the 'milk round' became ubiquitous: an annual routine search for bright new graduates to join the management trainee schemes of leading businesses.

Such management training schemes were typical of how large-scale businesses supported and developed their succeeding generations of management up to the late 1970s. Many smaller companies followed a similar process and most sought to adopt such development procedures as were within their reach. Management development was therefore achieved through practical in-company training and experience provided by the particular organization with more fragmentary support from external academic

---

3   Drucker in *Concept of the Corporation* quoted as summarised by Beatty, J., in *The World According to Drucker*, London: Orion Business Books, p. 57.

institutions. The managers who emerged from this process were therefore already imbued with the organization's culture and knowledgeable about its industry, its customers and competitors, and understood its technologies. The attractions of management being a completely generalized competence, instantly transferable from one environment to another quite independently of differing industrial environments, had not yet been accepted. The vast majority of senior management appointments were made from within the existing management ranks.

Environments differed radically from one industry to another. Various broad categories were used. 'Smoke stack industries' was a phrase used to describe declining heavy engineering, using 'old' technology to sell into mature markets. Steel and shipbuilding were typical of the category. The categorization seemed to explain why advanced economies might cease to be competitive in such activity, apart from small high-value high-technology niches. The continuing application of advancing technology in such apparently mature industries suggests the categorization may have been misleading.

At the other end of the industrial categories were the then new industries, in electronics, information technology and later internet communications which might require a different approach to management from that best suited to the traditional industries.

By the time Henry Mintzberg completed his doctoral study on managerial work in 1973 he was able to reveal that managers actually spent their time working under considerable pressure mainly on tasks which were brief and fragmented.

> *'Half of the observed activities being completed in less than nine minutes, and only one-tenth took more than an hour … Telephone calls were brief and to the point (averaging six minutes), and desk work sessions and unscheduled meetings seldom lasted as long as half an hour (they averaged 15 and 12 minutes respectively).'*[4]

The great majority of managerial time was spent communicating verbally directly with others, on the phone and face to face, in formal prearranged meetings and in informal spontaneous meetings. This was not the pattern of activities that might be assumed as necessary to the pursuit of command and control managerial functions identified by Fayol and others in less volatile

---

4   Mintzberg, H., (1973), *The Nature of Managerial Work*, New York: Harper & Row, p. 33.

times. But it did seem to fit with the more democratic approach at least partly shaped by 'human relations' inputs and the new imperatives resulting from rapidly changing technologies.

Innovating New Technologies

The connection between economic growth and technological innovation was apparent from the dawn of industrialization. The idea of long-wave economic cycles based on innovation was identified by Schumpeter in the 1930s.[5] He attributed the causes of the first 'wave' to the diffusion of steam power, the second to the railway boom and the third to the joint effects of the automobile and electricity. Kondratiev identified similar waves of innovation causing surges in economic growth occurring roughly every 50 years. The first such wave, from 1790 to 1840, was based on coal, steam power and new technology in textiles. A second wave, from 1840 to 1890, was based on railways and mechanization of manufacturing. The third Kondratiev wave, 1890 to 1940, was based on electric power, the internal combustion engine and advances in chemistry.[6]

Others have identified variations on the Kondratiev analysis. Piatier studied the whole life cycle of technologies, not just their birth and economic growth, but their maturity and resulting economic decline.[7] The first wave of innovations in coal, steel, railways, textiles and inorganic chemistry grew up and grew old together. For Piatier, the great depression of the 1930s was neither primarily a short-term economic crisis, nor a crisis of capitalism, but signalled the end of that great wave of major innovations.

Piatier's second conjunction of major innovations causing extraordinary economic growth had its embryonic phase in the 1930s. It was based on oil, motor vehicles, aircraft, sheet steel, organic chemistry and synthetic materials. The growth from this revolution was interrupted by the Second World War, but was realized in the period of post-war reconstruction in the 1950s and 1960s, slowing down in the 1970s, perhaps being brought to premature maturity by the oil price crises of the mid 1970s, but definitely in decline by the 1980s.

---

5   Schumpeter, J.A., (1939), *Business Cycles: A Theoretical, Historical and Statistical Analysis of the Capitalist Process*, New York: McGraw Hill.
6   Kondratiev, N.D., (1935), 'The Long Waves in Economic Life', *The Review of Economic Statistics*, November.
7   Piatier, A., (1984), *Barriers to Innovation*, London: Francis Pinter.

A third revolution, which was in its embryonic phase when Piatier was writing in 1984, appeared likely to be based on electronics, information technology, new forms of energy and energy substitute, biotechnology, molecular engineering, genetic engineering, ocean development and possibly new forms of transport or transport substitute.

Freeman tried to identify how these basic innovations caused the economic growth, seeking to identify, for example, the basic scientific advance, invention or innovation, that sparked off the first, steam power induced, Kondratiev upswing of around 1790.[8] Watt had not invented the steam engine, but merely improved it with the external condenser in 1769 and rotational power in 1781. It had been introduced by Newcomen in 1712, or in simpler form still by Savery in 1698. What it was that caused the explosive growth based on the diffusion of steam power in the industrial revolution was unclear. It was similarly so with the second wave based on the railways starting around 1844. Trevithick had built a locomotive for coal hauling as early as 1804; Stephenson's first locomotive came into operation in 1814 and the first passenger railway in 1825. The basic innovator was difficult to identify. Perhaps it even went back again to the steam engine itself. This lack of clarity was at the root of all such analyses.

Although there were various economic interpretations of the innovation and growth relationship, they were not in fundamental conflict. The stimulus to growth was caused or enabled by technological innovation, either in the shape of a single, all pervasive fundamental development, or by the coincidence of a number of basic innovations. On either analysis, the connection was sustainable if not open to detailed measurement. On either analysis, innovation was a contributory cause of economic growth and represented a powerful competitive tool. On either analysis there was a new generation of basic innovations breaking out of their embryonic phase by the late 1970s. At that time, only the electronics and information technology strands had reached the stage of substantial commercial exploitation, but that was rippling out from a core which was still bubbling with primary innovations.

In part, the investigations of innovation and growth sought to explain the real world booms and slumps of economic cycles which Say's law had excluded. But they were also interesting in that they recognized the importance of innovation not just at the macro level of the whole economy but also at the level

---

8   Freeman, C., (1977), 'The Kondratiev long wave, technical change and unemployment', the proceedings of the OECD experts meeting on structural determinants of unemployment.

of industries and the individual enterprise.[9] The management of innovation had therefore become a key focus of research interest by the time Burns and Stalker identified the appropriate characteristics of systems of management with their simple dichotomy. Just as industries were not adequately characterized in bipolar fashion as stable or volatile, so practical management needed to be more nuanced than simply mechanistic or organismic.

The post-war British government had funded the first empirical innovation study to be published identifying the requirements of 'the technically progressive firm', i.e. one that was 'keeping close to the best which could reasonably be achieved in the application of science and technology'.[10] Foremost among necessary characteristics were good internal and external communications, and a positive approach to the use of science and technology and to the recruitment and training of high calibre technical staff. These broad findings were replicated by many subsequent researchers. The lack of external communications, particularly in relation to market appraisal and marketing research, was found repeatedly to be associated with innovation laggards, while successful innovators were identified as having direct links between research and development and marketing, planned programmes of innovation and management being both technically effective and market oriented.

By the late 1970s some 3,000 empirical studies of innovation had been published,[11] so not only was there considerable knowledge of the economic impact of technological change but a lot of research had been focused on identifying the organizational characteristics of the most effective innovators.

This understanding was popularized by the two McKinsey consultants, Peters and Waterman in their review of what they referred to as 'excellent' companies.[12] It was indicated that they included in their study: 24 high technology firms, 17 consumer goods, six general industrials, seven service industry firms, three in project management and five in resource supply. They did not consider a single financial sector organization, focusing on wealth-creating activity rather than matters of ownership. Peters and Waterman

---

9 Rothwell, R., (1980), 'The Role of Technical Change in International Competitiveness: The Case of the Textile Machinery Industry', *Management Decision*, Vol. 15, No 6.
10 Carter, C.F. and Williams, B.R., (1956), *Industry and Technical Progress: Factors Governing the Speed of Application of Science*, Oxford: Oxford University Press.
11 Rogers, E.M., (1983), *The Diffusion of Innovations*, third edition, New York: Free Press.
12 Peters, T.J. and Waterman, R.H., (1982), *In Search of Excellence*, New York: Harper & Row.

emphasized the people orientation of management in their excellent companies, which contrasted with the then traditional rationalist, quantitative analytical approach of the less successful firms they reviewed. This focus on the support and development of people reflected the growing importance of people-based resources in an era of rapid technological change.

Nurturing Intangible Resources

The traditional business resources were land, capital and labour, but labour, largely unskilled or semi-skilled, was treated more as though it was a raw material to be bought in, or not, as the need arose. It was essentially a current item, hired by the day and paid by the hour.

More skilled layers of human resource could not be regarded in quite the same light. Craftsmen, professional specialists, scientists and engineers had to be recruited, retained and supported and were a significant part of any company's ongoing resource base. By the early 1960s the idea of a knowledge based business was beginning to diffuse into theoretical literature. Drucker, writing in 1964, suggested that:

> '*Business is a human organization, made or broken by the quality of its people. Labour might one day be done by machines to the point where it is fully automated. But knowledge is a specifically human resource. It is not found in books. Books contain information; whereas knowledge is the ability to apply information to specific work and performance. And that only comes with a human being, his brain or the skill of his hands.*'[13]

The cliché that 'our people are our most valuable asset' had by then, in that period of rapid technological change, become palpably true for most companies whether or not they realized it. They were not the most valuable asset because of their physical 'labour', but because of what they could create, both individually and in groups. For many companies by the middle of the twentieth century their creation, intellectual capital, had become a vital resource and the means of establishing and exploiting what was referred to as competitive advantage, i.e. what made the particular company different and in some way better than its competitors.

---

13 Drucker, P.F., (1964), *Managing for Results*. Oxford: Heinemann Professional Publishing, p. 104.

Intellectual capital comprised such things as patents, copyrights, trademarks and brands.[14] But the knowledge base went well beyond these formal items. It included such things as business processes, collective expertise, innovative capability, entrepreneurial and managerial skills, organizational culture and history and ways of doing things, all items resulting from the combined efforts and brainpower of individuals and groups of people and the way they worked together. These became embedded in the company as what was called structural capital, a permanent aspect of the company remaining in the company when the individuals contributing to its creation left. It was therefore not transitory but permanent and cumulative, even though it was not included with a valuation on any balance sheet.

From time to time attempts were made to establish ways of valuing intellectual capital. Brands were ascribed valuations and league tables of such valuations were published annually, but the valuations were unreliable and not accepted by international accounting standards. Attempts to control 'knowledge work' were also proposed as a way of quantifying and therefore valuing its results. Measuring the output of 'knowledge workers', and improving their productivity were also proposed[15] but no credible method of evaluation appeared and to this day none seems imminent.

The accounting profession, espousing principles of prudence and conservatism, was rightly suspicious of such dubious valuations of intellectual capital and consequently in the infrequent cases where an intangible item had an identified value, for example as a result of its acquisition, the rule was for its rapid depreciation on the balance sheet no matter how important it appeared to be.

The fact that such resources were not valued on accounting schedules did not in any way diminish their true value. Management had to be aware of their worth and understand how best to nurture, develop and exploit them by combining intellectual and structural property.[16]

Most company resources were relatively easy to copy, and if they appeared to be the source of competitive advantage they almost certainly would be copied

---

14   Stewart, T.A., (1997), *Intellectual Capital: The New Wealth of Organizations*, London: Nicholas Brealey Publishing.
15   Davenport, T.H., (2005), *Thinking for a Living: How to Get Better Performance and Results from Knowledge Workers*, Boston: Harvard Business School Press.
16   Edvinsson, L. and Sullivan, P., (1996), 'Developing a Model for Managing Intellectual Capital', *European Management Journal*, Vol. 14, No 4, pp. 356–364.

by competitors and their potential profitability competed away. However, intellectual property, such items as patents, trademarks and brands, was legally protected against competitive copying. Structural capital, as identified here, might also be valuable as the source of competitive advantage, and though it had no legal protection, it was nevertheless difficult to replicate because it was know-how embedded in the business processes and cultures that had evolved uniquely over time as the business developed.

The care and nurturing of these new resources, which was the responsibility of general managers, required competence beyond the technical and functional, to shape and develop a distinctive organizational culture in which intellectual and structural capital might flourish.

Shaping Organizational Culture

The traditional emphasis of management on command and control hierarchy failed when flexibility and innovation became critical. Management's alternative approach was to encourage people to contribute their knowledge, experience and enthusiasm at all levels of the organization. This change aimed to create a supportive, open, 'democratic' and progressive organizational culture and a substantial amount of research was conducted to establish how this could best be achieved.

Culture explained how people perceive the organization, and consequently determined how they behaved. It had been defined in many different ways, for example, *'the shared values, beliefs and ways of behaving and thinking that are unique to a particular organization'*.[17] But it was not simply homogeneous as was often assumed in such concepts as 'strong culture'.

Organizational culture could be the sum of many subcultures, each of which contributed its own nuances of meaning and its own rituals and images and even in some cases a specialist and exclusive language. Although there was a widely held view that culture was the glue that could bind an organization together,[18] it was equally clear that culture could in fact be divisive, just as easily as cohesive. In the absence of any dominant super-culture, the various

---

17 Child, J. and Faulkner, D., (1998), *Strategies of Co-operation*, Oxford: Oxford University Press, p. 230.

18 Deal, T. and Kennedy, A., (1982), *Corporate Cultures: The Rites and Rituals of Corporate Life*, New York: Addison Wesley.

subcultures could well be in conflict with each other. On occasion this conflict might become overt and sometimes highly dysfunctional, but more usually the conflict would be bubbling below the surface. Culture was thus described as a *'melange of cross cutting subcultures'*, continually reacting against each other in some more or less cohesive, or divisive, not necessarily stable, equilibrium.[19]

Peters and Waterman recounted how:

> *'stories, myths and legends appear to be very important, because they convey the organization's shared values, or culture. Without exception, the **dominance** and **coherence** of culture proved to be an essential quality of the excellent companies.'*[20]

The implication was that culture could in some way be controlled to make management's desired culture both coherent in itself and dominant over other subcultures. In the management literature, there were many stories, even legends or myths about the great and good, or not so good, originators of such organizations as IBM, Hewlett Packard, NCR, ITT, McDonald's etc. These businesses all shared 'strong', deliberately established and maintained, coherent, dominant 'cultures'. They had, it was argued, gained the active participation of all their members and their consistent concentration of effort on pushing their organization further in its intended direction.

The distinctive feature of these strong cultures was that they were shared by all organization members. The common assumptions about the organization, and the way to behave in it, represented a powerful means of getting to the 'hearts and minds' of all organization members. Thus, potentially, culture offered a way for people in the organization to focus their efforts, consistently to achieve a sense of direction and achievement, beyond the scope of more orthodox management approaches.

However, the creation of a strong culture was not without problems. Whilst it may have served to replace the control mechanisms once effectively wielded by powerful bureaucracies with something that appeared more congenial, it also replicated the problems created by those control mechanisms. Culture was by definition long lasting, and strong culture may have been particularly so. Thus all the old rigidities and loss of responsiveness that caused mechanistic

---

19 Gregory, K.L., (1983), 'Native-View Paradigms: Multiple Cultures and Culture Conflicts in Organisations', *Administrative Science Quarterly*, September.

20 Peters, T. and Waterman, R.H., (1982), *In Search of Excellence*, New York: Harper & Row, p. 75.

firms so much trouble when confronted with change, could be equally present in the strong culture businesses. Control was control, whether or not it came in the guise of a nineteenth-century bureaucratic structure, or a 1970s strong culture. In either format tight control implied lack of flexibility and ability to innovate.

Nevertheless, it was feasible that careful culture management could achieve what George Preston had referred to as the 'true spirit of co-operation between employer and employee'. Though he was speaking on behalf of labour, his plea surely applied through the organization hierarchy. Co-operation, rather than calculation or coercion, should surely always have been the preferred way forward for both employee and employer, though from time to time co-operation would be bound to break down when interests were competing too directly.

Barnard, after many years himself as a chief executive, had defined what he held to be management's essential functions:

> 'first, to provide the system of communications; second, to promote the securing of essential efforts; and third, to formulate and define purpose.'[21]

He emphasized the need for management to communicate an in-depth understanding of the internal and external situation of the organization and its relations with various stakeholders. His emphasis was on communication and persuasion, in order to gain the co-operation of people in achieving the purpose of the organization. For Barnard this communicative role of management to achieve 'morale' was paramount, involving the support of 'inducements' and 'supervision' as well as 'education and training.' He recognized the importance of what he referred to as 'communion, i.e. the opportunity for comradeship at work', as a major motivating force whereas 'material incentives' were weak once beyond the level of the bare physiological incentives. Though he did not use the term culture, he was an early advocate of its management – and not just to replace 'control' but to create a workplace where people could achieve some real fulfilment and enjoyment.

Running through the literature on organizational culture, as with most management literature, there was a fundamental ambiguity. Was management

---

21 Barnard, C.I., (1938), *The Functions of the Executive*, Cambridge, Mass: Harvard University Press, p. 217.

learning how to manage more subtly just in order to exploit the worker and so to maximize profits? This was not a theoretical question. Through the history of industrial management there have been the amoral exploitative robber barons and there have also been the enlightened, even idealistic, captains of industry. And no doubt coming up through the ranks of junior and middle management there were individuals of both categories. Training and education had given managers the opportunity to be effective, but they were not members of a profession which tied them to any notion of public service and they were not bound by any professional code of ethical behaviour. Managers had always had the choice to behave with integrity. Or not.

Managing with Integrity

From the perspective of labour, economic growth was achieved through the accumulation of capital resulting initially from the dispossession of the working classes and maintained through the profits sequestered from the workers' rightful compensation. It had been management that presided over that inequitable distribution of the economic benefits from industry. The interests of labour and the interest of management appeared therefore to be in fundamental opposition. The early mill owners had employed children from the age of six or seven working all the hours of daylight for just sufficient to survive in poverty. Engels had stood witness to working class starvation to death while the nascent capitalist grew ever more wealthy. Marx reported the smirk on 'Mr Moneybags'' face after his successful wage negotiation. Taylor persuaded Schmidt that a 60 per cent wage rise was sufficient reward for a 276 per cent increase in output. This past, if it were the whole truth, would surely have denied the possibility of Preston's 'true spirit of co-operation' and Robert Owen's 'Village of Co-operation'. These would certainly have deserved to have been dismissed as naively idealistic and unreal.

Furthermore, the typical modern mass production plant had become the social reality for many, carrying their dreams for equality of opportunity and personal achievement.[22] But mass production was the problem. Run by command and control with additional discipline imposed by machines, with the coercion of, for their day, high rates of pay for work produced, it took away worker autonomy, making them wholly dependent for survival on the mass-producing organization. Mass production made it difficult for the worker to achieve any dignity and self-respect and for the organization to build on human strengths.

22 Drucker, P.F., (1950), *The New Society*, New York: Harper & Brothers.

But that was not the whole story. Even within mass production organizations, individuals could find social compensations, comradeship and even fun at work. However, the brute fact of mass production was the dominant theme and it was management who presided over it.

But the idea of co-operation was seductive. Why should the various stakeholders in industry not co-operate with each other for the benefit of all? It would require a degree of trust among stakeholders, even between management and labour. But management could hardly expect to be regarded by labour as in any way worthy of their trust. From labour's perspective, it was unlikely that management would be wholly transparent and fair in their treatment of labour. Suspicion and conflict were the general rule rather than trust and co-operation, though there were exceptions.

The establishment of trust between stakeholders in modern organizations had been shown to develop a sense of community and, for example, had encouraged people to work together with less control and obvious hierarchy.[23] In large-scale business organizations, hierarchy could to some extent be replaced by trust and its reputation.

Jönsson studied the effects of trust on knowledge work. As the value of knowledge work increased and the work itself became more knowledge intensive, so the competence of command and control hierarchies to take decisions over that knowledge work became less feasible and less legitimate unless the decisions were taken in consultation with the relevant knowledge workers.[24]

The development of trust involved being accountable for deviations from the expected performance. So long as those trusted behaved in line with expectations, trust would be reinforced as a result of experience and built progressively over time. It did not need to involve belief in the good character or morality of the other party, merely their conformance to agreed action. The replacement of a command and control approach with a more democratic and communicative approach had to be based on establishing trust between the individuals and groups involved.

---

23 Misztal, B.A., (1996), *Trust in Modern Societies: The Search for the Bases of Social Order*, Cambridge: Polity Press.

24 Jönsson, S., (1996), 'Decoupling hierarchy and accountability: an examination of trust and reputation', in R. Munro and J. Mouritsen (eds), *Accountability: Power, Ethos and the Technologies of Managing*, London: Thomson Business Press.

What worked for knowledge workers was equally important for all other stakeholders including those broadly categorized as labour. If management appeared to be untrustworthy with one group, that perception of untrustworthiness would quickly leak to other stakeholder groups. Maintaining different levels of trustworthiness with different stakeholder groups was shown not to be feasible. The reputation for trust would sink to the lowest common denominator: in the end, 'the truth will out'.

Every management transaction with other stakeholders either enhanced or damaged stakeholders' perceptions of management's trustworthiness and this became recognized as a crucial aspect of a company's culture. Peters and Waterman found that one of the eight characteristics of their excellent companies was 'hands on, value driven', meaning management in open and regular interaction with other stakeholders governed by the need to develop perceptions of their trustworthiness. This was found to be particularly relevant to the newer forms of more loosely structured organization where the value-driven companies outperformed the more traditional ones that had tighter control and more rigid structures. And yet, managements were not always trustworthy.

Drucker highlighted the fact that there was much talk about making people feel their jobs were important, but not enough about making their jobs important; too much of the pretence of 'recognition' rather than real recognition of people's contributions to the organization; much clever technique to make people feel their working lives were meaningful and not enough effort to make their work have meaning. 'Management by walking about' (MBWA) became a recognized prescription. Senior managers were to interact with the workforce by visiting the shop floor or offices where the general staff worked. Not only would it cut through the vertical lines of communication in a hierarchical organization structure but it would also motivate by suggesting that senior management was taking an active interest in the workers. Thus MBWA was a technique to persuade the workers that senior management cared about them despite anything apparent to the contrary.

All such management approaches were shot through with the fundamental ambiguity: is the aim exploitative or genuinely co-operative? Barnard, talking about management's personnel role, focused on what he referred to as the 'central consideration' which was the 'development of the individual'. He argued that it was:

'not merely as a matter of tactics, nor merely or chiefly a matter of industrial efficiency. It will ultimately fail if it is merely a high sounding fiction for stimulating production and good morale. Hypocrisy is fatal in the management of personnel.'[25]

Barnard accepted that for most managers and management theorists the main purpose of personnel policies was to 'facilitate the working together of groups of people toward definite ends'. But while acknowledging the legitimacy of that aim, it emphasized for him the primacy of the development of the individual, the two aims – group working and individual development – being the entire justification for management in regard to personnel. And the reasons why so little had been achieved in both aims was:

'the lack of confidence in the sincerity and integrity of management. It is the lack of that confidence ... which insidiously thwarts the best efforts that are made in the industrialized world ... that discourages the most promising developments. And so the advancement of the interests of all is retarded.'[26]

The only answer to the apparent ambiguity of management – the 'key role in wealth creation' – as it operated at the sharp end of the business–labour relationship, was to *be* honest, transparent, consistent and sincere and so earn the trust of all stakeholders. But, though such managerial integrity was crucial to the advancement of all stakeholder interests, and widely acknowledged as such, neo-classical economic theory taught something quite different: that it was important for the economy and society at large for actors to act exclusively in their own self-interest. The 'Keynesian revolution', with the help of the Second World War, had achieved a more equitable distribution of incomes and wealth, but it did not replace amoral, wholly rational self-interest as the fundamental building block of economic theory. 'Economic man' denied the concept of integrity as the basis for managerial action, regarding all such concepts as irrational and therefore excludable exceptions.

The integrity of management, promoted by the early American management educators and their sponsors, further shaped by heroic practitioners such as Chester Barnard and Wilfred Brown and promulgated by the likes of

---

25 Barnard, C.I., (1948), *Organization and Management*, Cambridge, Mass: Harvard University Press, p. 8.
26 Ibid, p. 11.

Peter Drucker, was to be challenged and destroyed by the dismal theoretical constructions of Friedman and his political followers.

The Harrod–Keynesian Context

This chapter has so far reviewed management practice as it developed in the three decades following the Second World War. The war itself had created a distinctive economic and social context. Shop floor workers had been genuinely valued as never before, the interdependence of different social groups had been experienced as never before and economies which had previously been suffering the depths of the pre-war depression were now struggling to get established on a peacetime footing deploying all the new technologies that were becoming available. As always the progress of economic theory had a substantial influence on these developments.

Until the general acceptance of Harrod–Keynesian economics after World War Two, management had operated within a system dominated by neo-classical theory based on a set of propositions such as economic man, the efficiency of markets, domestic and international trade freed from government intervention, and the necessity for private property and profit. Keynes himself broadly agreed with these propositions adding weight to the rather subsidiary contention that economic progress should result in a progressively more equal distribution of income and wealth. His model was capitalism with full employment.

Keynes' concern to achieve full employment was both moral and technical. Full employment was the only way a more equitable distribution of income could be achieved. It was also the way to achieve the fullest sustainable use of the country's resources including its labour. These concerns were no doubt dominant at least in part because his experience had been of depression, war and post-war reconstruction. Depression caused unemployment while war and post-war reconstruction solved it.

His followers converted his short-term analysis into a long-run prescription for maintaining economic growth at a steady but sustainable level. This long-run 'Harrod–Keynesian economics' became the established orthodoxy, justifying high levels of public expenditure by national governments continuing after the war both in the United States and in Britain.

In Britain, unlike the United States, a left-of-centre government was established. The Labour party had emerged from the depression concerned that unemployment resulted from automation and that such technological unemployment was unavoidable but could be ameliorated by public ownership and socialist planning to convert unemployment into leisure.

Keynes himself had forthrightly expressed his view on nationalisation:

> 'There is no so-called important political question so really unimportant,
> so irrelevant to the reorganisation of the economic life of Great Britain,
> as the nationalisation of the railways.'[27]

Nevertheless, the Labour government went ahead with a broad programme of nationalization which included the railways. Harrod–Keynesian economics with its justification of ongoing government intervention, facilitated the socialist development of the welfare state and a truly mixed economy with the state taking over ownership and running basic industries.

The war itself had had other unforeseen consequences which impacted directly on management. Before the war, work on the mass production assembly line was described as:

> 'unnatural, disagreeable, meaningless and a stultifying condition ...
> devoid of dignity as well as of importance.' The worker was seen as 'not
> a human being in society, but a freely replaceable cog in an inhumanly
> efficient machine.'[28]

The war had changed that. It substantially raised the role and standing of the individual worker within society as a whole. Drucker cited evidence from Britain that:

> 'the war brought the industrial worker a satisfaction, a feeling of
> importance and achievement, a certainty of citizenship, self respect and
> pride ...'[29]

---

27 Keynes, J.M., (1931), 'Essays in Persuasion', p. 290, included in Vol. IX of *The Collected Writings of John Maynard Keynes*, (1972), (eds) A. Robinson, E. Johnson and D. Moggridge, London: Macmillan for the Royal Economic Society.

28 Beatty, J., (1998), *The World According to Drucker*, London: Orion Business Books, p. 45.

29 Ibid, p. 47.

After the war, these positive consequences gradually receded as the worker, devoid of value as combatant, resumed their pre-war low status with renewed alienation. But there was a critical difference. The power position of trade unions had been substantially increased by legislative protection and support.

In the United States this burgeoning influence of organized labour, encumbered as it was with some political intent, was a considerable concern. The continuing advance of communism from the Soviet Union, through Eastern Europe, China and elsewhere, caused considerable disquiet with mounting suspicions of communist infiltration of the State Department and concerns over the socialist influence in Western Europe and Britain.

Under this pressure the American Taft–Hartley Act was passed in 1947 reversing much of the trade union protection gained during the New Deal. Unfair labour practices by unions, restrictive practices, wildcat strikes, solidarity or political strikes, secondary picketing, closed shops, and monetary donations by unions to federal political campaigns were all outlawed and union officials were required to formally confirm their non-membership of any communist organization.

It was more than 30 years before any remotely comparable legislation was passed in Britain during which time trade unionism gained substantial influence and power in its relationship with government, business and management.

Keynes foresaw the problem of wage inflation if full employment was achieved and maintained. This was going to be especially difficult to control when collective bargaining was conducted between the newly powerful trades union movement and less powerful individual employers. But he saw it as a political problem for governments to deal with. He envisaged that enlightened governments would act decisively to control cost-push inflation driven largely by wage demands. He hardly acknowledged that democratic governments were in turn controlled by the market in votes and professional politicians would only be likely to do 'the right thing' if they felt they could persuade their voters to support it.

The classical alternative to the Keynesian approach would have been to let market forces replace the government's commitment to full employment and allow bankruptcy and unemployment to mediate the fight between employers and employed. But classical theory had been replaced by Harrod–Keynesian economics. While Keynes himself had studiously maintained a balance of approach between capital and labour, the struggle between employers and employed, often driven by political ideals rather than economic considerations, inflicted considerable economic and industrial damage in Britain and to a lesser extent in the United States.

Long-run Harrod–Keynesian economics encouraged the belief that full employment and the affluent society could be maintained for ever and that booms and slumps were things of the past. But it didn't work out that way.

The first OPEC induced oil price crisis in 1973 had a profound effect on the industrialized world, especially on those economies, including Britain and to a lesser extent the United States, which depended on oil imports. In Britain's case, the impact of oil price hikes was amplified by a strike of coal miners causing a restriction of industrial output to a three-day working week. The wage and oil cost-push inflation accompanied by slow, even negative, economic growth was a new phenomenon for which economic orthodoxy was ill-equipped. The prescriptions for dealing with inflation would inhibit economic growth while interventions to deal with stagnation would exacerbate inflation. By the mid 1970s, stagflation ruled and the good times appeared to be over.

The increasingly emboldened trade unions on both sides of the Atlantic were causing concern within both industry and government. Strikes – official, unofficial and wildcat – were resulting in ever increasing lost industrial production.

In Britain, the Communist Party had failed to achieve parliamentary representation and so focused on developing its presence and influence within the unions in order to influence strikes and industrial action motivated not so much by the best interests of their members as by the progression of their political aims, no matter how unrealistic, for 'regime change'. The opportunity to establish co-operation between employer and employee was effectively turned down, this time by organized labour.

The apparent state of the British economy, and especially industrial relations, under the left-of- centre administration, elaborated by an increasingly right-of-centre media, brought an end to Labour government for a generation. Subsequently the Carter presidency in the United States was replaced by the Reagan administration. Keynes had indicated that the problem of wage inflation supported by full employment would require a political solution. By the end of the 1970s, the Anglo-Saxon economies were set to find out if one was available.

PART III

The Educated Fall of Management

Management's rise as an autonomous category, independent of both capital and labour, placed it in a unique and powerful position. But management was not a coherent group as were the traditional professions. There had always been various routes of entry to management ranks including appropriate education and training as well as ownership by whatever means it was achieved. Management ranks were therefore mixed, having no agreed agenda, purpose or standards of behaviour.

Some acted in what they considered to be the long-term best interests of their company, others combined that concern with a broader concern for the good of the society in which they worked and lived, while some used their power position to maximize their own personal benefit at the expense of others. Thus while the period up to the late 1970s saw the rise in understanding of the role of management, the practical application of that understanding was uneven.

Its autonomy made management a potentially powerful source of good, both in terms of achieving economic growth and overseeing the distribution of its benefits equitably. However, that same autonomy always attracted individuals who were prepared to exploit their position for ill, even with criminality. Barnard, Brown and others had been well aware of this ambiguity which brought into question the fundamental legitimacy of management's position. With no democratic process and no professional gatekeeper it was unclear how the autonomous position of management could be justified. Some checks and balances were in place, some imposed by company law and professional accounting practice, some limitations imposed by organized labour, but day-to-day management were enabled to exercise more or less total power within their working unit. The legitimacy of this situation was troubling: the 'key role in twentieth-century wealth creation' was not without ambiguity.

This third part looks at how that management role was seduced and reduced as a result of a new focus on matters of ownership disguised as strategy, the renewal of neo-classical free-market economics with a more clinical focus on the achievement of wealth and its dogmatic application by government, and the malign effects of management academics and educators in promulgating these corrosive orthodoxies.

Chandler's 1962 account of the development of 'Strategy and Structure' in American industry recorded how diversification, often necessitated by the imperative to grow despite the restrictions of anti-trust legislation which limited market shares, multiplied the complexity of central decision making. It was this complexity which required structural change. Previously most large businesses had adopted a simple multi-divisional structure. The new structures dividing professional specialist staff functions from line management also divided management decisions into two categories:

> 'one – the strategic – dealt with the long term allocation of existing resources and the development of new ones essential to assure the continued health and future growth of the enterprise. The other – the tactical – was more involved in ensuring the efficient and steady use of current resources whose allocation had already been decided.'[1]

The distinction between day-to-day tactical and long-term strategic management implied a hierarchy of responsibilities with the 'strategic perspective' being paramount, distancing top management's primary interest from day-to-day concerns.

In due course, the top management focus on strategy, notably diversification, caused the development of a new specialism in strategic management. Initially this was driven largely by financial performance, criteria and language. During the late 1970s, management's focus was drawn more directly to maximizing the performance of company shares on the stock market. This 'strategic' perspective, driven partly by the threat from asset-stripping share raiders, led to a top management focus on immediate results which could more easily be

---

1   Chandler, A.D., (1962), *Strategy and Structure: Chapters in the History of the American Industrial Enterprise*, Cambridge, Mass: The MIT Press, p. 383.

achieved through mergers and acquisitions, rather than through the assiduous and constant management of existing business.

While management was thus changing its focus, the focus of economic theory was also changing. Keynes had recognized the dangers inherent in his primary concern for achieving and maintaining full employment. Collective bargaining by powerful unions, with government dedicated to full employment, would, Keynes had recognized, lead inevitably to continuously accelerating wage driven price inflation. Keynes had regarded the solution to this economic problem as a political matter, rather than one of economics. In this context, industrial management had been unable to constrain wage inflation. This failure and the stagflation of the late 1970s, presided over by Harrod–Keynesian economists, resulted in government changes in both Britain and the United States. The new conservative administrations accepted what Keynes had asserted was their responsibility. They dispensed with the commitment to full employment and brought inflation back under control inflicting substantial and symbolically important defeats on organized labour.

In doing so they had turned to the version of neo-classical free-market economics which had been progressed by von Mises, Hayek and colleagues of the Austrian school of economics. With the rise of Hitler they had migrated to Britain and the United States where their version of free-market capitalism was the available alternative to the failing Harrod–Keynesian model. Their influence on government policy was further intensified by the more populist approach of Milton Friedman of Chicago University. By the turn of the 1980s, the new neo-classical economics was becoming more or less totally dominant in Anglo-Saxon government and business as well as in management education, and it had many implications for the development of industry and for management.

Management's position had always been ambiguous, neither owner of capital nor representative of labour. It had been enabled to influence the distribution of incomes and wealth between the two, and able to do so with justice and fairness or with destructive exploitative intent. Management's fall from its higher aims was accomplished through the Friedmanite bribe to accept riches in return for acting exclusively as capital's agent and in so doing give up their autonomy and independence.

9

Seduction by the New Strategic Management

John Lombe's first ever water-powered silk mill was surely the product of strategic thinking, as was Arkwright's cotton-spinning mill. A century and a half later Henry Ford's mass production of the Model T established a virtuous cycle of massively reduced costs through standardization and mass production, enabling the decimation of automobile prices, thus creating the new mass markets to justify the new factories. More recently Microsoft, Intel, Amazon and Google, just as examples, have similarly blazed new ways ahead which surely represent the successful pursuit of strategy.

They all applied common sense to their business situations, as have so many other successful entrepreneurs. They did not have, and seem not to have needed, any formal knowledge of strategy as it is now taught in business schools. They were confronted with problems that needed solutions. They were not looking for intellectual challenge for its own sake. And they managed without all the panoply of analytical methods, models, tools and techniques now available.

Chandler focused on diversification as strategy. Successful companies were constrained by anti-trust legislation which limited their ability to dominate their markets, prevented competition-reducing acquisitions and sometimes resulted in companies being broken up if they became too dominant by organic growth. Growing businesses were therefore forced to diversify into new markets and new activities. Prior to the 1960s, diversification was the only aspect of strategy formally acknowledged in management literature and even then standard dictionary definitions of strategy were still only expressed in military terms as *'generalship'* or *'the art of war'*.[1]

---

1   *Concise Oxford Dictionary* third edition, (1964), p. 1273.

Subsequently the formulation and implementation of more general strategic plans began to diffuse across industry, such strategy being defined by one leading exponent as:

> *'the pattern of decisions in a company that determines and reveals its objectives, purposes, or goals, produces the principal policies and plans for achieving those goals, and defines the range of business the company is to pursue, the kind of economic and human organization it is or intends to be, and the nature of the economic and non-economic contribution it intends to make to its shareholders, employees, customers and communities.'[2]*

Strategic management was quickly adopted by leading firms of consultants as well as business school faculty. It was invested with some theoretical ideas and made amenable to quantitative analysis and became fashionable.

But the question remained as to its true substance. On the basis of his forty-year career at General Electric including two decades as CEO, Jack Welch expressed his doubts as follows:

> *'Forget the arduous, intellectualized number crunching and data grinding that gurus say you have to go through to get strategy right. Forget the scenario planning, year-long studies, and hundred plus page reports. They're time consuming and expensive, and you just don't need them.*
>
> *In real life strategy is actually very straightforward. You pick a general direction and implement like hell.'[3]*

However, picking a general direction and implementing like hell was not widely regarded as an adequate resolution of the strategy problem. It didn't satisfy the early specialist practitioners of the art nor the academic faculty who quickly engaged with the subject. It appeared to be a new and fertile field of management expertise engaging both consultants and academic faculty. By the late 1970s, its importance was becoming recognized and it achieved a leading position on the business school curriculum, attracting both high profile faculty and substantial funds for its research. This is what is referred to here as the

2   Andrews, K.R., (1980), *The Concept of Corporate Strategy*, Chicago: Irwin, pp. 18–19.
3   Welch, J., (2005), *Winning*, London: HarperCollins Publishers, p. 165.

new strategic management which replaced the old version, 'picking a general direction and implementing like hell'.

As an academic subject, it lacked provenance of any significance. In the spirit of true academic endeavour, faculty therefore sought to discover both strategy's history and its underlying theory. This discovery research was not carried out with the aim of improving management practice, but of raising the status of strategic management as an academic liberal arts subject within the perceptions of their academic peers.

Strategy's History

The earliest exemplars of writing about strategy date from around the fourth century BC. Sun Tzu was then scratching 'The Art of War' on strips of bamboo when China was divided into eight competing states and a number of minor principalities which were enduring a nightmare of lawlessness and chaos. War was conducted more as a way of life, a purposeless ritual governed by arcane rules and presided over by hereditary amateurs, punctuated by battles resembling disorderly mêlées which rarely produced a clear result.[4]

Sun Tzu recognized the futility of such warfare. He argued that war, which was always costly, should only be conducted in order to achieve a ruler's political aims. Generally, these would be related to the survival, security, expansion and/or prosperity of the ruler's state. For Sun Tzu there was no place for war for its own sake, or total war which would only be terminated on the complete destruction of the enemy. Such total war was unknown till the twentieth century.

Accounts of Philip and Alexander's strategy at the battle of Chaeronea, around the same time, have also been referenced in the modern strategic management literature.[5] Machiavelli too has received some attention,[6] but the next major contribution was in the early decades of the nineteenth century when von Clausewitz contributed *On War*.[7] At around the same time in the

---

4   Griffith, S.B., (1963), *Sun Tzu: The Art of War*, London: Oxford University Press.
5   Mintzberg, H. and Quinn, J.B., (1996), *The Strategy Process: Concepts, Contexts and Cases*, third edition, NJ: Prentice Hall International.
6   Machiavelli, N., (1521), *The Art of War*, currently available from De Capo Press, New York (1965) with an introduction by Neal Wood.
7   Clausewitz, C., (1832), *On War*, originally published in German with several English translations including an abridged version with an introduction by L.Willmot published in 1997, Ware: Wordsworth Editions.

United States the US Military Academy at West Point began teaching the military subject from its then curiously limited experience.

More recently Liddell Hart's 'Strategy' apparently drew the comment from Rommel (German high command in the Second World War) that:

> *'the British would have been able to prevent the greatest part of their defeats if they had paid attention to the modern theories expounded by Liddell Hart before the war.'*[8]

Military strategists tended to be methodical rather than theoretical, producing pragmatic and prescriptive guidelines as to how things should be done in order to achieve victory. Much of what passed for military strategy was devoted to what might more appropriately be regarded as tactics. Bulow defined strategy as relating to military movements which were beyond the enemy's cannon range or range of vision, tactics being such movements as were within that range.[9]

Overtaken by technology, the distinction between the strategic and the tactical or operational remained. Clausewitz argued that strategy was concerned with using battle for the purposes of war, which was 'simply the continuation of policy by other means,[10] while tactics were concerned with the use of armed forces in battle.

Military strategists produced many much-quoted gems concerning the conduct of warfare, the relations between the sovereign and the general and the management of armies. Sun Tzu advised generals to be subtle and insubstantial, silent and invisible. In order to win you must know when to fight and when not to, and you must know how to use both large and small forces. Moreover, a successful general must be able to unite all his troops to focus on achieving the purpose of the war. The prescriptions were translated in such general terms that they could be readily applied to modern business situations.

Though winning without fighting was perhaps the most widely quoted of Sun Tzu's ideas, most were actually concerned with the conduct of battle. He was concerned that generals should know and understand all they could about the enemy and the environment as well as the strengths and weaknesses of his

---

8   Liddell Hart, B.H., (1967), *Strategy,* second revised edition, London: Faber & Faber.
9   Paret, P., (ed.) (1986), *Makers of Modern Strategy,* Oxford: Clarendon Press, p. 186.
10   Clausewitz, C., (1832), *On War,* Ware: Wordsworth Editions, p. 22.

own forces. He emphasized that war and its battles were conducted only so as to achieve the political objective which was passed down to the military; it was not for the military to define the strategic objective.

The parallels between war and competition have been widely recognized and Sun Tzu's argument for what he referred to as 'moral action' motivated by enlightened self-interest seen as potent. Moral action drove relationships between different stakeholders such as the ruler, the general, the officers, the troops and the local population, not just between states. Such relationships were built on trust, and Sun Tzu advocated only the pursuit of objectives which could gain the enthusiastic support of all stakeholders. Such a leader would have to be 'wise, sincere, humane, courageous, and strict', a combination of characteristics with which Barnard, Brown, Drucker, Welch and many others may well have agreed.

Clausewitz was also concerned with 'such imponderables as the soldiers' morale and the commanders' psychology' and even Machiavelli held that, 'you will still need the goodwill of the people to keep a principality'.[11] Strategic aims, either an extraneous given, or a management decision, would not be achieved if the people in an organization were not acting in their pursuit. The effectiveness of the strategy process was dependent on the people in the organization, whether an army or a business.

Though military strategy did not offer a coherent body of theory applicable to modern non-military organizations, it did identify a simple strategy process, implicit in the writings of Sun Tzu, Clausewitz and others. The process started with the definition of the aim. This was the starting point for all the military strategists, given to them by their political masters. Sun Tzu then suggested success would depend on knowing the enemy, yourself, the ground and the weather. He emphasized the importance of military intelligence in gathering all this knowledge and understanding. Finally, based on this understanding, decisions were necessary as to the appropriate action to be taken. This then boiled down to a deceptively simple process which could be generalized as 'objectives – external analysis – internal analysis – action'. This four-stage strategy process was subsequently detectable in most published approaches to strategy.

---

11   Machiavelli, N., (1521), *The Art of War,* New York: De Capo Press, p. 27.

Strategy's Theory

Strategy's history was almost entirely military and not very profound. It hardly satisfied the needs of academic faculty any more than did Jack Welch's dismissive summary. Academic interest was therefore drawn to consider the possibility of underlying theory. Theory is perhaps a rather portentous term to describe the relatively lightweight underpinnings of strategic management. They ranged from practical routines, or even checklists, to those approaches extracted from economic theory.

The entrepreneurial model, for example, rested on the entrepreneur's originating identification of a customer need that the business was set up to satisfy in some way better, or at less cost, than existing competitors and the development of special capabilities to maintain and develop that superlative mode of satisfying the customer need.[12]

The life cycle model adapted from general systems theory was based on the phases of birth, growth, maturity and decline, through which all systems processed. It suggested the purpose of all systems was to achieve and maintain maturity, since that was when systems achieved maximum and most efficient energy conversion. In business terms, it was the phase in which most profit and most surplus cash were generated. The objective of the life cycle model would therefore be to ensure a succession of products or businesses which achieved the leadership position in their markets during their maturity phase. To do this would require knowledge of when the life cycle phases were going to occur, in particular when the growth phase would change to maturity. Such directional changes were notoriously difficult to predict, forecasts tending to be based on a continuation of current trends. Understanding the shape and size of the industry life cycle and the particular company's position on it would therefore be important in deciding the appropriate action to ensure leadership ahead of the change of phase to maturity.

The initial portfolio model introduced by the Boston Consulting Group[13] in the 1960s also followed the four-stage model. Its aim was to achieve a lasting and balanced portfolio of products or businesses. Its external analysis was concerned with the growth rate of the market and the position of the company's leading competitor. Internal analysis was focused on measuring the company's

---

12 Pearson, G., (1985), *The Strategic Discount*, Chichester: Wiley.
13 Boston Consulting Group, (1968), *Perspectives on Experience*, Boston: Boston Consulting Group.

experience, relative to that of its leading competitor, in producing and selling the product. And the actions were focused on decisions to buy, sell or hold products or businesses.

Porter's 'competitive strategy'[14] applied microeconomic theory to what he referred to as 'industry analysis'. Being based on economic theory, the model implicitly assumed profit maximization as the 'strategic' objective. The model was based on the not too profound equation that profit is equal to income less cost. Therefore, maximizing profit involved achieving either the lowest costs or the highest prices.

His external analysis assessed the extent to which the arcane assumptions of perfect competition applied in a particular market: the intensity of competition between existing competitors; existence of barriers to entry to and exit from the market; existence of substitute products; bargaining power of suppliers and customers. Porter's internal analysis focused on the direct and indirect activities of a firm and assessed the cost of each activity and, as though it was possible, the profit margin which each such activity contributed.

Strategy, for Porter, was then simply a matter of breaking out of the assumed position of competitors in a competitive market, for example by achieving lower costs or higher prices, or by focusing on a less competitive sub-segment of the market where some monopolistic characteristics might be achieved.[15]

A rather more sophisticated application of economic theory to business strategy was achieved through the 'resource based' approach. The weight of resource-based strategy was on the acquisition, development and exploitation of difficult to copy resources which might be the source of sustainable competitive advantage. The foundation of this approach lay deep within economic theory, going back to Ricardo, and was initially brought to the knowledge of academic strategists through the work of Edith Penrose in 1959.[16] It was later developed by Wernerfelt[17] and others in the 1980s and consistently promulgated in the pages of the *Strategic Management Journal*. As the importance of off balance sheet knowledge-based resources increased so the resource-based approach has

14 Porter, M.E., (1980), *Competitive Strategy – Techniques for Analyzing Industries and Competitors*, New York: Free Press.

15 Porter, M.E., (1985), *Competitive Advantage – Creating and Sustaining Superior Performance*, New York: Free Press.

16 Penrose, E.T., (1959), *The Theory of the Growth of the Firm*, Oxford: Oxford University Press.

17 Wernerfelt, B., (1984), 'A Resource Based View of the Firm', *Strategic Management Journal*, 5: pp. 171–80.

become more pervasive. All it lacked to become the overwhelmingly dominant strategic model among consultants, academic faculty and practitioners alike was some fashionable language and a memorable graphic.

A more widely used and quoted strategy model was that outlined by Prahalad and Hamel which straddled both resource-based and market-based approaches.[18] This model went beyond the simple economics of profit maximizing and acknowledged and responded to the importance of people in the achievement of strategy. The four-stage process was implicit in their approach: the strategic aim or intent being to beat competitors, external analysis involving a focus on technologies and competitors, internal analysis focusing on what they referred to as 'core competencies'. The strategic action for Prahalad and Hamel was to develop and exploit the 'core competencies' and create new 'competitive space' by a process of 'leverage and stretch'. This model not only analysed both markets and resources but its strategic action endeavoured to address progress in both, through the motivation, if not inspiration, of people.

The above brief outlines serve largely to emphasize the simplistic nature of strategic management theories and to confirm their adherence to the generalized four-stage strategy process. General systems theory, microeconomics, portfolio theory and resource-based theory all provide ample opportunity for interesting complication, but the reality is simple and is not at all dependent on quantitative sophistication or deep qualitative analysis. Practitioners were influenced by these various models with differing, though limited, strategic effect.

The most significant effect of the new focus on strategic management was to disengage top management from the day-to-day problems of running a business. Day-to-day management was concerned with the needs and aspirations of employees and customers, and the potential for technologies to satisfy those needs and aspirations. The focus of strategic management was quite elsewhere.

Long-Range Planning in Practice

Management's focus on strategy was born of necessity. The most successful of the large diversified companies which had been studied by Chandler, typically,

---

18 Hamel, G. and Prahalad, C.K., (1994), *Competing for the Future*, Boston: Harvard Business School Press. This book combined the content of four previous articles published in the Harvard Business Review.

had small central headquarters taking decisions relating to the allocation of scarce resources between business activities, decisions that could not be avoided. Initially this allocation role was achieved through a process of capital budgeting which agreed planned capital expenditures usually over a five-year time horizon.

Agreeing how to allocate resources between businesses necessitated those involved in the agreement to have some knowledge and understanding of the relative merits of the different candidate businesses. Business merits might logically include such issues as the inherent profitability of the business, its forecast future growth, the level and rate of its technological development, and some perception of the risk levels involved. Moreover, knowledge and understanding must also include some awareness of the relative strengths of the business within its industry in terms of its market or technological position.

The agreement of a 'long-range' plan of capital expenditure, critical as it was to the direction of a business, also had other ramifications. Expenditure on capital items when funds were limited could reduce the level of funding available to other business activities. Additionally, though it might have a beneficial impact on a firm's ability to maintain its position technologically and in the market and therefore to survive and prosper in the long term, the short-term profit impact of capital expenditure was invariably negative. It was widely held that major capital projects took around seven years before they produced the same level of profitability as an existing business; for completely new diversified projects the delay could be considerably longer.

It was only a small logical step to extend such capital expenditure plans to full five-year projections, involving not just capital expenditure but also full forecasts of the profit and loss account, balance sheet and cash flows. Such long-range financial plans became fashionable in large diversified businesses during the 1960s. At that time, electronic data processing was in its infancy. There were no personal computers and spreadsheets. Database-type programmes had been custom written for particular purposes, but were not generally available even on mainframes. Research universities, for example, devoted space to 'statistics laboratories' which had suites of physically huge calculating machines, far less powerful than a $5 pocket calculator of today, and which required a trained engineer to reset a machine if a user ever were to divide a number by zero. Computer programmes were still typically entered on punched cards for input to the computer. Though there were exceptions, for the most part mainframe computer systems were occupied in such administrative tasks as payroll calculation, order processing and inventory control.

Under these circumstances the development of a five-year corporate plan for a business of any complexity was a huge computational task, carried out, or at least supervised by, professional planning specialists then starting to be turned out by America's leading business schools. The completion of the corporate plan based on detailed five-year forecasts of all the inputs, showed a projection of profit and cash flow, the 'bottom line' of which may well not at first have been an acceptable result. Changes would have to be made, possibly the growth forecast increased, or capital expenditures delayed, in order to produce an acceptable projection of business performance. The recalculation of the five-year plan would involve the same manual accounting labour as the original. Recalculation three or four times or more became an annual nightmare requiring armies of accounting clerks working excessive hours of overtime to achieve rather pointless deadlines. The whole process had little to do with strategy and had limited impact on the way a company developed. The alternative approach was simply to miss out the whole planning process. Though equally short on strategic implications, this at least avoided the substantial costs and time wasted generating the plan.

However, the process did have some implications. Firstly, since the plans themselves were written in financial language, the importance of accounting was substantially raised in those companies which engaged with long-range financial planning. Secondly, it was not immediately obvious how devoid of strategic impact the plans were. They looked as though they mattered, projecting as they did the company's performance over a five-year period. They appeared to flag up potential problems and issues and helped with 'strategic communication' across the organization. They made the alternative, not planning, seem unprofessional and even irresponsible. This was especially so, as the financial projections were supported by qualitative analysis of the threats and opportunities facing a company and its strengths and weaknesses in dealing with the threats and opportunities. From this SWOT analysis then programmes of action could be specified which went far beyond long-range capital expenditures and five-year budgets. Thus a complete Ansoffian bureaucracy[19] was created with the inevitable resulting in what Mintzberg aptly described as 'paralysis by analysis'.

A further, more insidious impact of the new emphasis on long-range planning was to move the centre of gravity of management a little further away

---

19   Ansoff, H.I., (1965), *Corporate Strategy*, New York: McGraw Hill.

from the fundamental preoccupations of management with the resources at its disposal, notably its people. Managers who supervised the development, manufacture and marketing of physical products or services appeared to be distanced a little further from the top of large businesses where the important 'strategic' decisions were made. Those that headed up big companies, at least in the Anglo-Saxon world, were drawn not from those with industry-specific specialist technological training and graduate level expertise but more probably from those with higher level business school degrees or professional qualifications in accounting or the law. These appeared better fitted for assessing and deciding the sort of deals which the business portfolio approach required.

Portfolio Decisions

The leading management consultancies, such as Boston Consulting Group, McKinsey and Company, Booz, Allen and Hamilton and A.T.Kearney, were at the forefront of developments in strategic management. While practitioners laboured with the bureaucratic monster that their accountants had created, the consultancies offered streamlined versions which assisted management to focus on the key strategic decisions which were still seen as related to the allocation of resources.

The first consultancy model to achieve almost global acceptance was that devised by Boston Consulting Group based on its interpretation of learning curve data analysis for 24 undifferentiated commodities (e.g. transistors, diodes, crude oil, pvc, etc). Boston found, not surprisingly, that the more of a commodity that was produced by an industry, the lower the cost of its production. [20] They were more precise about the commodities they chose: unit costs reduced by between 20 per cent and 30 per cent every time total cumulative production doubled. In young, fast-growing industries, total production would be doubled quickly and costs therefore also reduced quickly. In mature, slow-growth industries, the reverse would be true. The competitor with the leading market share of a fast-growth industry would enjoy fastest decline in costs and therefore, assuming a set market price as would be the case for a commodity product and all other things being equal, they would be the most profitable competitor in that market.

---

20 Boston Consulting Group, (1968), *Perspectives on Experience*, Boston: Boston Consulting Group.

This was hardly revolutionary. Empirical evidence from the Strategic Planning Institute's PIMS (Profit Impact of Marketing Strategy) database had been published indicating a similar finding:

> 'a business's share of its served market (both absolute and relative to its three largest competitors) has a positive impact on its profit and net cash flow.'[21]

Boston went further, even developing a differential equation for evaluating the net present value of an increment in market share,[22] the spurious precision serving to camouflage the crude approximation or fundamental inaccuracy of the basic market share/profit relationship.

Drucker challenged the relationship pointing out that in many industries:

> 'the largest company is by no means the most profitable one ... the second spot, or even the third spot is often preferable, for it may make it possible for that concentration on one segment of the market, on one class of customer, or on one application of the technology, in which genuine leadership often lies.'[23]

From this simple if dubious foundation, the first portfolio model was derived. It enabled business headquarters to decide the allocation of resources on the basis of just two business characteristics: the growth rate of the served market, and the market share of the business relative to its largest competitor. These two dimensions defined a matrix divided into four quadrants and according to where a subsidiary business was positioned on the matrix so resources would be allocated to it. If it were high growth, it would consume a lot of cash just to keep up, but if it had a high share of that market, it would generate cash also (Boston labelled such as 'stars'). If it had a small share, it would be a net cash consumer ('problem children'). If the business served a mature low growth market, it would not consume so much cash, but if it had a low relative market share it wouldn't generate much either ('dogs'), though if it had a large share it would be a net cash generator ('cash cows'). The position on the matrix therefore enabled strategic management to categorize their various businesses: those to invest in, those to draw cash from, those to try to improve

---

21   Schoeffler, S., (1977), *The PIMS Letter on Business Strategy, No. 2,* Harvard: The Strategic Planning Institute.

22   Boston Consulting Group, (1968), *Perspectives on Experience,* Boston: Boston Consulting Group, pp. 102–107.

23   Drucker, P.F., (1964), *Managing for Results,* New York: Harper and Row, p. 38.

and those to be closed down or sold off. Those are the standard portfolio decisions of 'buy' (i.e. increase investment), 'sell' (i.e. reduce investment) and 'hold' (i.e. maintain investment).

These were important decisions for strategic management, and portfolio models – Boston was the first of several similar – enabled them to be taken on purely clinical objective grounds and at the same time cut the bureaucracy involved in the former financial planning system. At least that was how it was intended.

The reality was that it crystallized the divide between top strategic management on the one hand and day-to-day operational management on the other. Adoption of the portfolio system announced the rules of a strategy game which were as transparent to the subsidiary business managers as they were to the strategists at headquarters. Managers whose businesses were identified as 'dogs' would naturally wish to change that designation in order to increase financial support from the centre. A simple way to do this was to change the definition of the served market so that it could be seen as a higher-growth segment. All subsidiary management strategic effort would therefore be devoted to convincing top management of the new definition. Strategic planning therefore became a field of combat between strategic and operational managers, a dichotomy further exacerbated by the establishment of business school educated elites set up in headquarters' corporate planning departments, who had limited contact with the people and issues of general management and no necessity for talking directly to labour, yet being directly influential with top management to whose jobs they in due course succeeded. The more mundanely educated and industry trained operational line managers thereby lost expectation of succession to the top.

A further reality was that no business could be adequately understood simply through knowledge, even if it was accurate, of just two variables: market growth and relative market share. The decisions based on this partial understanding, or misunderstanding, were therefore likely to be seriously flawed. Nevertheless, the Boston portfolio successfully diffused through 1970s industry, and was the basis of many business divestment and closure decisions. As noted by Drucker and others, many of the divested businesses turned into exciting successes once freed of the portfolio-instigated repression.

Adopting this approach to strategy changed the nature of business itself. The strategic focus was no longer on the development of a coherent business direction, but on increasing the value of its diverse portfolio of businesses.

The new emphasis was on maximizing the real worth of the company's shares, an ambiguous concept which depended on both the firm's market capitalization and its ability to pay dividends, frequently interpreted as being a short-term, even immediate, concept, which certainly did not refer to management's responsibility to be concerned with the survival and long-term prosperity of the company as an autonomous entity.

The new strategic management role was to divest 'dog' business units, cut out surplus or underused assets where possible, identify and acquire under-valued assets or businesses and 'improve' them by cutting out any costs, such as research and development, which did not have an immediate payback. The relatedness or industrial logic of such combinations of business units in a portfolio was not of great concern since membership might only be temporary. The centre would limit its involvement in the business units to identifying surplus assets and deploying specialist 'locum' managers to sort out underperforming businesses, or organize their disposal or closure. Thus a deal-making mentality was established.

Such a portfolio business would minimize the costs of the centre by having only a small corporate staff, with business unit CEOs having a high degree of autonomy, being paid substantial bonuses for achieving clear financial targets with the expectation of low rewards, or loss of position, if targets were not achieved.

Such portfolio-based strategic business management was the first of many approaches to strategy implemented by the consultancies and adopted by academic business school faculty. Subsequent models added to the number of input variables and finessed the outputs beyond Boston's simple prescriptions, but the variations were of limited practical significance. Though the models became increasingly complex and apparently more precise in the spirit of Boston's own differential equation valuing market share, in truth the analysis remained crude and inaccurate, creating more the false impression of additional understanding, rather than any genuine new insight. However they clearly increased the focus on mergers and acquisitions.

Mergers and Acquisitions

Mergers and acquisitions (M&A) was the commonly used term, acquisition being where firm A acquired more than 50 per cent of firm B, and merger being where firm A and firm B joined forces to create firm C which was a new legal entity. Though the term M&A has persisted, the vast majority of such transactions have always been in the form of acquisition rather than merger.

Economists noted that new industries quickly attracted lots of small competitors which persisted through the industry's main growth phase. Then when growth slowed and the industry embarked on its mature phase there was a shake-out period with some firms leaving the industry and many others consolidating through M&A to form a smaller number of bigger operators. These then continued till the industry went into decline when there would be a further fall-out period of M&A leaving only a small number of competitors to dominate what was left.

Competitors engaging in the process of industry concentration through M&A might be driven by industrial logic. If competition law allowed, firms could achieve an improved market and technological position more rapidly by M&A than by normal organic growth. This would allow firms to achieve economies of scale in production, distribution and promotion as well as add to their financial strength and might also provide access to strategic patents and other intellectual capital. On the other hand, if prevented from that strategy by anti-trust legislation, firms would be forced to pursue their growth by diversifying away from the existing industry and would therefore acquire an established position and expertise in a new industry participating in its concentration process.

Such M&A had occurred in waves in the United States, the first being around 1897–1904, seeing a great industry concentration with the formation of, for example, DuPont, International Harvester and US Steel, among many other newly formed big businesses. This occurred despite the Sherman Antitrust Act of 1890. A second wave of horizontal industry-concentrating M&A lasted from roughly 1916 till the Wall Street crash of 1929. After that, M&A activity remained subdued for around three decades till a substantial wave of diversification and conglomeration M&A in the 1960s saw the formation of such firms as ITT, Gulf & Western, Litton Industries and others.

Parallel waves of M&A were experienced in Britain where, by the late 1960s, a form of acquisitive financial conglomerate (AFC) was emerging, largely controlled by individuals who had achieved a substantial element of ownership. Some of the AFC activity undoubtedly resulted in the turnaround of underperforming businesses. The true extent of such improvements is difficult to estimate, but its possibility is a justification for AFC activity which has often had a wholly negative effect both on the acquired business and the economy as a whole.

Companies managed by autonomous management, independent of both capital and labour, still prospered, but the new AFCs mingled among them. The AFC owner-controllers referred to themselves in the language of entrepreneurship. Their focus was not however on building a lasting enterprise, but rather more on achieving substantial personal wealth at the expense of other stakeholders. They were becoming more sophisticated in their relationship with the stock exchange, learning how to engage in creative accounting to boost price earnings ratios and therefore raise their share's price above sector average levels to better equip them for aggressive acquisitions.

Similar developments were apparent in the United States where in 1973 the first substantial hostile deal was completed with the merger of Inco–ESB followed by United Technologies' hostile acquisition of Otis Elevator and the Colt Industries takeover of Garlock. By the mid 1970s, hostile takeovers had become a substantial part of M&A activity and new ways of achieving hostile deals were being developed, aided by the professional advice and participation of investment banks.

The first British wave of 'asset stripping' acquisitions was underway from the early 1970s. Slater Walker Securities, for example, was the centre of one network of acquisitive satellites, whose main function was to acquire companies, dispose of disposable assets, frequently for a large proportion of the original cost of acquisition, 'release' the people who worked the assets, and retain, in most cases, just the core of the acquired business. This was held on a tight rein, starved of research and development and severely restricted in capital expenditure, before going on to the next big deal. Slater Walker was one of several such AFCs. Jessel Securities, Trafalgar House, Hanson Trust, Lonrho and many others were at that time in the same category. While business success required commitment to an industry, its technologies, its customers and suppliers and to achieving leadership within that setting, AFC success was dependent on having no such commitments but a willingness to move in and out of industries without hesitation if the immediate balance sheet impact was advantageous.

The distinctions between AFCs and corporations driven by industrial logic were best made by simply identifying which strategy was dominant: wealth creation or wealth ownership. From the macro perspective of the economy as a whole, it was clear that wealth creation was of greater importance. Provision for health, education, defence and social services were all financed by the proceeds of wealth creation and strategies for wealth creation. By comparison, wealth ownership provided few wider benefits. Indeed it was likely that the financial focus of firms driven by wealth ownership was likely to reduce wider benefits. This arose not only from the short-term cost-cutting focus which led to immediate rises in unemployment, but also to disinvestment and a direct focus on tax avoidance as a major component of corporate strategy and in some cases the prime reason for acquisition, for example Trafalgar's acquisition of Cunard, or the more recent machinations of private equity groups to reduce and avoid tax liabilities.

AFCs proved to be a short-lived means of enriching their founding owner-controllers, rarely outlasting the demise of their founding entrepreneur. Leading AFC operator of the time, Sir James Goldsmith, suggested the fate of all AFC's would be to die with their founders.

The fourth wave of American M&A activity, from 1984 to 89, had similarly little to do with industry concentration or industrial logic of any kind. It was characterized by 'the use of aggressive takeover tactics, leveraged buyouts and junk bond financing.'[24] The character of this M&A wave, like that of the British asset strippers of the 1970s, was driven by the accumulation of personal wealth at the expense of the other stakeholders and the destruction of the companies which fell victim to their raids.

This financial and non industrial approach to M&A action, though punctuated by the bear markets of the late 1990s continued through till the collapse of the credit bubble in 2007/8. The means of financing became more sophisticated and the avoidance of taxation more comprehensive, but the fundamental activity, the purchase of company shares funding for which was ultimately charged to the acquired company, the disposal of assets and people and the accumulation of substantial wealth by the business owner-controller-speculators remained fundamentally unchanged since the 1970s.

Drucker's views on hostile takeovers were clear:

> *'If enough stockholders take what amounts to a bribe, the raider captures the company and quickly unloads on it the debt he incurred*

---

24   Gaughan, P.A., 'The Fourth Merger Wave and Beyond', in *Readings in Mergers and Acquisitions*, (ed.) P.A. Gaughan, Cambridge Mass: Blackwell Publishers, p. 3.

in the takeover ... the victim ends up paying for his own execution.
... Fearful of raiders, companies began practicing defensive capitalism
... More and more of our businesses ... are not being run for business
results but for protection against the hostile takeover ...The fear of the
raider demoralizes and paralyzes.'[25]

The changing of management control without ownership to owner-controlling speculator was facilitated by the new top management strategic perspective which emphasized deal-making for quick results rather than the painstaking and progressive building of a business for the benefit of all stakeholders. The result was to 'hollow out' many traditional businesses leaving them without the resources which had been painstakingly accumulated over the years, but burdened with massive debt and unable to withstand even small downturns in demand without large-scale redundancy.

It was in large part justified by the promulgators of the new neo-classical economic theory expounded by von Mises, Hayek, Friedman and others who emphasized the importance of business to maximize shareholder wealth, shareholders being the owners of the private property which was the company.

Outsourcing

The deal making mentality and the focus on realizing and squeezing out value so as to make as much money for shareholders as possible led inevitably to the possibility of outsourcing 'non-core' activities previously completed within the company. The potential benefit might arise from the activity being completed better and at lower cost by specialists. Moreover it might enable some of the assets involved to be sold and the proceeds either re-invested more profitably elsewhere or returned to shareholders. Drucker himself argued for outsourcing on the grounds that mundane jobs such as cleaning, which offered no career structure if done in-house, might present opportunities for promotion if conducted by a specialist cleaning business. Outsourcing could therefore be good for the people involved.

Not only that, but the new neo-classical economic theory had a sophisticated theoretical argument in transaction cost economics which supported

---

25 Drucker, P.F., (1993), *The Ecological Vision: Reflections on the American Condition*, New Jersey: Transaction Publishers, p. 250.

outsourcing to 'the market' to provide goods and services if they could not be done better or cheaper in-house.

An early example of outsourcing was to management consultancy. Firms needing special expertise to solve a particular issue would not necessarily wish to employ that expertise permanently just to provide a one-off solution. Fred Taylor may have sorted out the best way to move pig iron, but Bethlehem Steel would not necessarily wish to retain his services as a permanent employee.

By 2004, management consultancy had grown to become a £115 billion-a-year global business, with Britain alone spending over £10bn. Spending on governmental and not-for-profit consulting in Europe was £8.1bn, of which £1.9bn was in Britain. Various studies have indicated a high degree of waste involved in this vast expenditure, as much as 60 per cent wasted because it was not implemented or not needed in the first place.[26]

Moreover, the waste was not limited to ineffective assignments. The consultants learned a lot on every job they undertook. Their careers developed through these invaluable experiences gained at the client's expense. They came, they learned, they charged and they took all their experience and learning away with them. And they left behind a management that was little the wiser for all the experience generated by the assignment, and probably including key members of the organization who were more than a little disenchanted by the exercise. Furthermore the use of consultants by top management who were becoming increasingly remote from day-to-day operations, only served to increase that distance and reduce the level of trust between the top and operations.

If an assignment was completed in-house by permanent staff, it would have been an opportunity for the organization's own people to gain a broader experience than they would ever have gained in their normal daily work. The benefit of this would be difficult to exaggerate: working on just one change assignment would have inculcated a critical approach to work. It would have invited people to challenge the accepted ways of doing things and to develop better ways and, most importantly, of implementing those improvements. That way, not only would the disenchantment have been avoided, but the learning would have stayed in-house. Moreover, the prospects of successfully implementing a solution would have been maximized if it were the organization's

26 Craig, D., (2005), *Rip Off: The Scandalous Inside Story of the Management Consulting Money Machine*, London: Original Book Company.

own people who were responsible from start to finish. Even if the right person, or people, were not available in the company to undertake the project, it would still most likely have been cheaper to recruit than to pay consultancy fees. In that way the skills and capabilities of the permanent staff would have been enhanced and they would have embarked on a morale-building virtuous cycle of improvement.

Elements of these positive and negative aspects of outsourcing are inevitably present in most such decisions. The Friedmanite insistence on the unavoidable inefficiency of public provision led in Britain to the mandatory tendering of many public services, notably within the National Health Service. But the problem in such private public provision was predictable in the clash of cultures. Cleaning hospital wards may be done cheaper by a profit-oriented organization, but less thoroughly. The rise in infections such as MRSA, which coincided with this outsourcing, resulted in the new mega-hospitals becoming, in the public mind, centres of disease and infection rather than being associated with the improvement of health and curing of disease.

Nevertheless, there are some real potential benefits from outsourcing. Offloading responsibility for back-office activity and getting it done at lower cost by specialists could allow a firm to focus all its attention on the core activity in which the firm has a distinctive competence which is the source of its competitive advantage. But the motivation for outsourcing is confused. The practical costs and benefits may not be persuasive one way or the other. But the opportunity to realize some assets provides a short-term benefit for shareholders which may often be the main justification.

The danger is that outsourcing can become a syndrome, the immediate benefits obscuring longer-term effects which may well be overwhelmingly adverse. The decisive issue is the integrity and motivation of those deciding on the outsourcing: is it for short-term cash benefit of shareholders, or for the long-term best interests of the organization and its stakeholders?

Automating Middle Management

Most of the specialist areas of management outlined in Chapter 6 have since benefited from advances in IT and computer systems as well as web-based facilities. Some functions, such as materials control, production scheduling and control, order processing and quality management and management accounting have been largely automated with the need for discretionary decisions becoming almost peripheral. In other areas, notably in marketing and marketing research, IT systems have been largely supportive.

The first steps in this automation process were taken in the 1960s when computers replaced punched card accounting machines in stock control, payroll, maintenance of personnel records and the like. From there it was a short step to envisaging all management information being automated in a single integrated management information system (MIS) which would record, control, simulate and report whatever was asked of it. However, the benefits from such systems proved elusive and the attempts at their implementation were expensive in terms of both hardware and software development and their operation frequently in excess of hardware capability.

The more practical way forward was to attack sub-units of such a system. Initially this was done by systems analysts capturing the essence of existing manual systems which was subsequently programmed in one of various computer languages. It was a laborious process, subject to considerable error of both systems analysis and computer programming. Such custom-written systems were subsequently replaced, in all but the very largest systems, by standard packages incorporating all manner of facilities which could be accessed for any particular application.

These standard programmes started off in manufacturing with separate stock control and order processing systems. They were subsequently integrated and combined with production planning and purchasing modules to form what was referred to as a materials requirements planning (MRP) system. The aim of such an integrated system was to replicate the management responsibilities of planning the purchase of materials, scheduling production activities, providing delivery schedules to ensure materials and products were available for production and delivery to customers, and consistent with that, maintaining the minimum levels of inventory and work in progress.

Further development of MRP as MRPII saw the added ability to handle monetary quantities including standard cost information which allowed the system to automate product estimates and quotations, analyze and report cost control information and provide the primary inputs to the management accounting systems as well as provide some business planning facilities.

These computerized systems, so long as the information fed into them was accurate, provided better inventory control and production scheduling which enabled improved delivery performance to be offered to customers. In addition, they also offered better quality control information and so improved quality at the same time as optimizing inventories and work in progress which reduced working capital requirements and enabled faster production and delivery. But as with all computer systems their success depended on the quality of data inputs: garbage in – garbage out.

MRPII was developed a stage further with Enterprise Resource Planning (ERP) which is still in use in 2009, based on a single common database holding all the information needed for a comprehensive set of business functions including manufacturing, supply chain management, full accounting and financial planning, human resource management and customer relationship management (CRM), vestiges of which are experienced by all customers of modern internet-based suppliers such as Amazon.

ERP is a modular software system rather than the originally envisaged management information system which was designed from the beginning as an integrated whole. ERP is intended to allow all business departments to store and access data in real-time. Standard ERP modules provide a wide variety of facilities so that any particular business can make use of whatever particular modules or combinations of modules are needed to control and improve the processes of their particular business. Problems arise when standard modules do not quite meet requirements and custom-written code is added which is not accommodated by subsequent versions of the standard product. For whatever reason, it is common experience that such computer-based systems still appear prone to error and under-performance, with the resulting shortcomings multiplying as the scale of system increases.

This brief explanation shows how progressively, and with mixed results, middle management was to a substantial degree automated out of existence, and with it were lost the real training grounds for future top management. Drucker had argued for the decentralization of large-scale business largely so that young managers might be trained and given experience in real decision-making and having real responsibility without taking company-threatening risks. But the automation of management in these various functional areas destroyed many of these job training possibilities. The ever flattening corporate management of the 1990s left Drucker concerned that the leadership-development purpose of decentralization was in the course of being lost; as he put it himself: 'flat organizations don't permit managerial farm teams'.[27]

Automation also changed the nature of the management task. Purchasing, materials control, production control and the other functions which were computerized still needed managing to ensure their satisfactory performance, but their management had become more technical and less interpersonal.

With such changes in management work becoming more pervasive and the consequent removal of opportunities for on the job training, managers were necessarily drawn increasingly direct from business schools and research universities with a management qualification such as a first degree in business studies or an MBA, but limited practical experience. Furthermore the management degrees were taught by academic faculty who themselves lacked practical experience, now being third and fourth generation academic management teachers, subjected to assessment according to academic criteria and who therefore found it necessary to use management texts replete with case studies and 'practical' exercises written by other academics similarly lacking in practical experience. And it was from these ranks that top managers had to be appointed, having had much less contact with real problems and real people in the workplace.

Strategic Management Mindset

The change in perspective from general to strategic management was fundamental to management's fall. Paradoxically it resulted in a change of perspective from the long term to the short. Hayes and Abernathy reported in 1980 how American managers' focus on short-term costs rather than long-term technology, and using analytical detachment rather than hands-on experience, was leading to what they referred to as a 'disinvestment spiral' where investment in new technology was delayed or avoided altogether for immediate cash reasons, which only led to a loss of competitive strength either through the lack of product performance or increasing marginal cost of production, which cumulatively led to 'economic decline'. This short-term orientation was further manifested by the way senior management were appointed largely from outside, and assessed over short time periods. Successful senior managers in America typically moved jobs within three to five years and so had to achieve

---

27 Drucker, P.F., quoted in Beatty, J., (1998), *The World According to Drucker*, London: Orion Business Books, p. 57.

success within that time period. As noted elsewhere major projects, especially ones involving significant innovation, only come to fruition over very much longer periods.

Hayes and Abernathy cited the portfolio system of central 'control' as inhibiting long-term investment in technological innovation. They contrasted technology's achievements, for example, the laser, xerography and transistors, with the trivia such as new-shape potato crisps and feminine hygiene deodorant, produced by the new orthodoxy, a risk-averse financial orientation to marketing.

The reasons why American managers had adopted this new orthodoxy were several. Firstly, there had been a dramatic increase in financial and legal executives getting to the top of American corporations in preference to those with technical or other industry-specific experience. Secondly, companies had increasingly hired top management from outside, often from outside their industry. Such managers had necessarily managed their companies simply on the basis of financial information and controlled their development without technical knowledge on the basis of oversimplified rule-of-thumb decisions such as to 'invest in businesses which dominate their markets and sell those that don't'.

These were the strategic managers and this was their mindset. The consequent focus on deal-making, particularly mergers and acquisitions, was therefore not surprising since the top managers' expertise was largely limited to finance. But it had done substantial damage to many of the United States' leading companies as well as Britain's, leading them to neglect their core technologies and rendering them vulnerable to attack by more technologically-focused competitors. The automobile industry was then, as now, a prime example.

Since then the short-term orientation of top management has been further emphasized. Firstly this was by the explosion in hostile takeovers driven wholly by short-term financial aims and justified by the new neo-classical theory; secondly by top management's growing detachment from industry and business arising from the new strategic management-led orientation to portfolio management; and thirdly by the seduction of that top management to follow the injunction to maximize shareholder wealth rather than accepting any broader responsibilities.

10

Friedman and Business-Friendly Government

Though Harrod–Keynesian economics had become the accepted orthodoxy after the Second World War, the group of Austrian neo-classical economists argued for tight monetary control of inflation and free-market capitalism. Ludwig von Mises and Friedrich Hayek denied the feasibility of Keynes' mixture of liberty and state intervention. For them socialism was the only real alternative to the classical model. That was the world they inhabited after the Second World War. Socialism, depending on the economy being controlled directly by government, would create a huge and expensive central planning bureaucracy which could never work as effectively as market forces. Comparison of American and Soviet living standards appeared to demonstrate this truth. Their arguments, supported by Friedman at Chicago university, became the alternative to Harrod–Keynesian economics, available for implementation whenever governments were so inclined.

By the end of the 1970s, electorates in both Britain and the United States were ready for change. Harrod–Keynesianism had resulted in wages-push inflation caused by organized labour emboldened by continuous years of full employment and led by increasingly powerful and ambitious trade unions. Keynes had indicated the solution to wage-push inflation would have to be political but successive governments had failed to impose one. Inflation combined with stagnating economic growth, 'stagflation', appeared to be the natural result of Harrod–Keynesian economics. Electorates in Britain and the United States turned to more conservative administrations for their alternative solution. They were not disappointed.

The new governments adopted the uncompromising restatement of the neo-classical free-market model. Thatcher had famously declared her 'belief' in Hayek's *The Constitution of Liberty* shortly after becoming party leader. In it Hayek identified the main points of the new neo-classical model which were subsequently expressed in more accessible form by Friedman. Initially their emphasis was on control of the money supply as the lever of economic regulation. The monetarist argument stemmed from the 1930s depression which was held by classical theorists to be caused by the Federal Reserve policy of restricting money supply. Monetarists rejected the Keynesian argument for full employment as the best way to stimulate demand and argued that by simply increasing the money supply, market forces would be enabled to do the rest. The inevitable consequent rise in inflation could be controlled by limiting money supply to a level which would support a rate of unemployment which was thought to be sustainable given industrial circumstances. To reduce unemployment further would require an increase in money supply which would lead to accelerating inflation which was not sustainable except in the very short run. The sustainable level of unemployment was a matter for political judgment, a level at which organized labour would be weakened but not necessarily destroyed and forced into covert or open revolt.

Control of the money supply was, however, no longer straightforward. New technology had added considerable complication. Effective control could only be achieved by precisely the heavy state interference which the new neo-classical theorists argued strenuously against. In later years Friedman accepted that monetarism had never worked as effectively as he had anticipated.

In reaction to the liberal[1] tendencies of Harrod–Keynesian economics the new neo-classical economic model went further than that of Adam Smith and his successors. Smith's argument for progressive taxation and spending its proceeds on public provision of education and welfare was reversed. All public provision was deemed to be inefficient and 'bad', private provision was efficient and 'good'. The argument against any avoidable public provision led to the mantra of 'competition and choice' creating artificial markets in public sector activity. For example, rather than the state providing schools, the state should provide vouchers enabling parents to pay for their children to be educated at a

---

1   The term liberal can have various meanings attached to it. The meaning intended here is the normal everyday meaning of a left-of-centre political programme which supports elements of the welfare state and a mixed economy. Friedman also used the word but attached quite different meanings going back to the nineteenth-century free-trade liberals who believed that freedom of the individual was dependent on governments minimising their involvement in economic life. Friedman's use of the term is more consistent with the ideas currently associated with conservatism. The confusion is sometimes addressed by the use of the term neo-liberal to define the modern right wing conservatism advocated by Friedman. Confusion is further added by the use of the term neo-conservative referring to the more extreme form of conservatism which was represented by some members of the George W. Bush administration in America.

school of their choice rather than their local state school. The choice would be influenced by reference to school league tables based on performance against measurable targets, the intention being to introduce competition into the education sector and so improve performance.

The new neo-classical approach was adopted by governments which were determined and committed to its implementation. Their first priority was to resolve the wage-push inflation caused by strong unions and the previous commitment to full employment.

Subsequently free-market ideas were focused on the withdrawal of government as far as possible from direct involvement in the public sector, their aim being to privatize public ownership wherever possible, minimizing the state's involvement which had grown up, notably in Harrod–Keynesian Britain. Where it was not politically feasible to privatize, government sought to control through a myopic system of targets intended to mimic what were conceived as private sector performance indicators, a process which tended to undermine any autonomous role for public sector management.

Friedman argued that Britain's economy demanded a shock treatment of government spending cuts and tax reductions while controlling money supply, accepting the unavoidable rises in unemployment which he argued would only be temporary. The United States economy being in a less parlous state required a less fierce treatment, but the direction was the same.[2]

Friedmanism

The new version of the neo-classical model was the product of many different contributors, not just those referred to here. But issues which related most closely to the business of management came most distinctly from Friedman. He took the model to its logical conclusion. Hayek had argued for a flat rate income tax, but allowed there should be a lower rate for the less well off; Friedman was more clinical, a flat rate was a flat rate. Friedman's exposition, though not necessarily the more intellectually secure was the more clear-cut and incisive. He explicitly excluded value judgment from his approach (ignoring the fact that 'economic man' was a rather sweeping value judgment), whereas Hayek appeared less dogmatic in his thinking.

2   Friedman, M., (1977), 'From Galbraith to Economic Freedom', *Occasional Paper* 49, London: Institute of Economic Affairs, pp. 48–51.

For convenience here the system has been labelled with Friedman's name, rather than Hayek's, in order to distinguish it from earlier manifestations of the classical approach.

The essential planks of Friedmanism were those of neo-classical economics with a heightened emphasis on monetarist control, fixed-rate non-progressive low taxation and the withdrawal of government from engagement in any public provision, as well as, most importantly in the present context, Friedman's assertion that:

> *'Few trends could so thoroughly undermine the very foundations of our free society than the acceptance by corporate officials of a social responsibility other than to make as much money for their stockholders as possible.'*[3]

From the perspective of management, this was perhaps the most corrosive Friedmanite doctrine. It was voiced in 1962, a time when the Soviet Union appeared to be strong and threatening to capitalist systems. The risk that corporations were being weakened by the acceptance of social responsibilities or corporate philanthropy had been highlighted four years earlier in the pages of the Harvard Business Review when Levitt argued that capitalism's future depended on business making money not 'sweet music';[4] social welfare was not an issue which should divert the attention of industrial management – it was the responsibility of government, paid for out of the taxes from successful business.

Government needed to be small because it was paid for from the taxation which was a burden on both individuals and on corporations. The high tax burden encouraged non-productive activity, notably in tax avoidance, which Friedman argued would not have been undertaken were the tax rates lower. He mistakenly anticipated that lower rates of tax would bring increased revenues to the exchequer by removing the incentive to avoid and evade.

Friedman's predecessors, Smith, Ricardo, Marshall and the rest, also including Keynes, had all argued the virtues of a progressive tax system where the higher paid would pay a higher proportion of tax. Friedman simply argued

---

3   Friedman, M., (2002), *Capitalism and Freedom*, 40th Anniversary edition, Chicago, University of Chicago Press, p. 133.
4   Levitt, T., (1958), 'The Dangers of Social Responsibility', *Harvard Business Review*, Vol. 36 No 5, pp. 41–50.

that income tax should be minimized and levied at a fixed rate irrespective of the level of income. Friedmanite governments largely followed his advice and reduced the level of taxation particularly on the richest, thus reversing the more egalitarian trends of the previous 50 years.

The new economic argument was, as Hayek had pointed out, fundamentally political.[5] If non-democratic regimes were to introduce economic freedoms then political freedom would inevitably follow, and conversely, that central control of economic activity would inevitably result in political repression. Von Mises and Hayek had argued that free-market capitalism was necessary though not sufficient for the achievement and preservation of individual political freedom. Friedman's concern was, however, only for freedom for what he referred to as 'responsible individuals' from which category he explicitly excluded 'madmen' and children. For them paternalism was inescapable.[6] He gave no consideration to other categories of individual who may not have been responsible through no fault of their own.

The year following his Nobel prize Friedman propounded his *'sort of empirical generalization that it costs the state twice as much to do anything as it costs private enterprise'.*[7] Though he provided several examples to support this belief they were not examined in any depth and it was not clear that the comparisons were fair or that there were not alternative explanations. Nevertheless the 'sort of empirical generalization' informed the philosophy stressing the advantages of the marketplace and the disadvantages of government intervention, and influenced the policies of conservative governments. From the 1980s on, Friedman's views on monetary policy, taxation, privatization and deregulation informed the policy of governments around the globe including the Reagan administration in the United States, Thatcher's in Britain, Pinochet's in Chile and many others, as well as that of international financial institutions such as the World Bank and International Monetary Fund.

His assertion of management's duty to maximize shareholder wealth lacked practical precision, just as did the profit maximization assumption of microeconomics. The microeconomic model ignored timescale, referring unavoidably to individual transactions, but it was clear that seeking to maximize the profit from an individual transaction, for example, the sale of a

5   Hayek, F., (1944), *The Road to Serfdom*, Chicago: University of Chicago Press.
6   Friedman, M., (2002) *Capitalism and Freedom*, 40th Anniversary edition, Chicago, University of Chicago Press, p. 33.
7   Friedman, M., (1977), 'From Galbraith to Economic Freedom', *Occasional Paper* 49, London: Institute of Economic Affairs, p. 57.

product to a customer, could compromise the longer term and the far greater profit to be generated from a lasting relationship with customers. Similar considerations applied to maximizing shareholder wealth. Nevertheless, the idea of maximizing shareholder wealth influenced management in particular ways in certain situations, for example, in the case of a hostile takeover bid.

Before Friedman, management might not unreasonably have construed their duty as being to preserve their company's autonomous survival in the short term and progress its longer-term prosperity for the benefit of all stakeholders. But Friedmanism suggested quite different priorities, for example, in the event of a takeover bid being received. Then their responsibility would be to get the best deal they could for shareholders, to gain an immediate windfall that would enable them to reinvest elsewhere so as to maximize wealth. The interests of other stakeholders such as employees or customers were not of concern. Thus Friedmanism fundamentally changed the role of management in such situations. Previously, management would have seen its role as to fight, fight and fight again, to preserve the company's autonomy in the best interests of all stakeholders and only to accept being taken over as a last resort.

The Friedmanite version of neo-classical theory was not just a minor adjustment of direction from Harrod–Keynesian economics for business, government and academia, but an about-turn which had unforeseen consequences. It reversed the previously closing income gap between the highest paid and the average, and created new inequalities. So much was inevitable and the old arguments justifying the inequity of the classical system were used in its defence. It undermined any notion that management might, in its autonomous role, mitigate the worst effects of the amoral pursuit of shareholder value. The task of industrial management was to maximize shareholder wealth at any cost. To this practitioners and theorists alike were persuaded to submit.

Economic theorists added to the apparent sophistication of the free-market capitalist argument with three sub-plots which directly impinged on the role of management. Firstly, agency theory, not so much a theory as it applied to the management situation, more a simple assertion, provided an explanation of the role of management which had previously been missing from economic theory. It held that management were the agents of shareholders and must therefore act in their interests above everything else. This was the prime theoretical justification for requiring management to maximize shareholder wealth. Secondly, the development of transaction cost economics was the justification for the existence of firms as opposed to sourcing from the open market. This was used to legitimize the deal-making strategies and in particular the outsourcing movement referred to in the previous chapter. Thirdly, the definition of a theory of competitive management control, an open competitive market in corporate management, justified what was referred to as the 'financialization' of managers and their action to achieve short-term gains for shareholders, including those from hostile takeovers.

Together these three justified the pursuit of Friedmanite ideas to their logical conclusions. All three were flawed if not wholly false, and they gave rise to consequences which undermined the autonomous role of management, were economically destructive and were inequitable in their effect. Chester Barnard's earlier comment on the dominance of economic thought in management was pertinent:

> 'Though I early found out how to behave effectively in organizations, not until I had much later relegated economic theory and economic interests to a secondary though indispensable place, did I begin to understand organizations or human behavior in them.'[8]

But economic theory and economic interests continued to play a primary role in both government and business and continued to obscure understanding of organizations and human behaviour in them.

Conservative Government

Since the Second World War the political ideologies that led British and American governments had diverged and only came together again with the almost simultaneous installation of the conservative administrations of Ronald Reagan and Margaret Thatcher, since when a right-of-centre consensus has ruled on both sides of the Atlantic. Their conservatism which was renewed by those governments was essentially Friedmanite in character with a fundamental debt to Hayek and to a lesser extent von Mises. In Thatcher's case, it replaced the former one-nation, middle-of-the-road Conservatism which sought to stabilize the economy, exercising control equally over wages and dividends. In Reagan's it was a renewal of domestic Republicanism after the more international focus of post-war administrations.

---

8   Barnard, C.I., (1938), *The Functions of the Executive,* Cambridge, Mass: Harvard University Press, p. xi.

Thatcher had been instrumental in setting up in 1974 the Centre for Policy Studies, a right-wing think tank to promote Friedmanite free-market economics, privatization of state-owned industries, lower taxation with emphasis moved from direct to indirect taxes, and a reduction of the size of the welfare state.

When she came to power in May 1979, she had claimed her experience both as a housewife and as a daughter of a grocer had taught her the importance of good housekeeping and her duty to make sure that every penny raised in taxation was spent wisely, giving good value for money to the taxpayer in return.

Reagan came to power less than two years later with a very similar commitment. Though America's record of industrial disputes had been less stormy than Britain's, Reagan was faced with a critical and decisive strike barely six months into his presidency. The Professional Air Traffic Controllers Organization (PATCO), despite having a 'no strike' clause in their employment contract, felt themselves to be in a powerful position and went on strike for more money, less work and better pensions. Reagan, knowing that all public sector workers would follow suit if PATCO succeeded, ordered them back to work or to face dismissal. The Federal Aviation Administration (FAA) improved its offer but developed a contingency plan in case it should be rejected. The vast majority of PATCO members did reject the improved offer and were dismissed. Much to most people's surprise the FAA plan worked and over 11,000 PATCO members stayed dismissed and the union was fined heavily for organizing an illegal strike. Reagan's handling of the strike had impressed the United States electorate and other unions alike.

It had also impressed Margaret Thatcher. In her famous claim that there was no such thing as society, she was declaring her profound belief in the individual and self-help over any collective groups having state support. This commitment would have surely led her into direct conflict with trade unionism anyway, but the ground for such battles was being prepared by the unions themselves.

Industrial unrest had prompted the previous Conservative government to call, and lose, a single-issue 'Who Rules Britain?' election in 1974, and had been a continuous aspect of economic life throughout the subsequent period of Labour rule till a final eruption of public sector disputes in the winter of 1978–9 were at least partly instrumental in bringing down the Callaghan government, paving the way for Thatcher.

The crunch eventually came with the coal miners' strike of March 1984 led by the National Union of Mineworkers whose president was a one-time member of the Young Communist League. The strike continued for a full year ending with the miners' defeat. It was probably due to Thatcher's personal determination and stubbornness that the strike was defeated. Two years later the print unions, refusing to accept the implications of new technology, were similarly defeated by News International following their move to new premises at Wapping equipped with new technology. That strike action also lasted, at least nominally, for over a year.

Braverman, in his work on the erosion of craft skills and degradation of work,[9] had noted, prior to the Wapping strike (or lock out), that Britain did not de-skill labour in the same way as the United States; craft skills were broken down, redefined and often protected through trade unions. The Wapping dispute showed Britain in a different light, merely a time interval behind the United States in its inevitable acceptance of new technology. For Braverman it was not the inevitable progress of technology, but a conspiracy of owners and their hired agents to dispossess and dominate the workers.

The real economic significance of strikes and other industrial action is in dispute. Amateur and incompetent management certainly played its part, but the unions were widely portrayed as the major cause of decline in several British industries such as machine tool manufacturing, automotive, motor cycle manufacturing, shipbuilding, coal and textiles. They certainly had a high profile in the largely right-of-centre media where they were portrayed as crucial. Whatever their real significance in monetary terms, they were certainly important symbolically.

It appeared that British management had failed to manage industrial relations effectively. Some trade union leaders were driven more by political aims, rather than simply the pay and working conditions of their members. Such politically motivated union militancy was then broken by the conservative government in both the public and private sectors.

The defeats had been inflicted on unions which were fighting for ideas which had ceased to be tenable. Yet, in 2008 the National Union of Mineworkers website referring to its 1984–5 strike concluded:

---

9   Braverman, H., (1974), *Labour and Monopoly Capital: The Degradation of Work in the Twentieth Century*, New York: Monthly Review Press.

'The strike had not been about wages, better conditions or any material gain. It had been waged on principle; the principle that miners' jobs were held by each generation of workers in trust for those who would come after them, and must not be wantonly destroyed .... This strike had set a new example in working class struggle, marking another milestone in a long road. It had been hard, bitter, painful, and as in 1926, there were those who said that never again would the British trade union movement see such a conflict. As in the aftermath of 1926, only time will tell.'[10]

Similar sentiments might have been expressed regarding the print workers' defeat at Wapping, or about the activities of the Luddites faced with Arkwright's new cotton-spinning machinery. In competitive markets, the progress of technology is always unavoidable and direct opposition is in the long run bound to fail.

The Friedman ideology which informed the administrations of Reagan and Thatcher succeeded in controlling the money supply, deregulating markets and reducing the power of organized labour. In Thatcher's case too, nationalized industries were privatized, elements of the welfare state were reduced and in the short term at least, unemployment was allowed to increase rapidly. As a result, they succeeded where their predecessors had failed in lowering inflation and reviving the economy. That was in the 1980s. Those same policies were not necessarily appropriate to different situations, but the Friedmanites espoused them as generally valid in all situations, just as the Harrod–Keynesians had with their opposing prescriptions following the 1930s recession.

So the accumulation and investment of capital resulting in an inequitable distribution of benefits had been successfully re-established. The opportunity had been made available once more for government and for industry, led by management, to demonstrate some magnanimity in their victory. But the opportunity was not taken.

Since the 1980s, governments of all colours, Republican or Democrat, Conservative or Labour, have accepted Friedmanite ideas and used them to shape their tax, monetary, trade and business policies. This universal acceptance was given further impetus with the collapse of communism so that raw free-market capitalism was almost universally accepted across the globe as the one best way of organizing all economic activity.

---

10   See the web site: http://www.num.org.uk/?p=history&c=num&h=13

Governments had themselves become increasingly involved in promoting international trade in latter day mercantilist ventures. Promoting trade was the unspoken top priority of diplomatic services everywhere. Ex-diplomat Carne Ross showed how the whole machinery of government was deployed to maximize business because 'it's the economy, stupid!' He explained it as follows:

> 'It is assumed in places like the Foreign Office and in governments world wide that trade is what their countries "want". But this of course is a very big assumption. The foundation of this assumption is what underpins neo-classical economics, namely that individuals seek to maximize utility through consumption, ie people want more things. Writ on the national scale, this assumption is expressed as more trade and more growth. But there is growing evidence – good hard empirical data too – that this is not in fact the case.'[11]

The evidence Ross refers to[12] suggests that the pursuit of wealth does not result in greater happiness once above a basic level of income. Research among so-called neuro-economists suggested basing economic action not on the simple amoral, self-interested utility maximizing 'economic man' assumptions but on what actually goes on in the heads of real people.

Though more difficult to model, the approach at least indicated that the priority that governments and their civil services gave to the economic interest might be inappropriate. Nevertheless, the orthodox wisdom remained, true or not, that governments must be seen as business friendly if they were to be re-electable.

Political parties of all hues had become nervous in case they should be construed as in any way 'anti-business'. Political leaders were not infrequently drawn to escort groups of senior business people, including the tax-haven-based super-rich, on international business jamborees. Such governmental initiatives were grounded on Friedmanite theory which could even draw governments into support for apparently dubious, if not wholly corrupt, export activities, of which there were several examples in both Britain and the United States.

---

11 Ross, C., (2007), *Independent Diplomat: Dispatches from an Unaccountable Elite*, New York: Cornell University Press, p. 116.
12 Layard, R., (2003), 'Happiness: Has Social Science a Clue?', The Lionel Robbins Memorial Lectures at London School of Economics.

Unquestioning acceptance of the necessity to be business friendly was a weakness of democratic government which the business lobby could only be expected to try to exploit. Business would naturally avoid paying taxes if it could, using tax havens where available so long as their actions were legal. The role of government was traditionally construed as being firm and fair, for example, closing tax loopholes where the ingenuity of business appeared to defeat the original intention behind the law. The business lobby would of course be expected to complain bitterly, but their real concern would be that they were not disadvantaged compared with their competitors.

Government's traditional task was to provide the level playing field. But under the continuing influence of Friedmanite dogma and an ever increasingly active business lobby pressure, government lacked the moral conviction and possibly the expertise to resist and fulfil their political role.

Friedmanism made no distinction between the industrial business sector in products and services and the financial sector which, though it had begun as the means of arranging debts and loans in support of the business sector, had long outgrown that limited role. The financial sector still depended on real business as exampled in recent years with the emergence of the Chinese sovereign fund as a substantial financial resource. China's traditional problem was how to feed its population. The sovereign fund emerged not from the brilliance of Shanghai's financiers but as a by-product of China's low labour-cost manufacturing industries. Without Chinese manufacturing its financial sector would have remained a minor player. Marx would no doubt have remarked on this expropriation from industrial labour and found it surprising in what was still nominally a communist country.

Financial sectors were not concerned with creating new wealth so much as matters of its ownership. Governments, failing to distinguish between business and finance, between creating wealth and capturing it, were anxious to be seen to be as friendly to Wall St and the City of London as they were to real business, if not more so.

Management, Ownership and Risk

The creation of wealth has always been the driving force in growing economies and its distribution the source of aggravation. The financial sector's contribution, originally simply to provide the financing of growth, latterly succeeded in reversing the process, expropriating the wealth accumulated through business operations. The process of expropriation was supported by the Friedmanite theory of an open market in corporate management, aimed particularly at managements which retained the traditional focus on making things rather than making money. The core theoretical prop justifying this reversal was agency theory.

Agency is the assertion that corporate management, in the shape of company directors, are the agents of the shareholders, who are the principals in the relationship. Management must therefore work solely in shareholder interests. But agency theory is palpably false. The principal in this particular relationship is actually not the shareholder, but the company. This was always the case. When joint stock companies were first established they were created as separate legal entities. They were sometimes referred to as 'legal persons' as opposed to natural persons. Company directors were empowered to act for and on behalf of the company and acting in good faith, which they were legally bound to do, meant acting in accord with the company's best interests. Directors, like all other employees, had contracts directly with the company, not with the shareholders. It was simply not the case, and never had been, that managers or directors were agents of the shareholders.

For agency theory to be valid, it would be necessary to deny the company its legal status.

> *'The mechanism agency theory used to break the connection between the manager and any notion that he or she owed an obligation to the firm was to argue that the firm itself was a legal fiction, a ghost of the mind. The organization according to early agency theorists Armen A Alchian and Harold Demsetz[13] was merely "the centralized contractual agent in a team productive process – not some superior authoritarian directive or disciplinary power."'[14]*

But in company legislation across the world the company, or the corporation, is accorded its separate legal existence with rights to make contracts and behave in many ways like a person, with directors acting for and on behalf of

---

13 Alchian, A.A. and Demsetz, H., (1972), 'Production, Information Costs, and Economic Organisation', *American Economic Review*, Vol. 62, p. 778.

14 Khurana, R., (2007), *From Higher Aims to Hired Hands: The Social Transformation of American Business Schools and the Unfulfilled Promise of Management as a Profession*, Princeton: Princeton University Press, p. 469.

the corporation. It is neither a 'legal fiction' nor a 'ghost of the mind', nor is it merely a centralized contractual agent.

The untruth which is agency theory had unfortunate effects, not only in perverting the overall objectives of business and its managers, but in more specific circumstances such as a hostile takeover bid, where the theory can be used to justify action to the detriment of the company and its employees, suppliers, customers and other stakeholders.

The effects of the Friedmanite focus on shareholder wealth have been almost exclusively destructive of the management project and negative so far as the wider social impacts are concerned. Even though it is based on a flawed analysis, agency theory remains curiously strong as what Galbraith[15] referred to as an 'institutional truth', that is not a truth at all, but an overarching lie which has to be bought into if an individual is to survive and prosper in a particular setting.

Furthermore, if the company was to be regarded as a 'legal person' then it could not, in the normal sense of private property, be owned by anyone. Not since slavery was abolished have persons been legally owned. The shareholders' position is therefore somewhat different from other forms of ownership. Shareholders own share certificates which give them certain entitlements, but they do not own a proportion of the company; they may not go to the company and demand that they take away their proportion of its assets. Shareholders' ownership position is peculiarly limited compared to normal ownership rights of private property, more akin to the temporary ownership of betting chips in a casino. They don't give part ownership of the casino itself but the right, at some risk, to a potential share of the surpluses it generates.

The nature of shareholding changed when joint stock companies were quoted on stock exchanges enabling investors to dispose of their shares and so avoid having their financial fortunes locked into a particular enterprise. They had the freedom of exit at any time. Their financial interests were not restricted to investing in the particular company, but rationally took account of all investment opportunities. Thus a wealth-maximizing shareholder might readily sell their shares to a hostile bidder for a quick profit in order to invest their newly enlarged capital in other opportunities. Any other response would be irrational. Their interests did not necessarily coincide with the best interests of the company in which for the time being they had invested. They had no responsibility, or

---

15 Galbraith, J.K., (1989), 'In pursuit of the simple truth', Commencement address to women
     graduates of Smith College, Massachusetts.

owed any duty, to the company. If they were dissatisfied with their company's performance they could make representations to the firm's management, they could try to engage the interest of other shareholders at the firm's annual general meeting, or they could sell their shares and invest elsewhere.

Nevertheless the fable, the untruth, remained that shareholders owned the business and employed directors and managers as their agents to run it on their behalf. This plugged a gap in the economic theory which could only ascribe to managers the amoral self-interested motives which would drive them to maximize their own pay and perks and minimize their inputs. Economic theory did not accommodate the autonomous role of management working in the best long-term interests of the company and its various stakeholders.

The problem for Friedmanite economists was how to persuade these amoral self-interested managers to make as much money for shareholders as possible. The obvious answer was to convert them into shareholders by remunerating them with share bonuses. They would then act in their own amoral self-interest on behalf of shareholders. This would determine how company directors should respond, for example, to take-over bids. If the bid resulted in the shareholders receiving an immediate payback then it should be accepted with the caveat that the directors should endeavour in such deals to ensure the shareholders received the best value for their shares. The directors should not in these circumstances give consideration to the interests of the company itself or of other stakeholders. Remunerating directors in part through share options was to ensure they fully endorsed the Friedmanite injunction and deserted their independent position as professional managers. Those that conformed might quickly join the ranks of the super-wealthy.

This was a different kind of management from that addressing the tasks and responsibilities described in earlier chapters, where the managers were focused on making things, rather than the acquisition of money. Previously their prime responsibility was to act in the best interests of the company. Their responsibility to the shareholder would have been best interpreted as managing the share performance, so as to be in the shareholders' best interests while they remained shareholders, but not extending to acting against the interests of the company, much less to sacrificing its independence or its existence altogether, in order to maximize shareholders' financial gain.

The Friedmanite theory and particularly the imperative to act solely for the shareholder had a number of consequences. Firstly the theory was used to justify substantial escalation of management compensation through stock option bonus schemes. These schemes had little effect in terms of raising real management performance,[16] but in conformity to the theory they did serve to convert the manager-as-agent into a shareholder-as-principal and thus, it was argued, to accept the objective of maximizing shareholder wealth.

The *'option loaded CEOs had a relatively high likelihood of delivering big losses'* because they were encouraged to go for riskier projects because their options had no downside and if all went wrong they were still likely to *'benefit from a lucrative exit payoff if they are fired.'*[17] In 2007 extraordinary examples of such payoffs included the CEO at Merrill Lynch, who presided over an $8bn write-down, precipitating the bank's ultimate failure, but was given a $161m payoff, and the CEO at Citibank responsible for $11bn write-downs being rewarded with a $100m payoff.

The same principles applied in industry where director-shareholders were also insulated from the risk attached to any particular strategy and were thus encouraged to adopt high-risk high-return projects which caution would have prevented them adopting in normal circumstances. This influence was further magnified by the increased pressure to take a short-term perspective and so achieve the quick results which would activate the share bonus payments. Under other circumstances, management would have been more likely to adopt a longer-term view of the business.

The short-term perspective and reduced concern for risk reinforced top management's deal-making mentality resulting from the 'strategic' approach described in the previous chapter.

The notion that companies exist solely to maximize shareholder wealth has become ubiquitous. Satisfying a customer need is merely an operational means to achieving the overarching goal. So embedded has the notion become that many company directors have the duty formally spelled out in their service contracts, even though this is likely to be in contravention of company law, and certainly against its spirit. Thus the end result for management of Friedmanite economics has been the reversal of the financial and industrial positions. Financiers aggressively attack the industrial sector with the avowed aim of

---

16 Jensen, M. and Murphy, K.J., (1990), 'Performance Pay and Top Management Incentives', *Journal of Political Economy*, Vol. 98, pp. 225–264.

17 Caulkin, S., (2007), 'Buccaneering bosses are the worst of all options', *The Observer, Business & Media Section*, 18 November, p. 10.

realizing, extracting, even 'squeezing out', value that industrial management has accumulated and retained within their companies while they attended to customer needs rather than those of shareholders. The vehicles for achieving this process, the investment banks, private equity funds, sovereign funds and other professionally managed financial resources, have little concern for the industrial strengths, capacities and futures of the firms they acquire and deplete.

Governments have remained, perhaps naively and gullibly, in thrall to business, failing to distinguish between the wealth-creating industrial sector and the wealth-expropriating financial sector, fearful that they should be seen as business-unfriendly by either. In their final execution of the Friedmanite project, governments have sought to impose on the public sector what they conceive as the discipline and efficiency of private for-profit business.

Public Sector Competition and Choice

Public sector management is a separate topic, no doubt warranting its own brief history. But in recent times the attempt has been made by government to impose private sector methods on public sector organizations. This section is really a footnote on the unfortunate effect of government's application of the Friedmanite dogma on the public sector. It had a profound impact.

The overriding idea was that the public sector should be privatized where possible and the parts that remained would be much improved in terms of cost and value for money as well as the quality of its delivery, by imposing on it the management methods, systems and criteria that government believed had worked for the private sector.

This followed Adam Smith's 'economic man' logic which guided the most efficient use of resources in a nation's economy, with public welfare coming as a happy by-product. Today, the Friedmanite Adam Smith Institute, which concentrates exclusively on the free-market strand of Smith's contribution, describes itself as:

> *'the UK's leading innovator of free-market economic and social policies. It researches practical ways to inject choice and competition into public services, extend personal freedom, reduce taxes, prune back regulation, and cut government waste.'*[18]

---

18   See the web site at: http://www.adamsmith.org

The first imperative was to privatize whatever could be privatized. The Thatcher government effectively dismantled Britain's mixed Harrod–Keynesian economy, privatizing water, gas, electricity generation and distribution, landline based telephones, railways, airports, and nuclear energy plus a number of smaller disposals and secondary offerings disposed of later including British Steel, British Airways and British Leyland.

Initially regulation of the newly privatized industries was done with a light hand and the businesses easily beat their targeted results which had been deliberately set at undemanding levels. Thereafter regulation tightened. The real impact of privatization was difficult to assess. Where there was a natural monopoly, as with utilities, there seemed to be no pressing practical reason to privatize, only the doctrinaire Friedmanite motivation. Where there was natural competition there seemed to be no real reason for public ownership, other than to rescue a lame duck which might have the potential for a long-term future. Perhaps the difference between public and private ownership was less significant than widely believed, the critical issue being the degree to which politicians, who increasingly lacked non-political experience, engaged with detailed management. Where they have so engaged they have almost invariably failed.

A further aspect of Friedmanite thinking was the dogmatic imposition of 'competition and choice' on those areas of the public sector which could not be privatized. And there was the attempt to measure and report the value for money being delivered, usually expressed in terms of league tables of performance against government set targets.

In principle there might seem to be no reason why private sector management principles should not also be applied in the public sector. The division of management labour described previously identifies several specializations that are equally relevant to public sector organizations, as well as the basic approach of making best use of resources.

But there was a problem. The dichotomy between the public service guardian culture and the commercial culture is fundamental.[19] These two cultures are not only very different, but incompatible, as they have developed over age-long practice. The British government notoriously highlighted the difference by imposing private industry criteria on the public services, for

---

19 Jacobs, J., (1992), *Systems of Survival: A Dialogue on the Moral Foundations of Commerce and Politics*, New York: Random House.

example providing monetary incentives for general medical practitioners (GPs) hoping to persuade them to focus on certain government-set targets.

> *'the disastrous results of the GP contract can be traced directly to the government's determination to turn an essentially guardian organization into a commercial one. GPs have responded to incentives in textbook fashion, by finding ways to meet the targets. The government had changed their motivation from intrinsic (the work itself) to extrinsic (outside rewards). But, as a patient, which GP would you rather consult, one motivated by money or by doing the best medical job?'*[20]

Such an apparent lack of governmental understanding of the cultural orientation of its health service employees has been repeated many times over, with inappropriate targets distracting attention from the primary aims of the service. The government's perspective on what motivates people is wholly based on the 'economic man' assumptions; we are all wholly amoral and only interested in maximizing our own utility which is defined in purely monetary terms. Friedmanite governments find no finer motivations credible. Yet the existence of the traditional professions and the public areas of health, education and social security are operated by people, many of whom are driven by different, some would say, higher, motivations.

Moreover, performances against target all needed measuring, recording and reporting, with the costs of the requisite bureaucracy detracting from the health service's primary provision. Friedmanite governments repeated their doctrinaire prognoses in UK public service areas such as education, social services, the police, the fire service and the probation service, with similarly dysfunctional, if not disastrous results.

The critique of the free-market approach to public services has become so extensive and so well documented it will not be repeated further. Quality guru Deming held that target-setting was hostile to quality because they (i.e. targets) were goal-focused not process-focused; they addressed ends not means. An organization could resort to any means to accomplish virtually any end wants. For Deming, a *'quota is a fortress against improvement of quality and productivity. I have yet to see a quota that includes any trace of a system by which to help anyone to do a better job'*. As an example Deming cited the policeman who must issue a quota of parking tickets every day.[21]

---

20 Caulkin, S., (2008), '198 reasons why we're in this terrible mess', *The Observer, Business & Media Section*, 9 March, p. 10.
21 Beatty, J., (1998), *The World According to Drucker*, London: Orion Publishing Group, p. 112.

Direct governmental involvement with public sector provision has generally proved counter-productive because politicians are largely innocent of Deming and the last 50 years or so progress in quality management and the approach to building quality in rather than inspecting it out. Also attempts to create artificial markets, competition and consumer choice have generally provided no real benefit and could be disastrous. For example, British governments have expressed the desire to privatize the Royal Mail (including the Post Office) for doctrinaire reasons, Friedman having attacked the United States Post Office's legal monopoly. But British governments failed to override public opinion which was in favour of retaining the service in public ownership. So they subsequently sought to introduce competition and choice to various monopoly markets served, with private sector delivery services being encouraged to cherry-pick profitable services in which to compete (for example, inter-city deliveries), but not required to provide a universal service including delivery to remote locations. This inevitably reduced the overall viability of the service to which the government responded by closing many rural post offices which provided a service but no profit. The logical conclusion of this Friedmanite approach is to suspend mail deliveries to unprofitable destinations, or at least to charge the full cost price which would have the same effect.

The Royal Mail in these activities, like the NHS, was operating within the guardian culture, not the commercial. Friedmanite economics don't work in these situations – there is no one best way. Public provision does not require direct engagement by government and the imposition of inappropriate targets which only add bureaucratic overhead and non-productive cost.

The Friedmanite Legacy

Prior to the Reagan and Thatcher administrations adopting Friedmanism, the neo-classical project had been kept alive by a number of dissident academics in various research university departments. The accepted orthodoxy was the Harrod–Keynesian elaboration of what Keynes himself had advocated, which justified continuous and significant government regulation of the economy in Britain, though less so in the United States, in order to maintain full employment which led to wage-push inflation and stagnant economic growth.

The Friedmanite version of classical theory emboldened the new conservative governments to confront organized labour head on. Their victories over union militancy resulted in a prolonged period of much improved industrial relations as measured by working days lost from strikes and industrial action. Organized labour itself appeared, subsequently and for the time being at least, to share the view that industrial action was a weapon to be used sparingly and with greater care than previously to avoid doing damage to labour and its cause.

The Friedmanites wholly accepted Hayek's argument that free-market capitalism led to political freedom for the individual and that government intervention in the economy led inevitably to tyranny and totalitarianism. This was the basis of what was sometimes referred to as neo-liberalism. It remains a theory, so far falsified by the examples, in their different ways, of both China and Russia as well as European social democracy.

Friedman's belief that private enterprise was good and public delivery bad, because the latter cost twice as much, may have had some approximate truth regarding things which are wholly dependent on cost for their justification. But where they were also dependent on non-cost issues the point was only partially relevant. Judging public service by private criteria and vice versa was only rarely appropriate.

Friedman's belief that low flat-rate taxation would increase tax revenue to the Exchequer was wrong. He argued that it *'would make it unprofitable for people to resort to the tax gimmicks and loopholes they now use'*.[22] Tax avoidance and evasion have grown substantially since 1977 at the same time as tax rates for the higher earners have been substantially reduced. The really rich have paid expensive tax consultants to eliminate their taxes altogether.

Friedmanism minimized tax and rejected the idea of progressive taxation. It denied the professional culture driven by ethical codes of practice, and the guardian culture of the public sector, and therefore sought strenuously to reduce them to the basic amoral, self-interested 'economic man' concept to which all economic actors are persuaded to conform.

The aggravation which inequity caused has been remarked time and again since Defoe's record of peasants pulling up the stakes around new enclosures. The grievance of the poor and excluded is never far below the surface. The 'super rich' of Friedmanite economies have taken inequality to a new level. Drucker had suggested in 1996 that the ratio between the top executive's pay and that of the average hourly paid worker:

---

22   Friedman, M., (1977), 'From Galbraith to Economic Freedom', *Occasional Paper* 40, London: The Institute of Economic Affairs, p. 50.

*'could be no more than twenty to one without injury to company morale
... Few top executives can imagine the hatred, contempt and even fury
that has been created – not primarily among blue-collar workers who
never had an exalted opinion of the bosses – but among their middle
management and professional people.'*[23]

Drucker had quoted J.P.Morgan as supporting this view. In 1960, the ratio between CEO and average hourly paid pay in the United States was already far above the twenty to one ideal at 41 times. By 1996, according to a *Business Week* survey, it had grown to 209 times, and by 2005 the ratio was 262 times.[24] This inequity, encouraged by Friedmanite governments everywhere, had certainly caused the 'hatred, contempt and even fury' to rise and had debased management itself.

A final element in the legacy of Friedmanism arose more from the changing world circumstances. When Friedmanite governments came to power the main concern was how to resume economic growth and the creation of wealth seemed a reasonably appropriate preoccupation. By the turn of the twenty-first century, the notion of wealth creation was widely challenged. Industrial production, it was argued, did not create wealth so much as extract it from the earth's store and convert it with varying degrees of inefficiency. By then it had become plain that the earth's resources were not only finite but were being consumed at a rate which was both unsustainable and accelerating. In addition, there was now a more or less total scientific consensus that industrial pollution was adding substantially to, if not the prime cause of, a catastrophic level of global warming.

In these changed circumstances Friedman's injunction for industry not to be concerned with any other social responsibility than to make as much money as possible for shareholders was seen as destructive and dangerous.

Despite these adverse considerations and unforeseen consequences, Friedmanism remained the orthodox economic wisdom across the world. And a major source of its success was because it had been promulgated through American business schools and research universities and from there to the rest of world leadership.

---

23 Beatty, J., (1998), *The World According to Drucker,* London: Orion Publishing Group, p. 83.
24 Mishel, L., (2007), 'CEO-to-worker pay imbalance grows', Economic Snapshots web site: http://www.epi.org/content.cfm/webfeatures_snapshots_20060621

11

Business Schools versus Management Education

Management presided over the process of industrialization and the resulting rise in living standards as well as the frequently inequitable distribution of industry's surpluses. In the early days of the twentieth century, management educators saw the role as of heroic importance, impacting not only the working lives of people, but the economic welfare of nations. Management had developed a new and decisive role in decision-making of unprecedented importance. Independent of both capital and labour, its impact had been revolutionary.

The early attempt to establish management as a profession with its own ideals and standards of behaviour as well as credentialed knowledge and expertise inevitably failed. There could be no such constraint on the entrepreneur or enterprise. Management education was therefore provided on a voluntary basis rather than as the provision of qualifications which were a mandatory requirement for entry to the profession. Nevertheless, as educational standards rose generally, the accepted qualifications for entry to management roles in big business became increasingly focused on the acquisition of university degrees in management subjects.

Approaches to the education of managers were divided between the objective of 'training the intellect' as Cardinal Newman had put it, or providing them with 'what might be useful' as John Locke had suggested. This dichotomy was present from the beginning of management education and is still a concern today with business school faculty dividing their concerns between improving management practice and achievement in terms of purely academic criteria at the expense of management practice.

Despite the blandishments of the new strategic management and the almost universal acceptance of Friedmanite thinking, many, if not most, managers have actually worked with integrity for the best interests of their companies and all stakeholders. But business school teaching made it ever more difficult to maintain the values and practical approach of a profession. Such non-conformist behaviour would seem quite puzzlingly irrational to any business school educated manager, taught to make as much money as possible for shareholders, rejecting social responsibilities and with the notion of business ethics being shown to be quite unrealistic.

The Management Curriculum

While the first business school was established in the United States in the late nineteenth century, the first British business colleges were not established until after the Second World War and the first university-based business schools not until 1965. Oxbridge did not join the fray till the 1990s. British universities were slow to follow the United States lead, but when they did they closely copied the American model, establishing postgraduate MBA degrees based around the American curriculum and pedagogic methods and adopting the voluminous American management literature.

Khurana's sociological perspective[1] traces the development of the United States management curriculum from the initial drive to establish American management as a high profession alongside medicine and law. The aim was to teach not just efficiency and effectiveness but also how management might fulfil its responsibilities for the greater good of society.

Early on, business schools adopted economics as the main underpinning theory of business though initially institutional economics, which paid more attention to practical realities and was more flexible and less quantitatively tractable than neo-classical theory, was accepted as more relevant to management education. However, as business school faculty became more academically sophisticated the neo-classical theorists, encouraged by the Ford and Carnegie foundations which funded much business education, gradually became dominant.

Initially university-based management education was delivered by people with experience as management practitioners but limited academic standing. So there was considerable pressure for management faculty to achieve academic respectability through research rather than to focus on teaching to improve

---

1   Khurana, R., (2007), *From Higher Aims to Hired Hands*, Princeton: Princeton University Press.

management practice. For the same reasons business school faculty sought to establish management as a scientific subject in its own right, quantitative, rational, technique-based, focused on planning, forecasting and controlling.

This coincided with the establishment of large-scale diversified conglomerate corporations resulting from anti-trust legislation. Management was then established with a general expertise which was deemed to be applicable to any situation, industry or technology. Finance and accounting provided the common language for managing these diversified corporations and maximizing profit became accepted as the single common objective.

The funding foundations favoured the 'scientific' approach to management and encouraged research in economics and business administration, giving priority to schools which focused on the application to management problems of neo-classical economics, behavioural sciences, statistics and mathematics. The foundations funded expansion of doctoral programmes, thus increasing the academic orientation and quality of business faculty. Having developed a scientific basis, management programmes became progressively less concerned with the realities of practice and more with the establishment of academic credibility.

The management that was generally taught in business schools was focused on tools and techniques, systems, quantitative methods and financial manipulation with little regard for technical competence related to any specific industry and little acknowledgement of the value of practical experience.

Business schools adopted Friedman's focus on maximizing shareholder wealth before it extended to government. It justified the priority given to short-term deal making ahead of long-term general management. And it was taught along with the supporting topics of agency theory, transaction cost economics and the open market in corporate managements.

Whether or not this was realistic, its influence extended beyond management education, business and government. Khurana quotes even the Business Roundtable:

> 'the paramount duty of management and of boards of directors is to the corporation's stockholders; the interests of other stakeholders are relevant as a derivative of the duty to the stockholders. The notion that the board must somehow balance the interests of other stakeholders fundamentally misconstrues the role of directors. It is moreover an

unworkable notion because it would leave the board with no criterion for resolving conflicts between the interests of stockholders and of other stakeholders or among different groups of stakeholders.[2]

In a note on the above quotation Khurana quotes Holmstrom and Kaplan that the shareholder value orientation:

'had become institutionalized inside the culture and structure of American corporations'

and

'that managers became aware of the potential benefits of pursuing shareholder value by observing the success of LBOs (leveraged buy outs) and takeovers in the 1980s. Helped along by generous stock option programs, management came to endorse shareholder value in the 1990s and to pursue it with vigor.'[3]

Even those who opposed the notion of shareholder value used it to rally objectors and reinforced it as an accepted truth. For example, the film *The Corporation* asserted that all publicly traded corporations were structured through a series of legal decisions to have a peculiar and disturbing characteristic:

'they are required by law to place the financial interests of their owners above competing interests ... even the public good.'[4]

Though this was untrue, it was proclaimed by Friedmanites and accepted by their opponents, taught by business schools, and became universally accepted. It legitimized the asset stripping activities of the financial sector including investment banks and private equity funds which were then able to attract management students who accepted their own amoral self-interest as taught.

The business schools themselves were then acting according to the logic of what they taught. They were in the market place, subject to all manner of

---

2   Khurana, R., (2007), *From Higher Aims to Hired Hands*, Princeton: Princeton University Press, p. 321.
3   Holmstrom, B. and Kaplan, S.N., (2001), 'Corporate Governance and Merger Activity in the United States: Making Sense of the 1980s and 1990s', *Journal of Economic Perspectives*, Vol. 15, No 2, pp. 132–133.
4   *The Corporation*, (2003), a documentary film by Achbar, M., Abbott, J. and Bakan, J., see the website www.thecorporation.com

league tables which determined their market position. Students were attracted on the basis of the return they would get from their MBA degree. One published league table calculated the internal rate of return from MBA courses.

The management curriculum taught in such business schools had by then departed from any serious interest in improving how managers fulfilled their responsibilities. The concerns were to sell their courses to make as much money as possible for their owners, the universities, and along the way to achieve the academic standing which would redound to their own self-interest as well as that of their employers.

The Quest for Academic Respectability

The study of management in academia had adopted an underlying theoretical foundation in neo-classical economic theory. It had produced some interesting empirical research into practice and developed some local theory about organization structure and human behaviour in organizations. In so doing, it had borrowed from psychology and sociology. It had also encompassed some professional credentials in the form of finance, accounting and law. But it did not appear to be an academic subject in its own right, capable of attracting high calibre academic faculty.

MANAGEMENT'S 'SCIENTIFIC' FOUNDATION

Based on its economic and quantitative components, management's scientific content was emphasized, drawing on theory from other spheres, notably natural science and mathematics. But the application of mathematical phenomena to explain issues in social science is almost invariably spurious, if not disreputable. Chaos theory, for example, has been a popular mathematical theory applied to the management problem, but its application has no real truth, as demonstrated by acceptance of the famous spoof article by Sokal and Bricmont:

> *'Unfortunately it is often difficult to find a mathematical model that is sufficiently simple to be analyzable and yet adequately describes the objects being considered. These problems arise in fact whenever one tries to apply a mathematical theory to reality.*
>
> *Some purported 'applications of chaos theory – for example to business management or literary criticism – border on the absurd. And, to make matters worse, chaos theory – which is well-developed mathematically*

– is often confused with the still emerging theories of complexity and self organization.'[5]

There are no examples in the literature of an 'analyzable' chaos model which adequately describes objects in business management. Discussing management issues in terms of chaos, complexity, string theory or any other developing strand of mathematics appears to be insubstantial, once described as 'pretentious froth'.

Game theory has been used to aid understanding of the logic underlying decision processes. For example, Nobel laureate Schelling's insight that a country's best safeguard against nuclear war is to protect its weapons rather than its people, the logic being that an enemy is less likely to strike first if it believes you can strike back after a nuclear hit, rather than simply that you can survive the hit. Examples of game theory models of competition exist but their real contribution tends to be rather more academic than practical. In any case, these are fairly slight inputs to management theory compared to the claims of some social theorists to use mathematics and natural science to model social systems.

Game theory apart, the only way in which these mathematical theories could make a useful input to management would be as metaphor. But metaphor is unnecessary when the real thing is at hand. In the case of neo-classical economic models, the mathematical application makes no pretence to be metaphoric. They are mathematical equations which have their own existence quite independently of any pretence to model reality. Nevertheless they embody a pretence to be applicable to real situations and have been so applied with malign effect.

Ghoshal referred to Elster's distinction between the explanations of behaviour in science and the humanities.[6] In natural science, the explanation is simply causal: combining a with b causes c. In biological science, there may be functional explanations: an organism behaves in a particular way to enhance its reproductive fitness. In the case of management, individual actions are largely explained by the intentions of the actor which may be based on some long-term aim rather than an immediate result. Management theories, such as the profit-maximizing model, are assumed to be causal or functional and do not accommodate individual intentions as an explanation of behaviour.

5   Sokal, A. and Bricmont, J., (1998), *Intellectual Impostures*, London: Profile Books, p. 135.
6   Elster, J., (1983), *Explaining Technical Change*, Cambridge: Cambridge University Press.

The attempt to make management theory scientific therefore meant that moral and ethical considerations had to be excluded as incompatible with the underlying approach.[7] Explanations which could not be reduced to numbers were excluded.

MANAGEMENT'S MORAL FOUNDATION

However, moral and ethical considerations have been widely acknowledged as essential aspects of management education and in fact also provide another thrust for academic standing. Business ethics, based around the teaching of applied moral philosophy, is a standard MBA course and the existence of corporate social responsibility (CSR), a more narrowly defined procedural approach to business ethics in practice, as an even fashionable part of contemporary management. Though they may cover necessary aspects of management, they have generally been added to the curriculum as separate modules which do not infuse or interfere with the basic shareholder value dominated curriculum. Moreover they are usually offered as options which students may avoid if they so choose. The Friedmanite theories underpinning management education have been allowed to remain untouched, the core curriculum unaltered.

The alternative of conflating the various management studies subjects with an ethical ingredient would strike right at the heart of the dominant theory and require its substitution with something different. The psychological commitment to the status quo is as yet too weighty to make such a modification feasible.

The question of whether or not there should be an element of moral education in management courses has long been debated. Objections are raised that it is not the job of an MBA teacher to proselytize some particular moral perspective to their students, or to try to influence their personal values. On the other hand the promotion of the Friedmanite thesis does just that. And a short course on business ethics hardly offsets the preponderance of business school amorality.

While there may be various approaches in teaching business ethics, there appears to be some consensus on three issues. First, that the ethical performance of business needs to be improved. Second, that improvement depends on raising the ethical values of people in business, and, third, it will only be achieved

---

7   Ghoshal, S., (2005), 'Bad Management Theories Are Destroying Good Management Practices,' *Academy of Management Learning & Education*, Vol. 4, No 1, p. 79.

through a process of moral education. Together they are the foundation of the business ethics curriculum.

De George highlighted various themes which underlie the standard approach to business ethics. The first and perhaps most crucial of these is that:

> 'business – national or international – can be no more ethical than the persons who run the firms. Companies that act with integrity are a function of individuals within them who act with integrity'.[8]

This is a basic tenet of business ethicists and has long been part of the orthodox wisdom:

> 'What matters most is where we stand as individual managers and how we behave when faced with decisions which combine ethical and commercial judgments.'[9]

The approach of business ethics is therefore personal, the intention being to inform, educate and indoctrinate so that the ethical standards of the individual recipients are raised and the business organizations in which they operate are therefore also 'improved'.

Ethicists can tend to be unrealistic suggesting, as they often do, that managers can't be genuinely ethical unless what they do in no way serves their own interests, i.e. ethics must hurt. Stark reported the following assertion:

> 'To be ethical as a business because it may increase your profits is to do so for entirely the wrong reason. The ethical business must be ethical because it wants to be ethical.'[10]

The unworldliness of such statements – idealistic or simply wrong-headed – stems from their theoretical roots in moral philosophy. They contribute little to the practice of business management. A typical business ethics course covers, at a necessarily superficial level, aspects of moral philosophy, such as utilitarianism and universalism, and defers to Mill, Bentham, Kant and others

---

8   De George, R.T., (1993), *Competing with Integrity in International Business*, New York: Oxford University Press, p. v.

9   Cadbury, A., (1987), 'Final Report of the Committee on the Financial Aspects of Corporate Governance', published by Gee, South Quay Plaza, London.

10   Anon quoted in Stark, A., (1993), 'What's the Matter with Business Ethics?' *Harvard Business Review*, May/June.

as well as the ancient Greek philosophers, all of whom were totally innocent of modern business and the dilemmas it poses.

The idea that the ethical performance of a business depends on the moral values of its managers would be a major limitation. Managers are temporary post holders, whereas the integrity which the business needs its stakeholders to perceive is permanent. It needs to be built into the culture of the business so that it not only survives changes of senior managers, but is also robust and impervious to any who might, either deliberately or inadvertently, put the company's reputation at risk.

The practical application of ethics to business practice is also problematic. Several different vehicles have been tried. Corporate philanthropy was advocated, but the object of the philanthropy, according to ethicists, must not be associated with the activities of the business. Otherwise, it would not be philanthropic, but merely self-interested publicity. Whether or not such considerations have any value, they appeared to weaken the appeal of corporate philanthropy as a management initiative.

Corporate social responsibility (CSR) is another approach which has established itself as a fashionable management routine which has penetrated deep into the reporting of business practice:

> 'It would be a challenge to find a recent annual report of any big international company that justifies the firm's existence merely in terms of profit, rather than "service to the community". Such reports often talk proudly of efforts to improve society and safeguard the environment.'[11]

In the pursuit of CSR some businesses have invested in schools or health facilities as, for example, Shell have done in the Delta region of Nigeria to partially mitigate the adverse impacts their operations have had on the local population. In Shell's case the net impact of its Nigerian operations on corporate reputation has nevertheless been overwhelmingly negative. Despite all this, the basic Friedmanite philosophy remains dominant.

> 'The proper business of business is business. No apology required.'[12]

---

11 Crook, C., (2005), 'The Good Company', in 'A Survey of Corporate Social Responsibility', *The Economist*, 22 January.

12 *Economist, The*, (2005), 'The Ethics of Business', in 'A Survey of Corporate Social Responsibility', *The Economist*, 22 January.

To enable business to avoid social responsibilities it would be up to government to guard the public interest, to regulate business only so as to protect its citizens and to attend to the minimum demands of social justice, to provide essential public goods and collect the taxes to pay for them. Governments tend sometimes not to be good at discharging these responsibilities. But that does not mean business should pay voluntarily instead. Friedman's insistence that business must seek to maximize shareholder wealth and Levitt's warning not to make 'sweet music', express the dominant fear that free-market economy businesses risk being sidetracked into ineffectiveness by business ethics and CSR.

From the academic perspective, business ethics has considerable attractions. While it can be adopted as a separate subject area it does not necessarily damage the main curriculum. Moreover, it brings to management educators the provenance stemming from the great and ancient philosophers which is helpful to management faculty in establishing their credentials to their academic peers.

Management Faculty and Academic Criteria

In the United States and also subsequently in Britain, great investments were made in raising the academic standing of business school faculty and the academic quality of business school research and publication. Inevitably, this strengthening of the academic focus resulted in a divorce from management practice. As De George expressed it forthrightly about business ethics:

> 'the legitimacy of business ethics as an academic field does not depend on its ...being effective in changing the climate of business in the United States. As an academic field it stands or falls on the quality of the research done in it, on the body of knowledge developed, and on its success as an academic liberal arts subject.'[13]

University departments, including business schools, are formally assessed as to the 'quality' of their 'research', by which is meant very largely the number of publications in academic journals of appropriate standing. And they are funded accordingly. Faculty members are therefore driven to achieve against

---

13   De George, R.T., (1991), 'Will success spoil business ethics?' in *Business Ethics: The State of the Art*, Freeman, R.E. (ed.), Oxford: Oxford University Press, p. 45.

the academic criteria of research and publication rather than by teaching to improve management practice.

Harvard Business School, for example, proclaimed on its 2009 web page:

> *'Each academic year, the faculty authors or co-authors about thirty-five books, produces more than 300 academic papers, and writes a broad array of articles for general business publications.'*[14]

Practice is similar in Britain where the Higher Education Funding Council for England is responsible on behalf of government for the allocation of research funds to universities. It sets criteria and establishes procedures by which to evaluate universities' research activities, i.e. publications, and funds are allocated according to the ratings which result. The funding is important. In Britain, there is much less private benefaction and endowment of university activity than there is in the United States. In 2007–8 public funding of £4.6bn was provided for teaching students, which was the basic university support and on top of that a further £1.5bn was targeted at research universities according to the quality of their research, which was assessed primarily on the amount and quality of their publications.

Consequently, the primary purpose of management educators, since this system of assessment and funding was first instituted in the 1980s, has been to publish academic papers rather than contribute to the improvement of management practice. Business school faculty now tends to have limited practical management experience other than as occasional advisors or consultants with no line responsibility for results. Nevertheless, they dominate the mainstream subject area aimed at practitioners. This is exampled by the *Financial Times* supplements on Mastering Management[15] which contained 55 articles by management specialists. Of these contributions, 51 were by academics, two by consultants and two by practitioners. Parallel supplements on Strategy[16] contained 78 articles by strategy specialists. Of these contributions, all bar two were by academics and the two exceptions were by 'educators' (one on-line and one consultant); not a single contribution was from a practitioner. This dominance by academia is of prime importance in the promulgation of theoretical ideas to the practical and political worlds.

---

14 See website: http://www.hbs.edu/about
15 Pickford, J., (ed.), (2001), *Financial Times Mastering Management: Your Single Source Guide to Becoming a Master of Management*, London: Financial Times Prentice Hall.
16 Dickson, T., (ed.), (2000), *Financial Times Mastering Strategy: The Complete MBA Companion in Strategy*, London: Financial Times Prentice Hall.

The need for business school faculty to publish their research is facilitated by the publication of academic journals. The EBSCO database on which, it is claimed, 'academic institutions worldwide depend … as their core resource of scholarly information', contained in 2008 full text for more than 2,000 journals, including more than 1,550 peer-reviewed journals, covering virtually every area of academic study. The EBSCO business database 'includes nearly 1,100 business publications, including full text for nearly 500 peer-reviewed business publications'. Most of these journals comprise articles written by academics, are edited by academics and whose readers are also academics. The purpose of such journals is not to be read but to be vehicles for the allocation of research funding. Their relevance to management practice is incidental and limited.

The quality of such academic journals is variable as is the calibre of the academic peers who review contributions. All have a vested interest in the publication of journals and journal articles, irrespective of their limited readership and lack of relevance to real world practice.

Determining the subject matter of management according to academic, rather than practical, criteria, has led it into abstruse and problematic areas which offer the opportunity to contribute an article on a subject which has not previously been exhausted. Such abstruse topics serve academic ends, for example, the reputation building of young faculty plus perhaps the provision of some intellectual challenge against which students can be tested in order to achieve their educational qualification. They have little practical interest or content.

The Damage from Management Teaching

Sumantra Ghoshal argued that management theory taught in business schools based on the 'economic man' assumptions was not only incorrect but in many different ways damaging to management and the managed, to industry and to society as a whole.

One example of the damage being done was in the encouragement of management greed and crookedness which had surfaced in corporate scandals such as Enron, Worldcom, Tyco and a hundred others, revealing how the upper reaches of management practice had been perverted. Prior to their downfall, many of these firms had featured in 'highly laudatory' business school case studies. Though the cases were rapidly withdrawn or rewritten and a renewed emphasis laid on the delivery of modules in business ethics and corporate social responsibility, the old Friedmanite ideas persisted as the mainstream orthodoxy.

According to Ghoshal:

> '*Many of the worst excesses of recent management practices have their roots in a set of ideas that have emerged from business school academics over the last 30 years.*'[17]

He argued that a refocus of management education was necessary:

> '*Business schools do not need to do a great deal more to help prevent future Enrons; they need only to stop doing a lot they currently do. ... we – as business school faculty – need to own up to our own role in creating Enrons. Our theories and ideas have done much to strengthen the management practices we are all now so loudly condemning.*'

Keynes had pointed out that economic and political ideas were more powerful than commonly understood:

> '*Practical men, who believe themselves to be quite exempt from any intellectual influences are usually the slaves of some defunct economist ... It is ideas, not vested interests, which are dangerous for good or evil.*'[18]

But the ideas of neo-classical thinkers such as Friedman conditioned 'practical men' always to suspect vested interests; to do otherwise would be naïve and naïveté would be an unforgivable error for 'practical men' such as managers.

The teaching of Friedmanite economics supported by the explanations of agency theory, transaction-cost analysis and the open market in corporate management, legitimized some management behaviours and de-legitimised others, even for managers who had not personally had the benefit of an MBA education but who had ingested the ideas and spirit of those who had.

---

17 Ghoshal, S., (2005), 'Bad Management Theories Are Destroying Good Management Practices', *Academy of Management Learning & Education*, Vol. 4, No 1, pp. 75–91.
18 Keynes, J.M., (1936), *The General Theory of Employment, Interest and Money*, London: Macmillan & Co, p. 306.

The management behaviours which theory legitimized through the Friedmanite injunction to maximize shareholder wealth supported by all the other neo-classical paraphernalia included the exploitation and abuse of employees, customers, the local community and the environment, the grasping of stock ownership for themselves where possible and the manipulation of rewards to stockowners at the expense of the longer-term future of the business and its other stakeholders. Drucker exampled the exploitation and abuse of employees when he expressed his contempt for those managers who removed the jobs of employees and then paid themselves extraordinary bonuses for so doing.

The management behaviours which Friedmanite theory de-legitimized included the exercise of balance in the distribution of benefits among stakeholders, investment in the local community or environment at the short-term expense of shareholders, all long-term investment, and the pursuit of social responsibilities and the adoption of any moral or ethical consideration other than maximising shareholder wealth and short-term economic gain.

In natural science, a theory does not change reality. As Ghoshal put it: *'if a theory assumes that the sun goes round the earth it does not change what the sun actually does.'*[19] In social science, theories which are successfully promulgated tend to become self-fulfilling. Despite lack of supporting evidence, they may be successfully promoted by sufficient adherents and so achieve a critical mass at which point they present the appearance of a scientific law. But while a scientific law has no impact on reality, merely reflecting it, a successful theory in social science can have a profound impact on behaviour. The Friedmanite orthodoxy reached critical mass around the end of the 1970s.

Espousing that version of the dismal science, so useful in establishing the academic status of management studies as a fully fledged social science subject, management students are led inexorably to the denial of moral or ethical considerations. Business school 'educated' managers are thus freed from a sense of moral responsibility in their subsequent management practice. So the theory is self-fulfilled.[20]

---

19   Ghoshal, S., (2005), 'Bad Management Theories Are Destroying Good Management Practices', *Academy of Management Learning & Education*, Vol. 4, No 1, p. 77.
20   Gergen, K.J., (1973), 'Social Psychology as History', *Journal of Personality and Social Psychology*, Vol. 26, No 2, pp. 309–320.

Instead, managers were taught using new models of strategic management, how to maximize short-term shareholder gains by expropriating the resources which manufacturing businesses and mutual societies had managed to accrue over many years. They learned the quick benefits of deal-making as opposed to managing.

With management having no professional affiliation or commitment and subverted by business school education, decisions were taken which maximized short-term shareholder value and largely ignored more profound longer-term impacts. And these longer-term impacts were considerable, including the depletion of the earth's resources, the pollution of its atmosphere and destruction of its climate. Industry and its management were not only the prime cause of these ills, but also the only real hope for their solution. But under Friedman's baleful influence there would be little reason to expect management to fulfil these heroic responsibilities.

PART IV

Management for New Responsibilities

Just as management first came into existence from necessity, an additional cost but an overwhelming benefit, so now its renewal is also a necessity. It presents the best, perhaps the only, opportunity for the earth's resources to be conserved and its climate protected. Continuation along the Friedmanite route is leading to disaster and renewal is by no means certain.

Management's competence is specific: waste reducing, cost minimizing, efficiency maximizing, people centred, profit seeking, technologically innovative and competitive. Of themselves these characteristics will not resolve the problems referred to above. The global playing field must not only be level but it must be slanted against the polluters in favour of the environmentally friendly. Free-trade capitalism may remain the foundation, but government intervention to ensure markets take full account of the long-term effects of economic activity, to fund appropriate projects and outlaw others, will necessarily have to be accepted as legitimate.

The continuing vitality of technological innovation within the commercial and business setting, initiated by management, has often been demonstrated in every industry, new and mature.[1] There is the capacity to respond to situations such as climate change and resource depletion, if effectively managed, to use that creative vitality for the greater good as well as that of the individual enterprise.

Corporate legislation reasserts the autonomous position of management with the responsibility to act even-handedly between all stakeholders in the

---

1   Pearson, G.J., (1989), 'Factors which facilitate and inhibit innovation in a mature industry', PhD thesis submitted to the University of Manchester.

best long-term interests of the enterprise. Yet custom and practice continues to break both the letter and spirit of the law in many different ways.

Renewed concern with the higher aims of management will show to future students the extent to which their predecessors were corrupted, and management educators misled, by their blind acceptance of what Ghoshal referred to simply as 'bad theory'.[2]

---

2   Ghoshal, S., (2005), 'Bad Management Theories Are Destroying Good Management Practices,' *Academy of Management Learning & Education*, Vol. 4, No 1.

12

The Emerging Perspective

The fall of management resulted from a combination of causes. The development of 'strategic' thinking, which paradoxically resulted in a shorter-term, deal-making orientation, was a necessary pre-condition. The automation of much middle management, and therefore the elimination of management training grounds, greatly assisted the divorce of top management from the practicalities of running a business. So, isolated from their organizations and their people, management became vulnerable to the rampant progress of Friedmanite ideas and were seduced from their previously autonomous role by the possibility of unimagined riches, into becoming the agents of shareholders and the puppets of neo-classical, amoral self-interest. The immediate but unsustainable result was measurable in terms of generally higher living standards, an explosion in the inequalities of wealth and income, massive pollution and the depletion of the earth's resources.

Friedmanism was dominant for around three decades. Its participants prospered while communism was seen to fail across the globe. It had been a fundamental shift from the more pluralistic approach of the Harrod–Keynesians which had preceded it.

Friedman himself had said that it was only in crisis that things change:

> *'Only a crisis – actual or perceived – produces real change. When that crisis occurs, the actions that are taken depend on the ideas that are lying around.'*[1]

That had been the experience in the late 1970s. A nucleus of academic researchers and thinkers had been at work for decades in Vienna and later Chicago. Following this long slow period of incubation, when the crisis was

---

1   Friedman, M., (2002), *Capitalism and Freedom*, 40th anniversary edition, Chicago: University of Chicago Press, quote is from the 1982 preface.

reached things had happened fast. Friedmanism was achieved after the crisis or tipping point, signalled in Britain by the 1978–9 'winter of discontent' which ushered in the Thatcher government, and in the United States with the inauguration of the Reagan administration. From that point, the change had been swift.

The financial crunch of 2007–8 and the ensuing economic distress and the inauguration of the Obama administration in the United States may be just such another tipping point after which change, seen in many areas as in urgent need, may be rapid, with the search being already joined for the suitable ideas that might be 'lying around'.

Management's renewal now might be achieved by the different ideas being discussed in research universities and business schools. These include a modification of the fundamental 'economic man' idea by what has been labelled 'behavioural economics', based on empirical studies of real human behaviour. It is unlikely to provide a mathematically tractable model of economic activity, but its importance lies in its rejection of the reductionist version of human motivation projected by Friedman.

A more equitable model of free-market behavioural economics incorporating some notion of social balance both within and between existing populations but also between this and future populations, could emerge as a new economic orthodoxy. But it would require different economic and management curriculum to be taught in business schools and research universities.

Accepting the legally defined duties of top management would also require a refocusing of management itself, addressing the needs of all stakeholders with integrity and transparency.

Business, Resources and Pollution

In 2008, it was still possible, and in fact common practice, to separate thinking about economic growth from thoughts about the damage being done to the planet by economic activity. Media reporters, in their perennial search for disaster stories, turned from the dire consequences of a reduction in GDP growth-rate projections to reports of the more dire consequences of the melting of the polar ice caps, to reports, for example, of the planned opening of a third runway at Heathrow to accommodate projected growth in air travel which, without the third runway, might go elsewhere. The topics were treated as separate and unrelated, as though the thought that they might be connected was too uncomfortable even to be entertained.

For Friedmanites, it may be too uncomfortable. To misquote the man himself: few trends could so thoroughly undermine the very foundations of human life on this planet than the rejection by corporate officials of any social responsibility other than to make as much money for their shareholders as possible. It seems that Friedman's assertion of management responsibility has to be refuted and reversed if humanity is to survive and prosper.

When the Republican administration came to power in the United States in 2000 it denied the reality of climate change and the global warming impact of human activities. Public perceptions may respond only slowly to the weight of published evidence, but the position has changed radically in the new century.

> *'In 2002, Watson (now the British government's climate change tsar) was ousted as Chairman of the Intergovernmental Panel on Climate Change (IPCC) after pressure from the Bush administration. Lobbyists from the American oil industry reportedly pressed the new president to replace Watson at the earliest opportunity for a heinous crime: claiming that humans were contributing to climate change by burning fossil fuels, and then getting a 2,500-strong group of experts to produce influential and carefully constructed scientific reviews to prove it.*
>
> *The oil men hoped to change the course of the IPCC, and stop the world waking up to some of the awful truths about climate change. Five years on they must feel a little dejected: a series of reports by the IPCC this year [ie 2007] unequivocally linked climate change to human activity.'*[2]

President George W. Bush's opening position on climate change was not long tenable. In his second term, he was forced by the weight of scientific evidence and opinion, to reverse his former denial.

Industry causes, directly and indirectly, the vast bulk of man-made climate change which is contributing to global warming with as yet unknown, but generally believed to be catastrophic, result. Industry must also produce the solutions. Until governments, internationally, intervene to provide the

---

2   Jha, A., (2007), 'Facing down the heat', *The Guardian, Society Guardian Environment*, 24 October.

necessary regulatory framework and financial support it will be difficult for individual businesses to take decisive action, even with their own carbon footprint, because of the probable response of unencumbered competitors.

Industry's activities have always polluted the environment and consumed limited resources and in the past companies have rarely paid the full price for these 'externalities'. Sometimes it has been because the adverse impacts were not known or not fully understood. Businesses have usually been reluctant to admit the extent of the damage they were doing, and when whole industries were involved, they have typically tried every means of avoiding paying for the consequences of their activities. Early industrializers polluted without restraint, doing grievous damage to the local communities and to their local environment. And such damage is being repeated, increasingly in the underdeveloped and emerging economies where the pressures to raise standards of living are greatest.

The asbestos companies provide an example of the polluting process and its outcome. They responded only slowly to the increasing awareness of their health impacts. In many cases, they carried on operations almost regardless of consequences for as long as they could. The reputation of the major operators was destroyed and the cost of compensating the damage they had caused bankrupted the industry.

While asbestos had a particular virulence, the impact of industry as a whole on the earth's climate is a far more serious proposition. Hardly any industry has a clean record. Global resources such as water, oil and various metals are being used up. Air is being contaminated; land and oceans are being polluted with chemicals, toxins and heavy metals, and ever more waste is being created with no apparent means of its safe reprocessing. Biodiversity is being lost in both vegetation and animal species on land and in the oceans. And all these problems are going to get worse before they can ever start to get better.[3]

Pollution in general, and the level of greenhouse gas emissions in particular, is in a state of flux. Projections from the US Energy Information Administration, for example, indicate that world coal consumption is expected to grow by 74 per cent over the 25 years to 2030 during which time coal's share of international

---

3   Esty, D.C. and Winston, A.S., (2006), *Green to Gold: How Smart Companies Use Environmental Strategy to Innovate, Create Value, and Build Competitive Advantage*, New Haven: Yale University Press, p. 287.

energy consumption will have marginally increased from 26 per cent in 2004 to 28 per cent in 2030.

China, already the world's largest coal consumer and enjoying GDP growth around 10 per cent p.a., is a major cause of the increase in coal consumption and greenhouse gas emissions. But China's per-person energy use and greenhouse gas emissions remain far below levels found in richer countries, for example, roughly one-eighth of that in the United States.[4]

> 'Even if we were to stabilize the concentration of greenhouse gas emissions at today's levels, which is impossible, we would still see a further half degree or so just built up on past emissions ... It's absolutely inevitable we're going to see 1.5C°, so our challenge is to try to limit it as close as possible to 2C° above pre-industrial (1850). Some level of adaptation is going to be needed and, clearly, to limit at 2C°, you need significant global action to reduce the projected emissions over the next 50–100 years.'[5]

When disaster has been predicted in the past, for example Malthus' prediction that population growth would outstrip food supply, it has been technology, rather than government that came to the rescue. And it is apparent that technology is the only feasible means of resolving the current environmental threat. Ensuring that polluters are taxed and the necessary technology is subsidized is a substantial global political problem.

Company managers are today charged, quoting the British Companies Act of 2006 which is fairly typical, with the legal duty to 'have regard to the impact of the company's operations on the community and the environment'. The severity of punishment for polluting is bound to increase as the climate change threat becomes more severe and the probability of punishment will also increase as public interest becomes more pervasive. Whatever are today's incentives not to pollute, they will substantially increase over time.

The problem represents a substantial opportunity and motivates green innovations in products, processes and services to which industry is capable of responding. Industry's eternal creativity is illustrated by, for example, the

---

4 Bradsher, K., (2003), 'China's Boom Adds to Global Warming Problem', 22 October: http://healthandenergy.com/china_burning_more_coal.htm

5 Watson, R., (2007), interview reported in Jha, A., (2007), 'Facing down the heat', *The Guardian, Society Guardian Environment*, 24 October.

ancient technology of car engines which are likely as a result of technological developments currently being worked on to double their efficiency, while other innovations in the application and use of cars could multiply that improvement several times over. Such projections seem possible in every industry. It is difficult to see a limit to the potential of technological innovation, but the possibility of an economic return would be essential for it to be accomplished.

The reward for fuel efficiency is clear when fuel prices are high. On the other hand, the application of technology to reducing pollution does not provide this promise of economic return unless governments intervene to punish polluters and reward green products and processes and fund green research and development. Such intervention and regulation might be anathema to Friedmanite free traders, but will be essential to future development.

Similarly, the active enforcement of corporate legislation which directly contradicts the Friedmanite contention is vital to the future development of industry.

Directors' Legal Responsibilities

Most corporate legislation, right across the globe, confirms the status of the joint stock company as a separate legal entity. This is so in the United States (e.g. the Delaware General Corporation Law) and in Britain (as expressed in the Companies Act of 2006). If the company is a separate legal entity this invalidates the application of agency theory and thus much of the dismal science's perspective on business and management. Both shareholders and management in the form of directors have contracts with the company, but there are no contracts directly between management and shareholders, defining one as the agent of the other.

The shareholders' contract with the company has changed quite radically from the time when they invested in overseas expeditions. Today their contract is simply related to the purchase of share certificates for which there is no guaranteed return of value. Their investment is known to be risky and as a consequence there is an expectation of an appropriate return, but no legal contract. Shareholders' liability on behalf of the company is limited to their initial investment and beyond that they have no responsibilities to the company. They are free to come and go as they please.

Management's contract with the company is defined in corporate legislation referring to the duties and responsibilities of company directors. Directors' transactions with the company are dealt with in some detail as clearly there may be a conflict of interest between when the director is acting in his or her own interest and when they may be acting for and on behalf of the company. Such conflict of interest may well arise in the case of a hostile takeover. The general injunction in such cases is to be completely honest and transparent.

There are also specific legal constraints on how a director may act for the company in a situation where they know it to be insolvent. Continuing to trade under such circumstance is fraudulent and the director may well face legal action. These apart, directors' duties tend to be identified rather tentatively and in some cases even ambiguously. There are indications that so long as directors act in good faith they may be unlikely to face legal action. Nevertheless, corporate law in the English-speaking world suggests a more enlightened approach to business and management than is suggested in mainstream management education.

The British Companies Act 2006, the most recently updated company law, identifies the director's duties as including the following:[6]

> *'to promote the success of the company for the benefit of its members as a whole, and in doing so have regard (amongst other matters) to—*
>
> *(a) the likely consequences of any decision in the long term,*
>
> *(b) the interests of the company's employees,*
>
> *(c) the need to foster the company's business relationships with suppliers, customers and others,*
>
> *(d) the impact of the company's operations on the community and the environment,*
>
> *(e) the desirability of the company maintaining a reputation for high standards of business conduct, and*
>
> *(f) the need to act fairly as between members of the company.'*

---

6   Companies Act 2006, Part 10, Chapter 2, paragraph 172.

The meaning of the 'success of the company' was not defined in the act, but a ministerial statement suggested:

> 'For a commercial company, success will usually mean long term increase in value.'[7]

This view of management's responsibilities is not new. As far back as 1844 legislation charged company directors with responsibility for the overall direction of the company's affairs.[8]

The legislation clearly indicates the company has responsibilities which extend to all its stakeholders: customers, employees, suppliers, shareholders, bankers, tax authorities, local community, environment (as proxy for future generations) and it is management's job to work for the best long-term interests of the company, balancing these various stakeholder interests. It is sometimes suggested that it is impossible to achieve such a balance without legal guidance as to priorities, but the law is quite specific that directors' top priority is the long-term interest of the company.

The Companies Act also flags up special requirements on the way directors should conduct themselves, including the duties not to exceed legal powers, to exercise independent judgment, reasonable care, skill and diligence, to avoid conflicts of interest, not accept benefits from third parties and to declare any interest in proposed transactions or arrangements. These last would include any projects that might influence any bonus issues or payments.

The law, as indicated above, requires directors to adopt a quite different role from that of the custom and practice of the past 30 years which has been largely shaped by Friedman's shareholder value contention.

Corporate Transactions with Stakeholders

The company's prime transactions are with its shareholders, its employees and its customers. Shareholders are not just the recipients of dividends and share price sensitive news. The company's shareholder communications

---

7   Goldsmith, Lord, (2006), Statement to the Lords Grand Committee, 6 February, 2006, column 255.
8   Read, A., (1971), *The Company Director: His Functions, Powers and Duties*, London: Jordan & Sons Ltd, p. 3.

include its annual and half-yearly reports, publicity through financial and general media, brokers' reports etc., product news and other items using the traditional and internet media resources. Some of these are directly controlled by management, others may be influenced by management, yet others may be beyond management's control or influence. Moreover, the messages that find their way to shareholders may be planned and deliberate or they may be unplanned, completely inadvertent and wholly unwelcome.

Similar considerations apply to transactions with all stakeholders. With customers, for example, transactions go far beyond the simple matter of delivery of product and receipt of payment and includes a wide array of communications, not simply advertising and publicity, but third party publicity (which may well be hostile), after-sales follow up and service and financial communications such as credit control etc. The interactions themselves may be continuous or one-offs, formal or informal, written or verbal, corporate or personal and controllable or not.

In each case, communications may be with past, present, future and potential stakeholders, communications with one category being likely to be received by the others.

Interactions with employees are especially rich and varied. Employment contracts vary hugely, some being largely informal, others detailed and formalized. The form and level of payment of wages and salaries, the nature of the work involved and the variety of forms of payment whether or not by results, are all subject to great variety. Transactions critically also depend on the degree to which the work done is measured as a basis for payment, or simply for the building of, for example, quality. Payment for work done is the basis of the employee relationship and can clearly be accomplished in many different ways, but employee communications include the way people are treated on a day-to-day basis, how they are supported and given opportunities for their personal development. The potential variety of employee interaction is almost infinite, including planned and deliberate, unplanned and inadvertent and wholly unwelcome communications with past, present, future and potential employees. Moreover, the legal structural arrangements with employees can be successfully extended to include elements of ownership. Highly successful co-owned organizations, such as W.L. Gore and Associates in the United States and the John Lewis Partnership in Britain, demonstrate the exciting potential for these more democratic forms of industrial organization.

The company's suppliers represent a broad category including not only suppliers of raw materials, finished parts and consumables, but also suppliers of various services that might have been outsourced, suppliers of technology, advisors and consultants, the providers of loan capital and financial services, banks and venture capitalists. Similar variety and considerations apply to these groups of stakeholders as to the ones previously discussed.

Directors' legal duty to have regard to 'the impact of the company's operations on the community and the environment' is made explicit. This is a direct contradiction of Friedman's injunction to be solely concerned with making as much money as possible.

Finally every company interacts with offices of local and national governments, including tax authorities, and the laws and regulations they enact, enforce and protect. This political–legal context is shaped also by various non-governmental organizations and pressure groups and where they are relevant to the company's operations, management maintain open communications also with these less direct stakeholders.

Management's legal responsibility for 'maintaining a reputation for high standards of business conduct, and the need to act fairly as between members of the company'[9] suggests interactions with all stakeholders need to maintain that reputation, be positive and supportive of the company's activities. An inappropriate interaction with one set of stakeholders will quickly be communicated to all others with potentially catastrophic effects on the business reputation.

Reputation takes long to build because it is the result of continued interactions with stakeholders which result in positive feedback. It cannot be simply created by some corporate publicity campaign. The most effect publicity or advertising can have is a marginal change in direction or emphasis.

Some aspects of reputation are newly decisive. The damage done to the environment has made pollution, perhaps measured as a company's 'carbon footprint', more important. Investors may shun buying shares in a company which has a poor environmental record, despite its financial performance to date. Partly this may be on the perfectly rational grounds that a poor environmental record today is going to adversely affect the company's future financial performance. And partly it may be on the, to an economist, irrational grounds,

---

9   British Companies Act 2006, Part 10, Chapter 2, paragraph 172.

that the investor simply doesn't wish to be associated with, or seen to support, a polluter no matter how profitable. Similarly, valued employees would, all other things being equal, prefer to work for a clean and green company rather than one which pollutes. Knowledge of the environmental record of the company is likely to have an increasing impact on how the company is perceived by all stakeholders, some significantly, others less so.

Being perceived by all stakeholders as part of the green vanguard, so long as this perception is real, will have a lasting positive effect on a company's reputation. An ever increasing number of major industrial concerns are recognizing this and the positive opportunities it represents, especially for companies traditionally committed to environmentally damaging technologies.

In carrying out these legally defined responsibilities, management may well be acting in the interests of the company, the local community and the environment, but it would not be following Friedman's injunction. Friedman himself argued that the only alternative to his virulent version of free-market capitalism was full-on socialism. That was his threat and his defence. But other possibilities were always available. Galbraith, for example, offered a more pluralist approach which would have been compatible with corporate law and the imperatives of climate change as well as preserving the essence of Smith's competitive capitalism.

Social Balance Economics

According to his fellow economists, Galbraith was the most famous, most widely read and most popular economist of his time. And yet, he appears not to have left a substantial imprint on economic theory. His time coincided with Friedman's, being born four years earlier in 1908, while both lived till 2006, but the Friedmanite legacy was by far the more substantial in their own lifetimes.

Galbraith feared for the fragility of economic growth which he saw as increasingly reliant on the production and purchase of goods which were not needed but for which demand was created artificially through sophisticated corporate advertising. The 'goods' which were in genuine demand were the public goods, such things as healthcare, education, a clean and healthy environment, increasing leisure and the public facilities for its enjoyment.

Today he would no doubt have added a livable and sustainable climate. He identified the problem as one of social balance.

At the start of his examination of the theory of social balance, Galbraith quoted from R.H. Tawney:

> *'It is not till it is discovered that high individual incomes will not purchase the mass of mankind immunity from cholera, typhus and ignorance, still less secure them the positive advantages of educational opportunity and economic security, that slowly and reluctantly, amid prophesies of moral degeneration and economic disaster, society begins to make collective provision for needs which no ordinary individual, even if he works overtime all his life, can provide himself.'*[10]

Writing four years before Friedman's *Capitalism and Freedom*, Galbraith pointed out that classical economic theory had been born in, and applied to, a world of poverty and was inappropriate to a world of affluence. He contrasted the United States affluence in the late 1950s in terms of privately produced and advertised goods, with its inadequate provision of public goods, most of which were fundamental needs, a point which still held true in 2008 with child poverty persisting even in the most advanced economy.

He fully accepted that the balance between different private goods, such as cars, steel, fuel and insurance, would be best maintained through the operation of market forces. Any attempt to plan such a balance would be likely to result, from the inevitable cock-up, in imbalance. But he was concerned with the balance over the whole area of products and services both private and public. Thus increased production of privately produced cars would require more publicly funded roads and if they were not provided in appropriate proportion the economy would suffer, e.g. through congestion and the consequent waste of fuel and time.

> *'The city of Los Angeles, in modern times, is a near classic study in the problem of social balance. Magnificently efficient factories and oil refineries, a lavish supply of cars, a vast consumption of handsomely packaged products, coupled with an absence of a municipal trash collection service which forced the use of home incinerators, made the air nearly unbreathable for an appreciable part of each year.'*[11]

---

10 Tawney, R.H., (1931), *Equality*, London: Allen & Unwin, pp. 134–5.
11 Galbraith, J.K., (1958), *The Affluent Society*, London: Hamish Hamilton, p. 210.

The following half century saw the problems of Los Angeles becoming more general and global. By 2008, for example, the Beijing smog had to be artificially held at bay for the duration of the Olympic Games.

Galbraith's social balance economics stood in contrast to the Friedmanite stance on private and public goods. Friedman had argued that public provision of goods and services was twice as costly as similar provision by private enterprise. This simple assertion escaped serious verification since it was so intuitively appealing to any who has experienced the inefficiency of public bureaucracy. Nevertheless, it was fundamental to Friedman's focus on eliminating the public provision of goods and services. Where elimination was not possible their supply would be minimized and organized and managed as nearly as possible according to the Friedmanite version of private sector practice with artificially created competition and choice.

Friedman's idea was clear and simple as an idea, whereas Galbraith's concepts were less clear-cut and led to some unattractive implications. The lack of social balance in the United States at that time was seen by Galbraith in the inadequate provision of health, education, public law enforcement and housing as leading to social dysfunction, increased crime and drug and alcohol abuse. This argument appeared to have some truth and the argument for achieving social balance between private wealth and public squalor was appealing. But Galbraith combined that argument with the simultaneous observation of the private wealth embedded in the subtle marketing of private goods of no great social value such as dubious media products, films, television, comic strips, pornography etc. His argument strayed too often into personal value judgments; in advocating an increased role for government, it risked becoming a justification for what is now referred to disparagingly as the 'nanny state'.

Moreover, Galbraith's view that the power of advertising could create an artificial demand for products that were not needed or wanted, probably overstated the power of advertising. Friedmanite corporate officials might have yearned for such a tool but none was available. Vance Packard's *The Hidden Persuaders* came out the year before Galbraith's *The Affluent Society* was published and ideas about sinister new methods of advertising were then prominent, which may have influenced Galbraith's judgment. He was prone to expressions of his own patrician tastes and was also criticized for his ill-informed and naïve explanation of how large enterprises were actually managed.[12]

---

12 McFadzean, F.S., (1968), *Galbraith and the Planners*, Glasgow: Strathclyde University Press.

And yet, the idea of social balance retains substance. After 30 years of Friedmanism, the disparity between what Galbraith referred to as 'private wealth' and 'public poverty' has only widened. The throw-away shopping culture has developed apace while the richest nation on earth still lacks a universal healthcare system and leaves its poorest citizens in slum dwellings and tenements unfit for human habitation.

That was the negative case for social balance. Galbraith also made the positive case. A community – a term with which Friedmanites might have had some difficulty – would have been better rewarded by having better schools, parks and recreation facilities than simply, as an example of private wealth, bigger cars. Galbraith argued that the private investment in marketing bigger cars influenced the choice of citizens away from the unpromoted public goods such as better schooling or hospitals. In the Friedmanite world, the engineer or scientists who focused on developing a new device to make cars go better was a hero, while a public servant who proposed a new public service was regarded as a 'wastrel'. Public expenditure was by definition bad, private provision good.

Galbraith's social balance was vulnerable to the false accusation that it required the state's imposition of subjectively based tastes and values. The truth was that it really only demanded that the public sector did those things which the private sector did not, would not or could not, do. The public sector's base task was to provide universal healthcare, education, social security, defence, and support for minimum standards of living, including critical housing. Arguments could also be made for the public provision of services which were natural monopoly necessities, such as gas, water and electricity. But as Keynes had pointed out there was no reason why there should be any benefit from the state being involved in industries such as the railways, or for that matter steel, coal, shipbuilding, cars, and aero engines, except in the short term to support lame ducks which had long-term potential or industries with strategic importance such as defence.

Galbraith also raised the consequent concern of social balance economics in the investment balance between material and personal capital. The distinction was fundamental. Public investment in material capital such as a school or a hospital was an increase in capital formation and a national asset. Investment in schooling increased the supply of educated human beings, of scientists and technologists on whom the nation's intellectual capital depended. But capital formation in human beings was 'off balance-sheet' and did not show up in any census of public capital formation. It was nevertheless of prime importance to a nation's future development and would be especially so in an era of high technology when solutions were sought to global warming and resource depletion and the most powerful resources were various forms of intellectual capital which were all dependent on the calibre of the people generating them.

Despite Friedman's quest to minimize government intervention and regulation it was from time to time essential to stabilize the economy, for example, to end the mass unemployment of the great depression of the 1930s or more recently to provide banking support during the 2007–8 financial failure and to create jobs during the subsequent recession. Keynes had advocated such interventions only in order to maintain full employment and Galbraith additionally advocated the maintenance of social balance to improve society, which in so doing would help address the 'hatred, contempt and even fury' engendered by the Friedman-induced disparity of income and wealth between the average earners and the highest paid.

Behavioural economics might encompass both the Keynesian and Galbraithian amendments to free-market economics applied pragmatically to maintain economic stability. The political problem was to address this change of economic orthodoxy in a global context when Friedmanite free-market globalization was no longer sustainable, and to get global acceptance of the necessity to exclude competitors from economies which did not conform to global standards regarding pollution as well as human rights and minimum worker pay and conditions.

The End of Friedmanism

The fundamental lesson of Friedmanism was that management took place within an economic system which was dependent for its success on managers ignoring all social responsibilities other than to maximize shareholder wealth. A discrete module on business ethics did not challenge that fundamental, but ignored it in favour of reference to the ancient Greeks and moral philosophy. Neither did teaching corporate social responsibility on the other side of the curriculum upset the fundamental Friedman idea which was invested with the long-standing authority of neo-classical economics supported by agency theory, transaction-cost analysis and the concept of the open market in corporate management.

The 'economic man' thesis teaches that people are – and should be for the economic good of all – amoral opportunists, prepared in the end to lie and cheat to achieve their self-interest, and that to prevent them exploiting the others, management must monitor and control, reward and punish. But, as with McGregor's Theory X, such a belief system is self-fulfilling; mistrust becomes endemic and opportunism is increased. The combined effect of agency theory with transaction-cost theory produces the worst possible outcomes, mistrust multiplies, monitoring and attempts to control have to be increased and so become more bureaucratic, repressive and costly.

But, even though this dominant model did not work, it would not be easily overturned. The barriers were high. From the structure of PhD training, to the requirements of publishing in top journals, the criteria for faculty recruitment and promotion were all built around the dominant model. Yet there were suggestions of an approaching crisis. The recurrent interest in behavioural economics, the review of Galbraith's concept of social balance and the imperative to re-enact public interventions to address the financial crunch of 2007–9, all suggested the dominant theory was in crisis.

Business school faculty was becoming more critical of the Friedmanite orthodoxy (e.g. the late Sumantra Ghoshal of INSEAD, London and Harvard Business Schools, and Rakesh Khurana of Harvard Business School, both quoted elsewhere in this text). The return to a more pluralist position would support the free-market model but with some necessary regulation and subject to the maintenance of a supportable level of employment. This level which might regulate wage-push inflation could facilitate the inclusion of social balance without undermining the idea of corporate social responsibility and corporate integrity.

Global resource depletion and climate change were also starting to pressure governments to regulate markets and technologies and new global infrastructure would in the end necessarily result in conformance from national governments. So much seemed inevitable. Management could energize this change, or seek to frustrate it, according to how they were taught and expected to behave.

The management curriculum was also subject to other contradiction. The Newman–Locke debate was between a liberal education and the teaching of specific skills and competences. The Newman argument was picked up by Barnard who argued for mental practice and challenge. But the subject of management is intellectually simple. And educators who sought to give mental challenge to students using management problems as the vehicle only served to confuse, for example, by teaching the usefulness of microeconomic models of the firm, or teaching spurious applications of mathematical procedures such as chaos theory. It might be better to provide a direct challenge to train the mind through science, technology, or philosophy or even literature, and to provide the skills and competences outside of university or in a skills and competencies module delivered in concert with industry practitioners to augment the practical experience gained on corporate management trainee schemes.

The management issue in the twenty-first century is how to recruit, retain, support and develop highly skilled and educated people, working in smaller numbers with a high degree of autonomy and with their rates of pay no longer the main cost drivers, but their individual and team contributions crucial to organizational survival and prosperity, and, at the same time, to engender a 'true spirit of co-operation' between employer and all employees. The emphasis has moved from control of labour and labour costs to innovation and the development and exploitation of ideas; from making as much money as possible for shareholders, to survival and prosperity for all stakeholders.

These changes are happening already. It remains to be seen whether they happen fast enough and go far enough.

Epilogue

This broad account of past progress and mistakes may provide some tentative suggestions as to how future development might be improved and some previous errors avoided. The somewhat tentative emergence, more confident rise and corrupted fall of management, clearly offers some pointers. But the regeneration of management could not be achieved by some sentimental journey back to that golden age led by the likes of Wilfred Brown, Chester Barnard and a youthful Peter Drucker. There was no golden age. The notion of recapturing some non-hierarchical, craft-based, localized, human-scale industry is nonsense. The world in 2009, for all its problems, is in so many different ways and for so many of its people, as good as the world has ever been. Moreover, its problems are now better understood, and though the time is now short, our ability to solve them greater than ever before. Now is the time: the problem really is an opportunity, the threat a challenge.

The 'bad theory' which justified the corruption of management and convinced the world there was no other way, is already in retreat as indicated in the previous chapter. It might be anticipated that Friedman's destructive logic will be replaced by the more pluralistic and socially oriented economic philosophy which will influence the business school orthodoxy, governments, industry and management.

But more will be needed if Anglo-Saxon management is to recover its former dynamic. The customs and practices which Friedmanism justified and helped establish need also to be changed. They appear to fly in the face of the law, seem palpably unfair and lead directly to dishonesty and corrupt practice. These final pages therefore raise questions about the legality, equity and integrity of industrial and commercial management behaviour. The questions are flagged up, alternative possibilities are considered and definitive answers will surely emerge in the course of time.

Firstly, attention is focused on legality and how accepted behaviour appears to be in flagrant conflict with the law. Problems may stem, in part at least, from the apparently ambiguous status of the joint stock limited liability company. The law is quite clear that the company, or corporation, is a legal entity in its own right, a virtual legal person. Its ownership must therefore be different in kind from the ownership of other categories of private property on which much law has been based. However, emboldened by economic theory of agency and concentrated by Friedman's insistence on maximizing shareholder wealth, the corporation has been treated in practice as no different from other types of property. Its owners, i.e. its shareholders, control it and may do with it as they will: break it up, strip it out, or close it down, just as they choose, without regard for the best interests of the company or other related parties.

Ownership of a small proportion of a company's shares does not involve ownership of the company itself or any of its assets. For such owners their interest is restricted to the rights they acquire with their share certificates. These include the possible benefit of dividends and the possibility of an increase in the share price, both being at risk. They also enjoy the right to vote on matters which are raised at the company's general meetings, including the appointment or dismissal of directors, the directors being formally subject to the approval of shareholders. However, this does not change the directors' legal duties to the company and their having regard to the interests of all its stakeholders. And it does not reduce them to being merely the agents of shareholders.

The status of ownership changes when the share exceeds 50 per cent and therefore becomes controlling, and control becomes total and absolute with 100 per cent ownership. But the law still requires that the directors of the company have a duty to promote its success having regard to the interests of all its stakeholders. This seems to be the nub of the problem, where custom and practice contravene the law. Where shareholders may, and do, decide on actions which are not in the best long-term interests of the company and its stakeholders, they are clearly acting against the law.

The difficulty arises because the non share owning stakeholders, who by definition have an interest in the company, do not have their interest represented when critical decisions may be taken or confirmed. This could be resolved by granting such stakeholders a proportion of the company's equity in non-beneficial shares, such shares having no face value and enjoying no rights to dividend, but having the right to vote in general meetings. If action was proposed against the company's interests there would at least be a voice that could be raised.

The Friedmanite focus on shareholder wealth maximization has so overpowered the law that company directors are led to believe it to be their duty to act solely in the interests of shareholders, where necessary against the interests of the company and its other stakeholders. This is what they are taught and is widely supposed. In the case of a 'hostile' (i.e. hostile to the best interests of the company) takeover bid, for instance, directors may be led to believe it is their duty so to act in order to maximize shareholder wealth, even if it means the break up of the company, desertion of its customers and redundancy of its employees. Such behaviour by directors, though common and unchallenged, appears to be in contravention of corporate law and a dereliction of their legal duties.

A further area where behaviour which is justified by reference to economic theory, conflicts with company law, relates to what is referred to as insider-dealing. A shareholder who takes advantage of information which is not available to all shareholders, stands to be accused of the criminal offence of insider-dealing. The director-shareholder is by definition an insider and any purchase or sale of shares by such an individual necessarily falls into the category of an insider deal. Similarly, the design of any scheme from which such an individual might benefit and which involves any share transactions such as issue, purchase or sale, would appear to fall into the same criminal category.

Economic theory has justified and encouraged the conversion of senior managers and directors into shareholders through the offer of share option bonus schemes, the aim being to persuade – bribe is a term that has been used elsewhere – such 'economic men' to act solely in the interests of shareholders should they have conceived of their responsibilities more broadly. Directors who benefit from such share option schemes not only have insider information about corporate strategies ahead of other shareholders, but in many cases they themselves actually design those strategies from which they will benefit. Moreover, it is widely understood that those strategies so designed will tend to be higher risk since their designers and prime beneficiaries will stand to gain hugely from successes but are not at risk from the failures. The term 'moral hazard' is the euphemism customarily used to refer to such situations, but criminality is not generally acknowledged.

Such abuses could be avoided by, for example, excluding directors of quoted companies from owning shares directly in their company. This is common practice in other fields, e.g. government politicians are required to avoid such conflicts of interest by disposing of shareholdings or placing them in trust till such time as they are freed from their executive roles.

The Friedmanite injunction to maximize shareholder wealth has also justified what has been referred to as 'creative accounting'. This is where accounting treatments are deliberately designed to deceive, for example, by keeping debts and liabilities from being clearly shown on a company's balance sheet. In that way, the company's riskiness is understated and it may be enabled to raise more capital from debt, the lower cost component of its capital, and so increase its exposure to risk. In the financial sector such 'creativity' was allowed to flourish for decades. Banks were traditionally required by the lender of last resort to maintain certain ratios of their resources to their lending, referred to as capital or liquidity ratios. Such ratios were calculated on the basis of the balance sheet figures. Keeping a proportion of liabilities off the balance sheet allowed banks to extend their business substantially beyond the level to which they would have been traditionally limited.

The off-balance-sheet deception became so widespread as to infect government and public accounts as well as the corporate and financial sectors, despite the fact that it involved contravention of the law.

The purpose of a balance sheet is to inform, not to mislead. And the purpose of auditing company accounts is not simply to confirm that the figures presented are accurate or that they have been prepared in accordance with applicable accounting standards, but that they are 'true and fair', i.e. they give a genuine account of the company's situation. Yet auditing firms, knowing the extent of potential liabilities was not reflected on the balance sheet, nevertheless routinely certified the accounts as true and fair in the full knowledge they were not in a position to state any such thing. Legal action against auditors for such negligence has so far been limited.

The audit process is becoming increasingly complex. Intangible assets such as patents, processes, structural capital, brand names and even people, are becoming an ever more important part of a company's asset base and there is no generally agreed means of their valuation. Add to this the pressure to deceive by taking real and potential liabilities off the balance sheet and the problem of assessing the extent to which a set of accounts is 'true and fair' becomes extremely problematic. It might be feasible to provide audited explanatory notes offering informal estimates of value in the accounts. Auditors are required by law not simply to sidestep these issues when they certify accounts and to refuse certification where this cannot be done.

The United States Sarbanes–Oxley Act of 2002 addresses some of these problems by prescribing limitations on audit firms, but its main thrust is to inhibit illegality through external regulation and internal processes. Its effect, it is widely argued, is unnecessarily bureaucratic and costly. A more effective solution might be to enforce the extant law with rigour rather than imposing additional regulation.

A second area of concern which any regeneration of management would require to be addressed is that of equity. The inequitable distribution of wealth and income has always been part of human experience and industrialization only exacerbated the situation, especially in terms of remuneration which Drucker referred to as 'a denial of justice and fairness'. He had suggested top executive pay should be no more than 20 times that of the average hourly paid worker.

> 'The resentment against the big salaries of the top executives poisons the political and social relations within the plant, aggravates the difficulty of communications between management and employees, and reduces management's chance to be accepted as the government of the plant.'[1]

That was over half a century ago when the problem of income disparity was much less than it is now. Today Drucker's ratio is approaching 300 times in America with Britain not far behind. The requirement for quoted companies to have remuneration committees to approve directors' pay has had limited effect, such committees being often led by consenting directors from other quoted companies.

In Britain, it appears that the market in company directorships of quoted companies has been cornered by an elaborate system of self-perpetuating, interlocking directorships. It would be possible to reduce this effect by restricting the number of public company directorships an individual could occupy.

In the past, taxation on income and wealth was progressive, reducing the unfairness of their distribution, and contributing a higher proportion to the provision of public services. Adam Smith and his successors, prior to Friedman, had all accepted the concept of progressive, redistributive taxation to compensate that fundamental inequity. However, under Friedman's influence, progressive taxation was more or less eliminated with a higher proportionate burden falling on the least well paid. The justification for that change was

---

1   Drucker, P.F., (1950), *The New Society*, New York: Harper & Brothers, p. 93.

never adequately argued. Friedman's own explanation was a rather doctrinaire admission:

> *'I find it hard, as a liberal* [as defined by Friedman, see the footnote on page 204], *to see any justification for graduated taxation solely to redistribute income ... The personal income tax structure which seems best to me is a flat rate (23.5 per cent) tax on income above an exemption.'*[2]

The broad argument seemed to be to reduce taxation and so reduce the burden on industry and individuals and at the same time reduce government spending, though which outcome was the real motivating force seemed to alternate according to circumstance.

Reversion to progressive systems of taxation could ameliorate the inequity problem, ensuring top earners, no matter what their detailed arrangements, always paid proportionately more tax than the basic rate tax payer, and could thereby contribute to some elements of social balance.

Within the global economy it has become more difficult for government regulation to operate in isolation. In the case of taxation, the fear is that individuals and companies would be lured in to migrating to where the taxation is lowest. Consequently there would need to be some minimum level of international agreement, a first step perhaps being to eliminate tax havens by excluding their residents, individual or corporate, from activity in mainstream economies. Some such consideration is now being joined in the United States. (The British role in the development and preservation of tax havens is curious: of the 35 OECD recognized tax havens, 10 are British colonial territories or dependencies and of the other 25, 14 were formerly British.)

A further aspect of equity which has been substantially damaged by the Friedmanite argument is industry's treatment of the environment in accord with the injunction to accept no social responsibility other than to make as much money as possible for shareholders. Up to now little has been done to protect the interests of future generations and industry has caused damage that needs now to be repaired and which the current economic downturn may make more attractive.

---

2   Friedman, M., (2002), *Capitalism and Freedom*, 40th anniversary edition, Chicago: University of Chicago Press, pp. 174–5.

Whatever is done in the short term, in the medium to long term governments will necessarily become more aggressive in taxing polluters, subsidizing green activity and funding green research. This is a global imperative, and as with the other taxation issue already noted, a coherent global response would be essential. Achieving this might necessitate some limitation on the free operation of global markets. Free trade can no longer afford to be blind to its consequences for climate change and resource depletion.

The third issue, the revival of management's integrity, is perhaps the most important of all to its regeneration. In an increasingly interconnected world the question of management's worthiness of trust, its basic honesty and transparency, are becoming ever more important.

Management's perceived integrity would be substantially raised if freed from the encumbrance of ownership. But then the question arises as to who or what controls or limits the exercise of management power which, as has often been demonstrated, can include the freedom to steal, bully and abuse. Managements are not voted into office through any democratic process and their period of office is not fixed or limited. What is it that could legitimate their undoubted and absolute power within their organizations, if it was not the power of ownership, or acting on behalf of owners?

Part of their legitimacy lies in their fulfilment of legal responsibilities to ensure the survival and long-term prosperity of their organization. This would depend on their effectiveness and efficiency in discharging their part of that responsibility which may or may not require some special expertise or competence. But the question remains as to their accountability. How are they accountable for the effectiveness and efficiency of their performance?

Management is formally accountable through the legal requirements for corporate reporting and disclosure which are professionally audited and made public. If the law in this area was rigorously applied this accountability would not be insubstantial. But that would not affect their internal accountability. Various approaches to internal accountability have been tried: worker directors, two-tier boards, various degrees of co-ownership, plus the possibility of the appointment of a stakeholder director representing the interests of stakeholder-equity holders.

Internal accountability could be extended through, for example, individual disclosure in annual reports by directors, non-financial reporting to stakeholders and the holding of stakeholder general meetings. These, plus the existing ultimate power of hire and fire by members, could be made sufficiently comprehensive to legitimate the role of autonomous management, that role being to create space for people at work which is interesting, challenging and fun. To achieve this, management will need to know their technologies, their customers and, above all, their people. That will require management to act at all times with legality, equity and integrity.

Bibliography

Adams, J.S., (1965), 'Inequity in Social Exchange', *Advances in Experimental Social Psychology*, Vol. 62, pp. 335–343.

Alchian, A.A. and Demsetz, H., (1972), 'Production, Information Costs, and Economic Organisation', *American Economic Review*, Vol. 62, pp. 777–795.

Alderfer, C.P., (1972), *Existence, Relatedness and Growth*, New York: Free Press.

Andrews, K.R., (1980), *The Concept of Corporate Strategy*, Chicago: Irwin.

Ansoff, H.I., (1965), *Corporate Strategy*, New York: McGraw Hill.

Ashton, T.S., (1955), *An Economic History of England: The Eighteenth Century*, London: Methuen & Co.

Atkinson, J.W., (1964), *An Introduction to Motivation*, London: Van Nostrand.

Barnard, C.I., (1938), *The Functions of the Executive*, Cambridge, Mass: Harvard University Press.

Barnard, C., (1948), *Organization and Management*, Cambridge, Mass: Harvard University Press.

Beatty, J., (1998), *The World According to Drucker*, London: Orion Publishing.

Bentham, J., (1789), *Introduction to the Principles of Morals and Legislation*, Oxford: Clarendon Press.

Berle, A.A. and Means, G.C., (1932), *The Modern Corporation and Private Property*, New York: Macmillan.

Boston Consulting Group, (1968), *Perspectives on Experience*, Boston: Boston Consulting Group.

Bradsher, K., (2003), 'China's Boom Adds to Global Warming Problem', available at http://healthandenergy.com/china_burning_more_coal.htm

Braverman, H., (1974), *Labour and Monopoly Capital: The Degradation of Work in the Twentieth Century*, New York: Monthly Review Press.

Briggs, A., (1983), *A Social History of England*, London: Weidenfeld and Nicolson.

Briggs, M. and Jordan, P., (1967), *Economic History of England*, sixth edition, Foxton: University Tutorial Press Ltd.

Brown, W., (1960), *Exploration in Management*, London: Heinemann.

Brown, W., (1962), *Piecework Abandoned*, London: Heinemann.

Burns, T. and Stalker, G.M., (1961), *The Management of Innovation*, third edition (1994), Oxford: Oxford University Press.

Cadbury, A., (1987), 'Final Report of the Committee on the Financial Aspects of Corporate Governance', published by Gee, South Quay Plaza, London.

Cairncross, A., (1978), 'Keynes and the Planned Economy', in *Keynes and Laissez-Faire* (ed.) A.P. Thirlwell, London: Macmillan Press.

Carter, C.F. and Williams, B.R., (1956), *Industry and Technical Progress – Factors Governing the Speed of Application of Science*, Oxford: Oxford University Press.

Caulkin, S., (2007), 'Buccaneering bosses are the worst of all options', *The Observer, Business & Media Section*, 18 November, p. 10.

Caulkin, S., (2008), '198 reasons why we're in this terrible mess', *The Observer, Business & Media Section*, 9 March, p. 10.

Chandler, A.D., (1962), *Strategy and Structure: Chapters in the History of the American Industrial Enterprise*, Cambridge, Mass: The MIT Press.

Chandler, A.D., (1965), *The Railroads: The Nation's First Big Business*, New York: Harcourt, Brace & World Inc (The Forces in American Economic Growth Series).

Chandler, A.D., (1977), *The Visible Hand: The Managerial Revolution in American Business*, Cambridge, Mass: The Belknap Press of Harvard University Press.

Child, J., and Faulkner, D., (1998), *Strategies of Co-operation*, Oxford: Oxford University Press.

Clausewitz, C., (1832), *On War*, originally published in German with several English translations including an abridged version with an introduction by L. Willmot published in 1997, Ware: Wordsworth Editions.

Craig, D., (2005), *Rip Off: The Scandalous Inside Story of the Management Consulting Money Machine*, London: Original Book Company.

Crook, C., (2005), 'The Good Company', in 'A Survey of Corporate Social Responsibility', *The Economist*, 22 January.

Croome, H., (1960), *Human Problems of Innovation*, Department of Scientific and Industrial Research pamphlet, Problems of Progress in Industry, No 5.

Davenport, T.H., (2005), *Thinking for a Living: How to Get Better Performance and Results from Knowledge Workers*, Boston: Harvard Business School Press.

Deal, T. and Kennedy, A., (1982), *Corporate Cultures: The Rites and Rituals of Corporate Life*, New York: Addison Wesley.

Defoe, D., (1722), *A Tour Through England and Wales, Vol. 2*, J.M. Dent & Sons Ltd, Everyman edition published in 1928.

De George, R.T., (1991), 'Will success spoil business ethics?' in *Business Ethics: The State of the Art*, Freeman, R.E., (ed.) Oxford: Oxford University Press.

De George, R.T., (1993), *Competing with Integrity in International Business*, New York: Oxford University Press.

Dickson, T., (ed.), (2000), *Financial Times Mastering Strategy: The Complete MBA Companion in Strategy*, London: Financial Times Prentice Hall.

Drucker, P.F., (1950), *The New Society*, New York: Harper & Brothers.

Drucker, P.F., (1964), *Managing for Results,* Oxford: Heinemann Professional Publishing.

Drucker, P.F., (1993), *The Ecological Vision: Reflections on the American Condition*, New Jersey: Transaction Publishers.

Economist, The, (2005), 'The Ethics of Business', in 'A Survey of Corporate Social Responsibility', *The Economist*, 22 January.

Edvinsson, L. and Sullivan, P., (1996), 'Developing a Model for Managing Intellectual Capital', *European Management Journal*, Vol. 14, No 4, pp. 356–364.

Elster, J., (1983), *Explaining Technical Change*, Cambridge: Cambridge University Press.

Emery, F.E., (1969), *Systems Thinking: Penguin Modern Management Readings*, Harmondsworth: Penguin Books Ltd.

Engels, F., (1844), *The Condition of the Working Class in England*, republished in 1969 by Panther Books with an introduction by Eric Hobsbawm.

Esty, D.C. and Winston, A.S., (2006), *Green to Gold: How Smart Companies use Environmental Strategy to Innovate, Create Value, and Build Competitive Advantage*, New Haven: Yale University Press.

Fayol, H., (1949), *General and Industrial Management,* translation by Constance Storrs, London: Pitman Publishing Company.

Follett, M.P., (1941), *Dynamic Administration*, H.C. Metcalf and L.F. Urwick (eds), New York: Pitman Publishing.

Freeman, C., (1977), *The Kondratiev Long Wave, Technical Change and Unemployment*, the proceedings of the OECD experts meeting on structural determinants of unemployment.

Friedman, M., (2002), *Capitalism and Freedom*, 40th Anniversary edition, Chicago: Chicago University Press.

Friedman, M., (1977), 'From Galbraith to Economic Freedom', *Occasional Paper* 49, London: Institute of Economic Affairs.

Galbraith, J.K., (1958), *The Affluent Society*, London: Hamish Hamilton.

Galbraith, J.K., (1987), *A History of Economics*, London: Hamish Hamilton.

Garvin, D.A., (1987) 'Competing on the eight dimensions of quality', *Harvard Business Review*, November/December, pp. 108–119.

Gaughan, P.A., 'The Fourth Merger Wave and Beyond' in *Readings in Mergers and Acquisitions*, (ed.) P.A. Gaughan, Cambridge Mass: Blackwell Publishers.

George, C.S., (1968), *The History of Management Thought*, Englewood Cliffs, New Jersey: Prentice Hall.

Gergen, K.J., (1973), 'Social Psychology as History', *Journal of Personality and Social Psychology*, Vol. 26, No 2, pp. 309–320.

Ghoshal, S., (2005), 'Bad Management Theories Are Destroying Good Management Practices,' *Academy of Management Learning & Education*, Vol. 4, No 1, pp. 79–91.

Gregory, K.L., (1983), 'Native-View Paradigms: Multiple Cultures and Culture Conflicts in Organisations', *Administrative Science Quarterly*, September, pp. 359–76.

Griffith, S.B., (1963), *Sun Tzu: The Art of War*, London: Oxford University Press.

Hamel, G. and Prahalad, C.K., (1994), *Competing for the Future*, Boston: Harvard Business School Press.

Hayes, R.H. and Abernathy, W.J., (1980), 'Managing Our Way to Economic Decline', *Harvard Business Review*, July/August, pp. 67–77.

Hayek, F., (1944), *The Road to Serfdom*, Chicago: University of Chicago Press.

Herzberg, F., Mausner, B. and Snyderman, B.B., (1959), *The Motivation to Work*, New York: Wiley.

Hofstadter, R.A., (1959), *Social Darwinism in American Thought*, New York: Braziller.

Holmstrom, B. and Kaplan, S.N., (2001), 'Corporate Governance and Merger Activity in the United States: Making Sense of the 1980s and 1990s', *Journal of Economic Perspectives*, Vol. 15, No 2, pp. 132–133.

Hughes, J., (1711), 'Nihil largiundo gloriam adeptus est', *The Spectator* No. 232, 26 November, available at: http://meta.montclair.edu/spectator/text/1711/november/spectator232.xml

Hume, D., (1729), *A Treatise of Human Nature*, republished in 2004 by the Dover Philosophical Classics imprint of Dover Publications Inc of New York.

Jacobs, J., (1992), *Systems of Survival: A Dialogue on the Moral Foundations of Commerce and Politics*, New York: Random House

Jensen, M. and Murphy, K.J., (1990), 'Performance Pay and Top Management Incentives', *Journal of Political Economy*, Vol. 98, pp. 225–264.

Jha, A., (2007), 'Facing down the heat', *The Guardian, Society Guardian Environment*, 24 October.

Jönsson, S., (1996), 'Decoupling hierarchy and accountability: An examination of trust and reputation', in R. Munro and J. Mouritsen (eds) *Accountability: Power, Eethos and the Technologies of Managing*, London: Thomson Business Press.

Kanigel, R., (1997), *The One Best Way: Frederick Winslow Taylor and the Enigma of Efficiency*, London: Little, Brown & Company.

Keynes, J.M., (1931), 'Essays in Persuasion', included in Vol. IX of *The Collected Writings of John Maynard Keynes*, (1972), (eds) A. Robinson, E. Johnson and D. Moggridge, London: Macmillan for the Royal Economic Society.

Keynes, J.M., (1936), *The General Theory of Employment, Interest and Money*, London: Macmillan & Co.

Khurana, R., (2007), *From Higher Aims to Hired Hands: The Social Transformation of American Business Schools and the Unfulfilled Promise of Management as a Profession*, Princeton NJ: Princeton University Press.

Koehler, W., (1938), 'Closed and Open Systems', included in *Systems Thinking*, F.E. Emery (ed.), Harmondsworth: Penguin Books, Penguin Modern Management Readings.

Kondratiev, N.D., (1935), 'The Long Waves in Economic Life', *The Review of Economic Statistics*, November, pp. 105–115.

Kotler, P., (1999), *Kotler on Marketing*, New York: The Free Press.

Lawrence, P.R. and Lorsch, J.W., (1967), *Organization and Environment*, Harvard: Harvard University Press.

Layard, R., (2003), 'Happiness: Has Social Science a Clue?', The Lionel Robbins Memorial Lectures at London School of Economics.

Levitt, T., (1958), 'The Dangers of Social Responsibility', *Harvard Business Review*, Vol. 36, No 5, pp. 41–50.

Levitt, T., (1960), 'Marketing Myopia', *Harvard Business Review*, July/August, pp. 26–38.

Levy, A.B., (1950), *Private Corporations and Their Control*, London: Routledge & Kegan Paul Ltd.

Liddell Hart, B.H., (1967), *Strategy*, second revised edition, London: Faber & Faber.

McClelland, D.C., Atkinson, J.W., Clark, R.A. and Lowell, E.L, (1953), *The Achievement Motive*, London: Van Nostrand.

McFadzean, F.S., (1968), *Galbraith and the Planners*, Glasgow: Strathclyde University Press.

McGregor, D., (1960), *The Human Side of Enterprise*, Tokyo: McGraw Hill Kogakusha, International Student Edition.

Machiavelli, N., (1521), *The Art of War*, currently available from De Capo Press, New York (1965) with an introduction by Neal Wood.

Mandeville, B., (1728), *The Fable of the Bees*, available within *The Enlightenment Fable* by E.J. Hundert (1994), Vancouver: University of British Columbia.

Mantoux, P., (1961), *The Industrial Revolution in the Eighteenth Century*, London: Jonathan Cape.

Marshall, A., (1890), *Principles of Economics*, London: Macmillan & Co.

Marx, K., and Engels, F., (1847), *The Communist Manifesto*, republished in 1964 by New York: Modern Reader Paperbacks.

Marx, K., (1867), *Capital*, An abridged edition was published in 1995 by Oxford World's Classics, an imprint of Oxford University Press.

Maslow, A., (1943), 'A Theory of Human Motivation', *Psychological Review*, Vol 50, pp. 370–396.

Mayo, E., (1933), *The Human Problems of an Industrial Civilization*, New York: Macmillan.

Mayo, E., (1949), *The Social Problems of an Industrial Civilization*, London: Routledge, quoted in *Organization Theory*, London: Penguin.

Mill, J.S., (1848), *Principles of Political Economy*, London: Longmans, Green & Co.

Mill, J.S., (1861), *Utilitarianism*, Chapter 2, paragraph 2, quoted in Warnock, G., (1967), *Contemporary Moral Philosophy*, London: Macmillan.

Miller, E. J. and Rice, A. K., (1967), *Systems of Organization: Task and Sentient Systems and Their Boundary Control*, London: Tavistock Publications.

Mingay, G.E., (1968), *Enclosure and the Small Farmer in the Age of the Industrial Revolution*, Studies in Economic History Series, London: Macmillan.

Mintzberg, H., (1973), *The Nature of Managerial Work*, New York: Harper & Row.

Mintzberg, H. and Quinn, J. B., (1996), *The Strategy Process: Concepts, Contexts and Cases*, third edition, New Jersey: Prentice Hall International.

Mishel, L., (2007), 'CEO-to-worker pay imbalance grows', Economic Snapshots website: http://www.epi.org/content.cfm/webfeatures_snapshots_20060621

Misztal, B.A, (1996), *Trust in Modern Societies: The Search for the Bases of Social Order*, Cambridge: Polity Press.

Murray, H.A., (1938), *Explorations in Personality*, Oxford: Oxford University Press.

Nelson, D.M., (1946), *Arsenal of Democracy: The Story of American War Production*, New York: Harcourt Brace & Co.

Newman, J.H., (1854), *The Idea of a University: Discourse 7. Knowledge Viewed in Relation to Professional Skill*, Newhaven, CT: Yale University Press.

Owen, R., (1857), *Life of Robert Owen Written by Himself*, London edition.

Owen, R., (1969), *A New View of Society*, Harmondsworth: Penguin Books. (First published 1814)

Paret, P., (ed.) (1986), *Makers of Modern Strategy*, Oxford: Clarendon Press.

Parker, M., (2004), 'Becoming Manager', *Management Learning*, Vol. 35, No 1, pp. 45–59.

Parker, M. and Pearson, G., (2005) 'Capitalism and its Regulation: A Dialogue on Business and Ethics', *Journal of Business Ethics*, Vol. 60, No 1, pp. 91–101.

Pearson, G., (1985), *The Strategic Discount*, Chichester: Wiley.

Pearson, G., (1989), 'Factors which facilitate and inhibit innovation in a mature industry', PhD thesis submitted to the University of Manchester.

Pearson, G., (1995), *Integrity in Organizations: An Alternative Business Ethic*, Maidenhead: McGraw Hill Book Co.

Pearson, G., (1999), *Strategy in Action: Strategic Thinking, Understanding and Practice*, Harlow: FT Prentice Hall.

Penrose, E.T., (1959), *The Theory of the Growth of the Firm*, Oxford: Oxford University Press.

Peters, T.J., and Waterman, R.H., (1982), *In Search of Excellence*, New York: Harper & Row.

Petty, W., (1691) *Political Anatomy of Ireland*, based on his experience in 1672 and published posthumously.

Phillips, J., (1792), *History of Inland Navigation,* p. 87, quoted in Ashton, T.S., (1955), *An Economic History of England: The Eighteenth Century*, London: Methuen & Co.

Piatier, A., (1984), *Barriers to Innovation*, London: Francis Pinter.

Pickford, J., (ed.), (2001), *Financial Times Mastering Management: Your Single Source Guide to Becoming a Master of Management*, London: Financial Times Prentice Hall.

Pitt, W. the Younger, parliamentary speech introducing 1792 budget, quoted in Galbraith, J.K., (1987), *A History of Economics*, London: Hamish Hamilton.

Plato, (~ 375BC), *The Republic*, Desmond Lee's 1955 translation available in Penguin Classics, London: Penguin Books.

Porter, M.E., (1980), *Competitive Strategy – Techniques for Analyzing Industries and Competitors*, New York: Free Press.

Porter, M.E., (1985), *Competitive Advantage – Creating and Sustaining Superior Performance*, New York: Free Press.

Preston, G., trade unionist, contemporary response to Scientific Management archived by the Samuel C. Williams library of the Stevens Institute of Technology, Hoboken, New Jersey, and can be seen in full at http://stevens. cdmhost.com/cdm4/document.php?CISOROOT=/p4100coll1&CISOPTR=44 2&REC=1 (The date of this document is handwritten and not clear)

Pugh, D.S., Hickson, D.J., Hinings, C.R. and Turner, C., (1968), 'Dimensions of Organisation Structure', *Administrative Science* Quarterly, Vol. 13, pp. 65–105.

Read, A., (1971), *The Company Director: His Functions, Powers and Duties*, London: Jordan & Sons Ltd.

Ricardo, D., (1817), *The Principles of Political Economy and Taxation*, republished in 2004, with an introduction by F.W. Kolthammer, by Dover Publications Inc of New York.

Rogers, E.M., (1983), *The Diffusion of Innovations*, third edition, New York: Free Press.

Ross, C., (2007), *Independent Diplomat: Dispatches from an Unaccountable Elite*, New York: Cornell University Press.

Rothwell, R., (1980), 'The Role of Technical Change in International Competitiveness: The Case of the Textile Machinery Industry', *Management Decision*, Vol. 15, No 6, pp. 542–549

Schmiemann M., (1999), 'The Link between R&D, Inventions and Innovations in Europe', *World Patent Information*, Vol. 21, No 1, pp. 43–45.

Schoeffler, S., (1977), *The PIMSletter on Business Strategy, No 2*, Harvard: The Strategic Planning Institute.

Schumpeter, J.A., (1939), *Business Cycles: A Theoretical, Historical and Statistical Analysis of the Capitalist Process*, New York: McGraw Hill.

Sismondi, J.C.L. de, (1819), *Nouveaux Principes d'économie politique, ou de la Richesse dans ses rapports avec la population*, Paris : Delaunay.

Skidelsky, R., (1977), 'The Political Meaning of the Keynesian Revolution', in *The End of the Keynesian Era*, (ed.) R. Skidelsky, London: Macmillan.

Smith, A., (1759), *The Theory of Moral Sentiments*, republished in the Dover Philosophical Classics imprint by Dover Publications Inc of New York in 2006.

Smith, A., (1776), *An Inquiry into the Nature and Causes of the Wealth of Nations*, republished as a selected edition in 1993 with an introduction and notes by Kathryn Sutherland in the Oxford World's Classics imprint by Oxford University Press..

Sokal, A. and Bricmont, J., (1998), *Intellectual Impostures*, London: Profile Books.

Stark, A., (1993) 'What's the Matter with Business Ethics?' *Harvard Business Review*, May/June, pp. 38–48.

Stewart, T.A., (1997), *Intellectual Capital: The New Wealth of Organizations*, London: Nicholas Brealey Publishing.

Sumner, W.G., (1914), 'The Challenge of Facts and Other Essays', (ed.) A.G. Keller, New Haven: Yale University Press.

Tawney, R.H., (1931), *Equality*, London: Allen & Unwin.

Taylor, F., (1910), *The Principles of Scientific Management*, available from Northern Illinois University's website at http://www3.niu.edu/~td0raf1/labor/Story%20of%20Schmidt.htm

Trist, E.A. and Bamforth, K.W., (1951), 'Some Social and Psychological Consequences of the Longwall Method of Coal-getting', *Human Relations*, Vol. 4, No 1, pp. 6–38.

Veblen, T., (1899), *The Theory of the Leisure Class: An Economic Study in the Evolution of Institutions*, New York: Macmillan.

Veblen, T., (1904), *The Theory of Business Enterprise*, New York: Macmillan.

Weber, M., (1904), *The Protestant Ethic and The Spirit of Capitalism*, London: Routledge Classics, republished in 2001.

Welch, J., (2005), *Winning*, London: HarperCollins Publishers.

Wernerfelt, B., (1984), 'A Resource Based View of the Firm', *Strategic Management Journal*, 5: pp. 171–80.

Woodward, J., (1965), *Industrial Organisation: Theory and Practice*, Oxford: Oxford University Press.

Zola, E., (1885), *Germinal*, Penguin Classics (2004) translated by Roger Pearson.

About the Author

This is Gordon Pearson's sixth book on management, the previous ones being mainly focused on strategy, innovation and ethics. His previous experience is divided more or less equally between industry and academia. His first degree was in Management Science at Warwick University which included final year options in financial analysis and marketing research. This was later followed by a PhD at Manchester Business School investigating what helped and hindered firms being effective innovators, published in *The Competitive Organization* by McGraw Hill.

His doctoral research identified two clusters of organizational characteristics to do with strategic orientation and organizational culture which was critically influenced by the perceived integrity of senior management. This aspect of the research was developed further through an enquiry among FTSE 100 firms, the results of which were published by McGraw Hill in *Integrity in Organizations: an Alternative Business Ethic*.

His other research interests centre on strategic management practice, focusing on what firms of different sizes and technologies actually do in relation to their long-term development and how effective it is, and the extent to which they engage in formal strategic management processes and the nature of those formal processes as well as any informal processes. This work has informed various journal articles and books, including *The Strategic Discount*, *Strategic Thinking* and *Strategy in Action*. These all focused on the practice and theory of strategic management, an area in which he has developed a distinctively practitioner-oriented position, reflected also in his many refereed journal articles.

His industrial experience started as a management trainee with Mills & Allen International where he was concerned mainly with operations management in electronics manufacture and culminating in general management of a subsidiary company in office equipment distribution.

After graduating he spent almost seven years with T&N plc, initially as a company planning specialist in the main UK subsidiary, subsequently as business planning manager responsible for business planning, analysis of strategic options, acquisitions, marketing research and new product investigation. Latterly he moved to corporate headquarters where he was responsible for the co-ordination of strategic planning of the main UK companies plus over 30 overseas operations. This role involved responsibility for shaping the strategic development of individual businesses, including strategic innovations and diversifications as well as acquisitions.

He subsequently joined RMC of Australia's main UK subsidiary as director of administration and strategic development. He was recruited to initiate the further development of RMC's UK interests as well as heading up the accounting, personnel and training, buying and IT functions. The role also included the initiation, negotiation and integration of acquisitions. During this time he also acted as general manager of a major quarrying subsidiary and a horticultural products business.

This practical experience informed his academic career. His teaching at both undergraduate and postgraduate levels has focused on strategic management, business ethics and innovation and change. His approach to teaching reflects his practitioner background and experience and tends to focus on the practicalities of implementation which he sees as the main problems in this area of management, rather than the theory.

Index

**If you have found this book useful you may be
interested in other titles from Gower Applied Research**

**The Durable Corporation:
Strategies for Sustainable Development**
Güler Aras and David Crowther
300 pages; 978-0-566-08819-3

**Terrorism, the Worker and the City:
Simulations and Security in a Time of Terror**
Luke Howie
208 pages; 978-0-566-08889-6

**Globalization's Limits:
Conflicting National Interests in Trade and Finance**
Dimitris N. Chorafas
360 pages; 978-0-566-08885-8

**Transformation Management:
Towards the Integral Enterprise**
Ronnie Lessem and Alexander Schieffer
376 pages; 978-0-566-08896-4

Risk Strategies: Dialling Up Optimum Firm Risk
Les Coleman
264 pages; 978-0-566-08938-1

**Wealth, Welfare and the Global Free Market:
A Social Audit of Capitalist Economics**
Ibrahim Ozer Ertuna
248 pages; 978-0-566-08905-3

**Convergenomics:
Strategic Innovation in the Convergence Era**
Sang M. Lee and David L. Olson
c. 170 pages; 978-0-566-08936-7

GOWER